TRADITIONALISM AND RADICALISM IN THE HISTORY OF CHRISTIAN THOUGHT

Traditionalism and Radicalism in the History of Christian Thought

Corneliu C. Simuţ

TRADITIONALISM AND RADICALISM IN THE HISTORY OF CHRISTIAN THOUGHT

BR
100
.S515
2010

First published in 2010 by PALGRAVE MACMILLAN® in the
United States—a division of St. Martin's Press LLC, 175 Fifth
Avenue, New York, NY 10010

Where this book is distributed in the UK, Europe and the rest of
the world, this is by Palgrave Macmillan, a division of Macmillan
Publishers Limited, registered in England, company number 785998,
of Houndmills, Basingstoke, Hampshire RG21 6XS.

Palgrave Macmillan is the global academic imprint of the above
companies and has companies and representatives throughout the
world.

Palgrave® and Macmillan® are registered trademarks in the United
States, the United Kingdom, Europe and other countries.

Library of Congress Cataloging-in-Publication Data

Simut, Corneliu C.
    Traditionalism and radicalism in the history of Christian thought /
    Corneliu C. Simut.
        p. cm.
    ISBN 978-0-230-10558-4 (hardback)
    1. Christianity—Philosophy—History. I. Title.

BR100.S515 2010

230.046—dc22   2010007415

Design by Scribe Inc.

First edition: September 2010

10 9 8 7 6 5 4 3 2 1

CONTENTS

INTRODUCTION

This book is the result of numerous conversations as well as confrontations that I had with my bachelor's and master's degree students in theology throughout the academic year 2008–2009 at Emanuel University. As I grew acutely aware that many of the newcomers, but also some of the more experienced students, neither know nor understand the fundamental differences between the theology of the past and that of more recent times, writing a book about this particular issue seemed appropriate in the first days of October 2008. Having just returned from a conference in Rome where I had some mild exchanges of ideas over what contemporary theology should be and what it should do as compared to what is generally perceived as traditional theology, I realized—again, for I do not know which time in the past few years—that a book dealing with traditional and radical theology would not only help my students but also at the same time serve those with serious interests in the welfare of the church in general.

There are, however, a number of things that must be carefully explained before anyone begins to read this work. First, it should be stressed that the purpose of the book is to present and explain the differences between traditional and radical theology as they emerged and developed through the history of Christianity. In doing so, a selection of authors and dogmatic aspects was made available for use as theological samples for a better description of the two types of theology as they developed through history. Personal reflection and criticism are not excluded, but—despite my obvious attachment to traditional theology—the work in its entirety is intended mainly to present rather than criticize theological traditionalism or radicalism.

Second, while the book is concerned with the presentation and analysis of certain dogmatic issues such as Christology, ecclesiology, pastoral work, anthropology, faith, and bioethics among many others—all meant to illustrate how Christian thought stands between traditionalism and radicalism—it is not primarily a dogmatic study but rather a highly selective historical overview. This is why each author and theological subject is discussed with specific reference to distinct historical periods: Gregory Nazianzen to late antiquity, Jean Calvin to early modernity, Ion Bria to postmodernity in general, Erich Fromm to early postmodernity, Paul Ricoeur to mid postmodernity, and Vito Mancuso to late postmodernity. It should be quite clear by now that the historical periodization and the authors reveal the structure of the book. Thus, the work has six chapters: the first three are dedicated to traditional Christian thought in Gregory, Calvin, and Bria, while the last three deal with radical Christian thought in Fromm, Ricoeur, and Mancuso. A brief concluding section at the end of the book intends to present—in a very succinct way—a summary as well as the results of the present research.

Third, a clarification of terms is needed, especially in connection with the organizing principle that lies behind the book. From the perspective of church history, and particularly of the individual person who attempts to understand the development of Christian doctrine from the beginnings of the church to the present situation, the question of establishing what is "traditional" and what is "radical" can become a thorny one. What should be clear nevertheless from the start is that traditionalism and radicalism represent a wide spectrum of theological views, not two blocks of dogmatic thought. In my understanding, traditional theology is the interpretation of the information contained in Scriptures, which allows for the actual ontological existence of metaphysical realities, such as the Trinity, the incarnation of Jesus Christ, his physical resurrection from the dead and ascension to heaven, but also the believers' resurrection and eternal life with Christ. This type of theology, though present from the beginning of Christianity to the present moment, was predominant from antiquity to early modernity, namely, from the time of the apostles to the Protestant Reformation. Radical theology is, by contrast, the interpretation of Scriptures that does not allow for the actual ontological existence of the above-mentioned metaphysical realities; in turn, these realities are either radically reinterpreted to fit the rational experience of contemporary people or given up altogether. Historically, this theology began to exert a high degree of influence starting with the Enlightenment and post-Enlightenment philosophy, blossomed during the liberal Protestantism of the late nineteenth century, and then continued to develop, especially in the academy, throughout the twentieth and twenty-first centuries. In my view, radical theology equals modern theology, which in turn is one and the same as liberal theology. To be sure, traditionalism and modernism are not two "eras" in church history but rather two polarities, within which Christian theology has swung through the centuries. Traditionalism and radicalism have coexisted and overlapped since the beginning of the church, but traditionalism was predominant before the Enlightenment, while radicalism has produced a growing impact after the dramatic cultural shift of late seventeenth-century rationalism. While I realize these definitions of traditional and radical theology are far from being perfect and may seem simplistic, it is my conviction that they can help achieve a better understanding of the points I want to make, especially if read by people who are not professional theologians.

Fourth, the historical periodization I work with should be explained. Thus, while concepts like late antiquity with reference to the fourth century and early modernity as attached to the sixteenth century may go unnoticed, postmodernity and especially its fragmentation into early, mid, and late postmodernity can indeed cause at least some degree of criticism. It needs to be pointed out here that this particular division of postmodernity is not primarily philosophical or intellectual but essentially historical. This is to say that despite being artificial in nature, my fragmentation of postmodernity is successful at least in conveying a sense of history, which can assist the reader in his quest to build a broader, more comprehensive perspective on the development of recent dogma history. Consequently, early postmodernity is ascribed to the first half of the twentieth century, mid postmodernity to the second half of the twentieth century, and late postmodernity to the years of the twenty-first century. At the same time, the philosophical-intellectual aspect of this periodization was not totally ignored because while, as briefly shown before, modernity refers to Enlightenment, post-Enlightenment, and Liberal Protestant thought until the end of the First World War, postmodernity describes the intellectual development ranging from the early 1920s to the present. Hence, the period between the early 1920s and the 1950s, which I term early postmodernity, witnessed a revitalization of liberalism under the influence of the Frankfurt School and its social critical theory with Marxist overtones. Then, from the 1950s to the late 1990s—a time frame I dub mid postmodernity—Western theology was heavily influenced by the overwhelming diversity of intellectual currents in hermeneutics, especially the movement away from the text with structuralism, poststructuralism, deconstruction, and reader response criticism, which almost turned theology into pure philosophy to the obvious detriment of the former and the overarching benefit of the latter. The last but not the least important, with the dawn of the third millennium late postmodernity—obviously not a coinage of my own but rather a widely circulated phrase in the past few decades—has witnessed a renewed interest in theology, seen as a discipline on its own, which should be radically reinterpreted to fit the experience of today's men and women. The results of late postmodern endeavors are not necessarily different from those achieved by early and mid postmodern efforts, but it has become increasingly evident that theology began to be treated as a distinct field of research alongside philosophy and other culturally oriented subjects.

Fifth, the choice of authors may also raise questions. I could have chosen a multitude of other names from the incredibly rich theological tradition of church history. Nevertheless, as I intended the book to be not only a detailed presentation of the differences between traditional and radical theology but also a personal analysis—with critical considerations kept to a minimum—the singling out of only six names became a necessity. For traditional theology, Gregory Nazianzen and Jean Calvin seemed evident choices, as 2009 was a commemorative year for both theologians: 1630 years since the death of Basil the Great (as formally celebrated by the Holy Synod of the Romanian Orthodox Church, which decided to honor all Cappadocian Fathers—Gregory Nazianzen included—within the same year) and the quincentenary for Calvin. As I traced traditional theology well into the twentieth century, I became increasingly aware that Eastern Orthodoxy remained a bulwark of theological traditionalism (although not always for the best theological and practical reasons), so an Eastern Orthodox theologian with a reasonable degree of openness toward Western theology like Bria presented itself as a good choice. Radical theology on the other hand could have implied an equally wide range of names, but I eventually chose Fromm for his psychoanalytical approach to Christology, Ricoeur for his impressive role in recent hermeneutics, and Mancuso for all the turmoil he ignited in Italy's contemporary theological setting because of his decision to rebuild Christian theology based on man's rational experience. At this point, one key aspect is in need of straightforward clarification and it has to do with my choice to omit traditional Catholic theology from my historical survey. Thus, Thomas Aquinas—undoubtedly the representative of Catholic theology *par excellence*—was deliberately avoided not because his theology is a little too rationalistic for my own taste but rather because he is much too present in historical surveys of Christian theology, a situation I was determined to prevent at all costs. I do not suffer from any anti-Catholic bias whatsoever; I am only concerned to produce a reading of traditionalism and radicalism that presents us with theologians of lesser fame whose intellectual and spiritual achievements are nonetheless vital for the development of Christian thought.

Sixth, the main features of traditional and radical Christian thought respectively are identified and briefly analyzed as they emerge from particular subjects detailed in some of the most representative works of each author. For instance, with reference to traditional Christian thought, I selected the Christological spirituality of Gregory Nazianzen's *Letter to Nectarius, Bishop of Constantinople*; the ecclesiastical discipline of Calvin's *Institutes of the Christian Religion*; and the pastoral ecclesiology of Bria's *Liturgy after the Liturgy*. Likewise, for radical Christian thought, I chose the psychoanalytical Christology of Fromm's *The Dogma of Christ*; the fallibility theory of Ricoeur's *Fallible Man*; and the faith reassessment of Mancuso's *Innocent Suffering, Rebuilding Faith*, and *The Soul and Its Destiny*. While at first glance all the names appear to fit their corresponding subjects and works quite naturally, some readers will probably find the choice of Calvin's ecclesiastical discipline an unfortunate oddity. I should admit here that one could be annoyed by and consequently question my decision to put Calvin's doctrine of church discipline under scrutiny, to the detriment of other more salient teachings of his impressive dogmatic volumes. In my defense, however, the selection of Calvin's doctrine of church discipline over other arguably more important classical doctrines—such as God, Christology, sin, and salvation—was triggered by my conviction that church discipline has been gradually and intentionally ignored in most ecclesiastical settings of today's church life, both traditional and radical. Dogmatically, however, Calvin's approach to church discipline shows its fundamental importance for traditional theology as well as its lack of importance for the radical vein. To take just one example, sexual minorities are not excluded from churches favoring radical theologies, while in traditional communities they are excommunicated or at least dealt with in a disciplinary way as the morality of their lives and the practical consequences of their behavior are considered biblically inadequate.

A final remark has to do with the reason why the title contains the phrase "Christian Thought" and not the more evident "Christian Theology," as probably one could rightly have expected. The decision to choose the former over the latter has to do with Paul Ricoeur who, despite his astute theological competence, was primarily a philosopher with interests related to phenomenology and hermeneutics. Nevertheless, due to his extensive research in biblical interpretation, Ricoeur can legitimately be included among the formidable intellectuals who have shown a distinct preoccupation with Christian thought, if not specifically with Christian theology.

CHAPTER 1

TRADITIONAL CHRISTIAN
THOUGHT IN LATE ANTIQUITY

GREGORY NAZIANZEN AND CHRISTOLOGICAL
SPIRITUALITY IN THE FOURTH CENTURY

INTRODUCTION

Writing in the second half of the fourth century, Gregory Nazianzen (330–389) provides us with one of the classic examples of traditional Christian theology. Decades after the Edict of Mediolanum (313 AD), Christianity was no longer preoccupied with the threat of imminent persecution, so the dangers from outside became increasingly a matter of the past. It was time, however, to confront the dangers from within or the quite impressive wave of teachings that originated in the Christian church but that did not reflect the dogmatic morrow of the faith handed down through almost four hundred years of history. It was in this particular historical setting that Gregory wrote his works, in close connection with what he believed to be the very core of Christianity, namely, the teaching about Jesus Christ and about God as Trinity. Keenly aware that the church's convictions about Christ resulted in a certain type of practical behavior, Gregory was convinced that the life of those who declare themselves Christians was a life of faith, which is, in other words, a life of constant spirituality. Such a life, however, needs confirmation, but this confirmation is in itself bound to a definition. Gregory's most essential definition of faith, which is also the basis of Christian spirituality, has to do with the fundamental tenets of the Nicene Creed and especially with the way he sees Jesus Christ. This means that the core of the Christian life is the image of Christ, namely, the way we understand Christ. Gregory is fully aware that our life is shaped by our perspective on Christ, so it is the correct interpretation of Christ's person and work that characterizes our spirituality. This is why it is utterly important to see Christ in light of Scripture; our lives are molded by our understanding of Christ himself. Man does not need a religious spirituality in general; what man needs is a Christological spirituality, namely, a life that is not informed by any image of Christ but a life heavily permeated by the correct image of Christ. This is what prompted Gregory to react against a series of antiorthodox teachings such as Arianism, Macedonianism, and Apollinarianism because a flawed interpretation of Christ leads to a crippled spirituality, while the correct interpretation of Christ is the very basis of our spiritual lives. It will be shown next how Gregory's reaction against these three teachings—and especially against Apollinarianism—prompted him to lay the foundation for traditional theology.

A BRIEF PRESENTATION OF ARIANISM, MACEDONIANISM, AND APOLLINARIANISM

Gregory wrote four letters concerning the dogmatic errors of the teachings proliferated by Apollinarius: the *Letter to Nectarius, Bishop of Constantinople;*[1] the *Letter to Cledonius the Priest against Apollinarius;*[2] *Against Apollinarius: The Second Letter to Cledonius;*[3] and the *Letter to Olympius.*[4] The letters are relatively short, with the exception of the *Letter to Cledonius the Priest against Apollinarius,* which is a little longer, but they convey Gregory's great concern about the spiritual damage that can result from the dissemination of erroneous teachings throughout the churches. The first, however, the *Letter to Nectarius, Bishop of Constantinople,* contains a very brief though illuminating presentation of the main dogmatic errors of Apollinarianism.[5] According to Gregory, who probably wrote the letter around the year 383 AD,[6] churches go through a very difficult time that can be described as real suffering. He even states that the situation of the suffering churches is so distinctively grave that the care or the love of God seems to have forsaken the very life of the churches. Gregory mentions his own physical suffering, which had it afflicted anybody else it would have seemed unbearable to him, but at the end of the day cannot even be compared to the suffering of the churches, which appear to have reached the brink of disaster. At this time, Gregory has not mentioned the very problem that triggered the suffering of the churches, but the reader begins to understand that it is a dogmatic problem at issue when he sees that Gregory almost immediately mentions the word "heresy." Thus he writes that the churches are in pain because some follow the heresies of Arius[7] and Eudoxius.[8] Gregory is evidently bothered by the heresy of Arianism, but he seems to be even more distraught by those followers who reportedly gained confidence in attracting more and more churches to their side. As far as Gregory is concerned, Arianism is a disease that causes a great deal of suffering to all churches.[9]

Thus, the first feature of traditional theology—as seen in Gregory Nazianzen—is its willingness to treat doctrine very seriously to the point that all the teachings that do not reflect the content of its doctrinal core should be treated as malignant. For traditional theology, doctrine is crucially important for the simple reason that it directly affects the life of the church and that of believers; this is why any teaching that does not reflect the doctrine of the church is literally believed to be a disease that impairs the church in leading a spiritually sound life.

In addition to Arianism, Gregory mentions a second heresy when he tackles the issue of Macedonianism.[10] As grieved as he was by Arianism, whose followers captured more and more churches under their bad influence, Gregory seems on the verge of losing his patience when he talks about the heresy of Macedonianism. For him, the teachings of Macedonius[11] are not seen as a mere disease but rather as madness, especially because some of the heretics not only cast their malignant influence over churches but also had the audacity to claim the title of bishop for their own ecclesiastical offices. In connection with the heresy of Macedonianism, Gregory mentions two other names, those of Eleusius[12] and Eunomius[13]; the former appears to have endorsed the appointments of some heretics to bishoprics, while the latter—whom Gregory calls "our bosom evil"—seems to have regarded himself as somehow persecuted for the sake of his own beliefs. It is quite clear that Gregory was extremely concerned about the situation of the churches afflicted by heresy, and he could not bear the heresy itself. Nevertheless, he was nearly infuriated by the actions of some of the heretics, who not only spread heresies widely but also did their best to find access to Episcopal sees. This is why Gregory writes with regard to Eunomius that he "is no longer content with merely existing," but he is now more and more confident in his attempts to attract people to his side while simultaneously complaining of being "injured" because of his theological convictions.[14]

Gregory's explanations bring us to the second feature of traditional theology, namely, its determination to label foreign teachings as not only malignant but also evil. This is a clear indication that doctrine and especially its content are not optional for the church. The church in general, and believers in particular, as members of the church, must not treat doctrine as a matter of personal choice but as a binding spiritual reality that bears unmediated influence over the personal and communitarian existence of the church. The church must always pay serious attention to doctrine as well as to all the teachings that circulate among its members, lest the quality of spiritual life be gravely diminished by heretical influences.

For Gregory, however, the two heresies he so tenaciously opposes—Arianism and Macedonianism—seem to be a bearable suffering. He himself and the churches with him look as if they had accustomed themselves to the situation. While Arianism had a longer history and Macedonianism a relatively shorter one at the time of Gregory's writing, both were pictured as problems that the church could eventually face with a certain degree of detachment because each of them downplayed the divinity of Jesus Christ and of the Holy Spirit, respectively, while keeping the reality of created humanity (in Jesus's case) within its originally designated limits, in the sense that the humanity of Christ, for instance, was believed to have had its starting point on earth as he was born into this world bearing the form of a human being. Thus both Orthodoxy and Arianism clung to the position that the humanity of Christ is a matter that pertains to his existence within the world's history. Regardless of whether Christ was seen as the eternal preexistent Logos of God (in Orthodoxy) or as a mere human being (in Arianism), his humanity had a starting point within human history. This seems to be the reason why, for Gregory, the heresies of Arianism and Macedonianism were somehow easier to handle: the beginnings of humanity were believed to have been confined to the realm of created history, while the idea of divinity remained untouched (even though not fully recognized with reference to Christ or to the Holy Spirit as far as Arianism and Macedonianism were concerned).

The third feature of traditional theology is therefore brought to light by Gregory, and this is the serious preoccupation with the historical life of Jesus Christ, with the accompanying realization that his earthly life was chronologically preceded by his metaphysical existence as the Logos of God. This does not mean that before we consider the actual and historical life of Jesus we could speak of a theoretical existence of a certain image of Christ that somehow could reflect—in advance—his own humanity or the humanity of men and women in general. On the contrary, Jesus's historical exis-tence was preceded by another type of existence—metahistorical but equally real, ontological, and actual—that presents him as a real per-son even before he began his physical life through incarnation.

Gregory's tone, however, changes radically when it comes to the presentation of a third heresy, which followed Arianism and Mace-donianism. This is the "boldness of the Apollinarians," which for Gregory became some sort of a personal issue. While Gregory's grief as produced by the heresy of Apollinarius cannot be questioned, it is true nevertheless that he was personally annoyed by Nectarius's decision to grant them the right to assemble ecclesiastical meet-ings.[15] One cannot lose sight of the fact that Nectarius was Grego-ry's own successor to the Episcopal See of Constantinople[16], and it was in this capacity that he allowed the Apollinarians to have church meetings. This is why Gregory elegantly accuses Nectarius of having overlooked the daring spirit of the Apollinarians, which eventually led to his decision to grant them the right to put together church meetings. Although Gregory expresses his lack of knowledge con-cerning the reasons why the very bishop of Constantinople even-tually came to such a decision, he does not seem to be primarily bothered by the bishop's decision to allow the Apollinarians to have their own church meetings, but rather by the fact that the bishop's action gave them the right to hold ecclesiastical assemblies that had the same status (or equality) with those overseen by Gregory him-self. This situation obviously placed Gregory in a position of equality with the Apollinarians, and vice versa, and it seems to have been this particular result that pushed Gregory to a firm response. He could not stand the idea that his own position was placed at the same level as that of heretics, so he informs Nectarius that he possesses a work written by Apollinarius himself (he does not give any further infor-mation about the work itself), which is very likely to have escaped Nectarius's attention. Gregory does not spend too many words on denigrating Apollinarius's work, which he evidently disliked, but he does say that its teachings go far beyond any heretical crookedness, which is just another way that Apollinarianism was, at least in his opinion, the chief of all heresies.[17]

Gregory's reaction outlines a fourth feature of traditional the-ology, which is always determined to present, explain, criticize, and therefore limit the influence of all the teachings that threaten the dogmatic integrity of the church. Thus, traditional theology is constantly vigilant, critical, and militant when it comes to counter-ing the weight of anti-orthodox teachings.

THE SPIRITUALITY OF A FULLY DIVINE CHRIST WITHOUT A HUMAN BODY BEFORE THE INCARNATION

At this point, Gregory begins to elaborate on the main tenets of Apollinarianism. As far as he was concerned, the heresy of Apol-linarius had three fundamental teachings. First, the preexistence of Christ's body in heaven pushes Gregory to a fierce criticism of Apol-linarius's creed.[18] It is interesting to note that Gregory's critique is a mixture of Orthodox affirmations and Apollinarius's ideas. Thus, in order to criticize Apollinarius's belief in Christ's preexistent body in heaven, Gregory writes that, as far as Orthodoxy is concerned, the body of Christ was assumed by the Lord in order to reshape our nature, but this reality happened within our created history. Apolli-narius, however, believed that the body of Christ, or the flesh of the Only-begotten Son (to use Gregory's words), which was assumed by our Lord for the remodeling of our human nature, is not a new reality for the existence of the divine Logos, in the sense that the divine, body-less Logos accepted a human body in order to shape again the very nature of all human bodies.[19] For Apollinarius, the concept of body, or the human body, is intrinsically linked to the everlasting existence of the divine Logos. In other words, the body, or the carnal nature, was in the Logos from the very beginning, from eternity to eternity. For Gregory, the teaching of the eternity of the body with reference to the divine Logos is nothing but a "mon-strous assertion" that, even if he does not say it at this particular point, represents the total failure to understand the inner reality of God's own nature. Gregory knows that the imposition of the idea of a preexistent body within the Godhead is a misrepresentation of God's own trinitarian being as well as of our own creation and salva-tion. Regardless of the paramount importance of the human body for Christ's incarnation but also for our salvation, the body cannot coexist with the divine Logos prior to the incarnation because the distinction between our creatureliness and God's uncreated exis-tence would be blurred. At the same time, and also as a consequence of this, the reality of original sin, which virtually destroyed the cre-ated human body to the point that it needed a thorough reshap-ing, is rendered useless. The very idea of creation, with reference to human beings, becomes equally useless if one accepts that the reality of the body is preexistent to our own history. Gregory was fully aware that it was either that creation needed a radical reassessment or that the being of God had to be rethought should Apollinarius be right in his conviction that the body of Christ was part of the Holy Trinity before the incarnation.[20]

Gregory also identifies two biblical texts used by Apollinarius to back his belief in the preexistence of Christ's body before incarnation. The first text is John 3:13, which reads that "no man hath ascended up to heaven, but he that came down from heaven, even the Son of man which is in heaven" (KJV), and the second is 1 Corinthians 15:47: "The first man is of the earth, earthy; the second man is the Lord from heaven" (KJV).[21] As far as Gregory is concerned, Apollinarius is wrong in asserting Christ's preexistent body because the phrase "the Son of man which is in heaven" does not mean that "man . . . is in heaven" before "no man . . . ascended up to heaven."[22] In other words, it does not mean that Christ had a body like that of any other man before the moment he began his ministry on earth. The Bible's affirmation that "the Son of man which is in heaven" is, for Gregory, a reference to Christ's eternal capacity of being the "Son of man," or the one who has always been appointed to carry out the salvation of humanity. Thus, the "Son of man" is a title rather than a designation of his inner nature. Moreover, it is clear in Gregory's mind, the biblical text that reads "no man hath ascended up to heaven, but he that came down from heaven" does not refer to a temporal sequence in the sense that "no man hath ascended up to heaven" but then there was a man "that came down from heaven." Actually, and it is here that Apollinarius got things wrong, the "he" from "he that came down from heaven" does not need to refer to a "man" or to a "bodily man" just to complete, somehow logically, the previous phrase "no man hath ascended up to heaven."[23] So the reference to the "man" in the first part of the verse does not necessarily imply a second reference to another "man"; the "he" in the second part of the verse could well be an indication of Christ, who bears the title "Son of man" in order not to present his inner nature but rather to disclose the nature of his salvific work. Gregory understood that juxtaposition of the idea of the body and the reality of Christ's preexistence as divine Logos was utterly false because the uncreated nature of God could not have been joined to the created nature of man from eternity. The same is true with reference to the way Apollinarius seems to have understood the second text because if the first man is of the earth and the second is the Lord from heaven, it is clear that Apollinarius did not understand the biblical references to the first and the second man as being part of a timeline; on the contrary, it appears that for Apollinarius the two references must be seen as simultaneously valid because there is a man who exists on earth (a reference to created humanity) and another man who exists in heaven (a reference to Christ before his incarnation). Such an understanding of the biblical material raises serious questions about the incarnation itself, and Gregory was not unaware of this. Let alone what the incarnation is in reality and what happened to the divine Logos as he assumed human nature/body within Mary's womb, Gregory seems to be more concerned about the very nature or even the quality of the man about whom Apollinarius said he had been in heaven from the beginning.[24]

It is now that a fifth characteristic of traditional theology arises in Gregory's thought, which is the awareness that Jesus Christ's human nature was not part of his existence before incarnation. Although Jesus Christ is the very same person before and after incarnation, his nonphysical existence before incarnation is distinct from his physical life after incarnation, and traditional theology is always willing to affirm this reality. Despite the obvious difference before his pre-physical existence before history and his physical existence in history, Christ has always been the Logos of God before and after incarnation. The problem with Apollinarius's first error is not primarily the dogmatic flaw itself but the fact that the image of Christ it attempts to provide leads to a spirituality that hails human nature to a point that has never been intended for it. The picture of Christ having a body or a human body from eternity pushes humanity near the very nature of God, in the sense that human nature is part of the God-head. Leaving aside the logical impossibility of such a situation given the uncreated and eternal being of God on the one hand, and the created and historical nature of human existence on the other, the real issue at stake here is the fact that our humanity can be wrongly thought of as being part of the divine nature. Such a perspective could lead to an overrated confidence in our own nature, which in turn leads to a problematic view of our relationship with God. If our bodies or our nature has always been part of God's nature, then the most problematic aspect that immediately results is the reality of sin. It is not an issue of how sin appeared or which are its consequences but the very fact that sin does not matter any longer, at least not to its full extent. If our nature has been with God and in God since the beginning, we can be confident that our innermost constitution has divine attributes. In other words, we can function as human beings in a way that can be defined as divine. Then we can fully rely on our minds as well as on our actions because what we are is ultimately and closely connected to the very being of God. We should no longer trust God for guidance but rather our own intellect, our own will, and our own feelings. This also means that the person and the work of the Holy Spirit of God are presented as having no use for us because if we can fully trust our own nature, there is no need for us to believe and rely on the daily guidance of God through the Spirit.

The last but certainly not the least of the problems caused by Apollinarius's teachings is related to the fact that, as we no longer need to place our entire trust in God, God himself becomes more and more distant from us despite the claim that our nature is part of God's nature. That may be the case for Apollinarius, but as we live in history and God is nowhere to be seen (plus the fact that the guidance as well as the assurance brought in our lives by the Holy Spirit is no longer a necessity), the odd result is a growing distance between ourselves and God. We no longer need God for anything because our own nature, which has been with God forever in the preexistent body of Christ, is sufficient for whatever we will, think, feel, and eventually do in our lives. Thus, our lives are guided based on a spirituality that no longer focuses on Christ but rather on ourselves. In this way Christ becomes an image of humanity, a symbol of what we are, and a model for what we need to do. In Apollinarius, the true spirituality of Christ is turned into an anthropological spirituality that is heavily influenced by what man thinks of himself. Therefore, man builds an image of himself that is far greater than the Bible allows for because Christ is perceived in terms that mix divine nature and human nature to the point of their total confusion. Gregory was aware of this, so the next step for him was to tackle the issue of the nature of the man/human nature, which has been, according to Apollinarius, with Christ from the beginning.

THE SPIRITUALITY OF A FULLY DIVINE CHRIST WITH A HUMAN MIND AFTER THE INCARNATION

This is how Gregory comes to the second teaching of Apollinarius, namely, the mindless body of the man in heaven.[25] As it turns out, it is not exactly a man about whom Apollinarius says he is in heaven, but rather a body that somehow shares a very close connection with the divine nature. Gregory writes that, in Apollinarius, there is a man who came down from above in order to enter our historicity. As if this were not enough of a dogmatic problem, Gregory underlines that Apollinarius works with the rather peculiar assumption that this man does not have a mind of his own.[26] What he has, as some sort of a replacement for his mind or his human mind, is the divinity of Christ. So it is the divinity of Christ or, to use Gregory's rendering, the "Godhead of the Only-begotten," that works as the mind of the man in heaven.[27] This creates a serious problem for Gregory because, according to his dual anthropology, man's constitution is made up by the body and the soul, but it appears that the divinity of Christ is the third aspect of man's being. The problem gets bigger as, according to Gregory, in Apollinarius the image of Christ before incarnation incorporates a body, a soul, and his own divinity but without the human mind, which is replaced by "God the Word."[28] So it is as if Apollinarius believed in a human carcass, in the sense of a physical body, which has a mindless soul. This is a real issue for Gregory because this not only impairs the divinity of Christ, which is pictured as stuck to humanity from the very start, but also seriously damages man's actual constitution as a human being. Consequently, Apollinarius got it wrong twice: first by crayoning a flawed divinity for Christ and second by presenting us with a partial humanity for the same Christ. It is as if Christ were seen as a seriously handicapped divinity in both his divinity and his humanity.[29]

Gregory does not elaborate on this dogmatic error at this point, but his analysis presents us with a sixth feature of traditional theology, which is the realization that Jesus Christ's divinity and humanity must be correctly linked to his prephysical existence before incarnation and his physical life after incarnation. This is why traditional theology will always oppose any image of Christ that distorts Christ's divinity, humanity, or both. The reason for such criticism is that a deficient presentation of Christ cannot produce a healthy spirituality within churches, so this is why they suffer greatly, as Gregory is very keen to underline. This portrait of a crippled divinity cannot lead to trust when it comes to man's salvation; on the contrary, it can have the reverse effect on people. Such a deity is not worthy of respect, let alone trust; neither God nor man, this theological "product" gives rise to pity and mistrust because it seems totally unable to handle the problems of humanity. If he does not have a human mind, he cannot sympathize with us, and if he does not have a full-fledged divine nature, he cannot solve our problems since he is only a little above us. It may be true that some people would prefer such a God because he can neither command nor help us. This leaves humanity itself and the world in its entirety to the discretion of human individuals, who feel powerful enough to act fearlessly because there is no higher justice to react against them. In others, however, the image of such a deity will never trigger any feelings of awe, respect, or reverence. At the end of the day, it cannot yield such emotions because he is himself totally incapable of them. The divinity of such a Christ can of course understand the notion of human feelings as well as grasp the full extent of man's daily problems, but without a human mind there seems almost nothing he can practically do for them, at least not in the real sense of the word, which involves the full participation of such a God in the reality of man's actual existence. A divine-human God without a human mind is of no use to a people who have a human mind and cannot lead their lives without making use of it. As damaged as it is by sin, the human mind needs to be recuperated by a God who has a human mind, and Gregory knows this very well. The churches seem to suffer because the people in them who accepted this distorted image of Christ probably found themselves in the very difficult position of having placed their trust in a God who is totally incapable of understanding them or their trust. Moreover, a God without a human mind is a terrifying construct because there cannot be a true reciprocal participation between divinity and humanity within such a being. The human mind is human awareness, and there is no logical reason why a divine mind should take the place of a human mind, given that the human body has always been with the divine nature itself. Why should the body be better than the mind? This is only one question that could cast a serious degree of doubt over Apollinarius's distorted image of the Son of man.

THE SPIRITUALITY OF A FULLY DIVINE CHRIST SEEN AS SOVEREIGN GOD

The third error made by Apollinarius, which for Gregory is "the most terrible of all," has to do with an issue that represents the coronation of his previous two mistakes. Thus, following his conviction that Christ, God's Logos, has had a body as part of his inner divine nature from the very beginning or from a time prior to the incarnation, as well as his belief in the fact that this particular body was without a mind, Apollinarius reaches the somehow logical conclusion that Christ, which evidently includes his divinity, is mortal.[30] As is quite clear in the way Gregory formulates his critique, he is absolutely bewildered by this last of Apollinarius's convictions but before presenting the error in itself, he takes time to present an image of Christ that, from the very start, is totally opposed to that of Apollinarius. Consequently, for Gregory, Christ is seen in a way that presents his absolute sovereignty over everything related to the fundamentals of human existence. This is why, in Gregory's majestic presentation, Christ appears as *the* God who presides over the furthest-reaching realities of man's life. Actually, Gregory makes use of three major phrases to present us with a victorious image of Christ.[31]

First, Gregory sees Christ as the Only-begotten God.[32] So far, when dealing with Apollinarius's first and second errors, he used only the phrases "Only-begotten Son" and "Only-begotten." Now, however, lest any misunderstanding should creep in, he writes that the Only-begotten Son and the Only-begotten who is in heaven are actually one and the same person, namely, the Only-begotten God.[33] Gregory knows that it is now time to present Christ in colors that leave no doubt about his divinity, so he makes it clear that the Son, the Only-begotten Son of God, is without any doubt whatsoever true God. It is now that one can fully understand that Gregory had an accurate perception of why Apollinarius's presentation of Christ as a human divinity or even as a crippled divine-human kind of God can indeed cause a great deal of suffering within the church. Apollinarius's Christ was not God in the true sense of the word; his deity could be neither trusted nor relied upon for anything at all. All those who placed their trust in such a deity would eventually end up in spiritual failure. Christ must not be seen as a superior kind of man with divinelike attributes, nor must he be presented as a God who is not in fact a full-fledged God; in order to be fully trusted, Christ must be presented as God, the true God, and this is exactly what Gregory had in mind when, in addition to his previous phrases, the Only-begotten Son and the Only-begotten, he eventually captured in a few plain words the very nature of Christ as God. Christ is the Only-begotten God; in other words, he is God and for that reason he can be fully trusted in all respects. This is the correct image of Christ, which builds in us a spirituality that does not end in spiritual suffering but in a life fully characterized by trust and confidence in Christ. Without a Christ who is God, true God, human beings tend to either distance themselves from a God who cannot understand them or focus on their own faculties and capacities, which they trust to be divine. This is why it is only the spirituality of Christ that leads humanity to the true God who sent Christ, also true God of true God, to enrich our lives. This reality leads to the awareness that there is a God above us whom we all must acknowledge as our final authority in all matters pertaining to life. There is someone above us to whom we owe respect and obedience.[34]

Second, in line with his presentation of Christ as God, Gregory depicts the Son of God as the "Judge of all."[35] It is clear that for

Gregory only God can be the judge of all human beings, so this characterization of Christ actually strengthens the first. This image of Christ is utterly crucial for humanity because it directly informs our spirituality as well as our way of life. The very essence of Christian ethics is encapsulated in the image of Christ as the Judge of all.[36] We must be painfully but also happily aware that the possibility of true justice does exist for us. It does not lie within this world or with the authorities of this world; it is in Christ and Christ will eventually impart true justice to everyone. We must all lead lives that do justice to this image of Christ because we are now allowed to behave or even believe as we please but only as it is just to behave and believe: we must all behave in full belief that Christ, our God, will judge us as well as everyone else in accordance with his full divine justice. This conviction must always be part of our inner spirituality as a constant proof that this God, Christ himself, really exists.[37]

Third, Christ is presented by Gregory as the Prince of life, but his image goes hand in hand with his fourth depiction of Christ as the Destroyer of death.[38] Life and death are definitely the essential coordinates of the human existence, and Gregory wants to make sure that Christ is above them in the sense that there is nothing within the created realm of humanity that escapes his sovereign rule.[39] Concerning our life, Christ is the Prince, the one who rules over it, owns it, and keeps it. Concerning our death, Christ is the Destroyer, the only one who can make it go away.[40] This is how Gregory pictures Christ as the Lord of life, the God who wants the best for us not only by ruling over our lives but also by putting an end to death, so that our existence may continue with a life totally surrendered to God.[41] This is the essence of Christian spirituality, namely, the conviction that Christ is God, the God who can both keep and save our lives from the impending death caused by sin. It should be highlighted here that, even if he does not say anything about sin in this letter, Gregory's entire manner of writing, as well as his choice of presenting Christ as God, confirms his deep awareness of human sin. Man's life is so permeated by sin that the only way to genuine life, the only way to true spirituality is belief in Christ as the God who judges us, keeps us, and saves us.

To sum up—and this is the seventh feature of traditional theology as elaborated by Gregory—Christ is fully divine, which means that he is fully God and fully man at the same time. Traditional theology confesses the complete divinity and humanity of Christ by presenting him as the Only-begotten God, then as the Son of God who has dominion over everything—it is here that the image of the judge plays a crucial role—and finally as the only being that can handle life and death as he pleases. This threefold Christological imagery is a confirmation of Christ's existence before incarnation, then of his ministry and death after incarnation, and finally of his resurrection and ascension to heaven. Traditional theology is based on this "cycle" of Christ's existence: metaphysical before his incarnation in history, physical in history, and metaphysical again—but with a human resurrected body—after his ascension.

PRACTICAL ADVICE TO NECTARIUS FOR THE SAKE OF HEALTHY CHRISTIAN SPIRITUALITY

Having exposed the three main errors of Apollinarianism, Gregory explains that there is no need to press forward with other dogmatic mistakes. These three should suffice for a concise presentation of the peril they represent for the churches. This is why, toward the end of his letter, Gregory takes a little time for some personal as well as practical advice to Nectarius.[42] Gregory's advice discloses his concern for the churches but also his desire to have the teachings of Apollinarius driven out of the churches. Thus, he tells Nectarius that what he needs to do is prevent the Apollinarians from gathering and teaching. In other words, he quite abruptly suggests that Nectarius should do two main things: first, cancel the Apollinarians' right to assemble as churches, and second, cancel their permission to teach their views within churches.[43] If these two actions are not taken, Gregory warns that two opposite realities may emerge: first, if the Apollinarians' right to meet as churches is not canceled, people will eventually understand that their erroneous teachings are more important than the Orthodox doctrines of the church, and second, if their permission to teach in churches is not dealt with, people will reach the conclusion that the Orthodox teachings of the church are in fact the ones that should be condemned.[44]

In order to make things clear, Gregory resorts to the natural principle that cannot allow for two opposite affirmations to be true at the same time. With reference to the teachings of Apollinarius, the hint is more than evident. It is impossible that their errors and the Orthodox teachings of the church should be true at the same time. This is why prompt action should be enforced with respect to the cancellation of their right to hold ecclesiastical meetings, as well as to the annulling of their permission to disseminate their teachings. Gregory is convinced that the Apollinarians' dogmatic errors are actually a great evil that must be corrected, so he urges Nectarius to act accordingly using his authority as bishop of Constantinople. It is evident that Gregory would like Nectarius to take action immediately, but he also realizes the implementation of such actions against the Apollinarians could cause unrest in some higher quarters beyond the realm of the churches and into that of imperial politics. Gregory seems to be painfully aware that it may be the case that the bishop himself could not act on his own against the Apollinarians, so he advises him to seek the emperor's help.[45] It must be underlined here that Gregory's suggestion that Nectarius should ask for the emperor's help is not put bluntly. What he does in fact is advise Nectarius to "teach" the emperor[46] that there is no profitable end to the permission given to the Apollinarians to disseminate their doctrines and hold their meetings.[47]

At this point—which brings us to the eighth characteristic of traditional theology—Gregory reaches a very delicate issue, namely, that of freedom of speech and its relationship with faith.[48] Is freedom of speech more important than the faith of the church?[49] To Gregory—as well as to traditional theology in general—the answer is clear and it is negative. Thus, in traditional theology there is nothing more important than the soundness of the church's faith because the church's faith is in fact the faith of each Christian believer. In addition to this, the faith of each Christian believer reflects his or her spirituality, which in the true church is the spirituality of Christ. Although he does not elaborate on this, it seems that for Gregory freedom of speech is a reality that does not apply to the church in the sense the world understands it. This is because the church is not free to say whatever she wants, and this is also true for Christians. We are not allowed, we are not free to say everything we want in churches. What we must say in churches is exclusively the words of the Gospel, which present Christ in the correct, biblical way. Going to church is definitely not compulsory, but confessing Christ in full accordance with his image as pictured in the Bible is. This is why traditional theology will always value the correct preaching of Christ for the edification of the believers' faith over the more or less politically correct freedom of speech.

This is the reason why, in the fourth century, Gregory insists that the Apollinarians had no right to teach in churches, because their doctrines about Christ were wrong. What they teach in churches is dogmatically erroneous and spiritually defective, so their tenets do nothing but cause suffering to the church as well as to individual Christians. This is why Gregory has no qualms of conscience when he advises Nectarius and, through him, the emperor himself, that firm action against the Apollinarians means in fact putting an end to the suffering of the church.[50] At the same time, Gregory seems convinced that the cancellation of the Apollinarians' right to teach and hold meetings is nothing but the result of well-informed Christian spirituality, which cannot be other than that of Christ seen as sovereign God over the entire creation—a confession that traditional theology has resolutely professed ever since.

CHAPTER 2

TRADITIONAL CHRISTIAN
THOUGHT IN EARLY MODERNITY

JOHN CALVIN AND ECCLESIASTICAL
DISCIPLINE IN THE SIXTEENTH CENTURY

INTRODUCTION

Although the Protestant Reformation sought to turn to the church of antiquity as the desired ecclesiological and theological model for the newly established Protestant communities, the vital issues of patristic theology as reflected in Gregory Nazianzen and his Christological focus were no longer a problem in the sixteenth century. The doctrine of God as Trinity and the key aspects of Jesus Christ's hypostatic union had been long established despite the constant claims of antitrinitarians and unitarians embodied, for instance, by the works of Michael Servetus. The very problem that bothered the Reformation was not Christology but rather ecclesiology. Everyone knew who Jesus Christ was, but not everybody was convinced about how he should be followed. The question of following Christ by attending the ancient Catholic church or by joining the new Protestant communities proved to be an issue needing a great deal of theological reflection. In addition to this, it was not enough to join either of the two main denominations; what really counted was how believers ought to behave in the churches they eventually decided to attend. This is why the doctrine of the church and the teaching of ecclesiastical discipline became a key aspect of Protestant theology in the sixteenth century and, at the same time, another classical example of traditional Christianity. It should be pointed out that Jean Calvin

(1509–64) presents ecclesiastical discipline as a necessity for the life of the church, as well as a feature of normality for all believers. Discipline should be applied on a regular basis for the benefit of believers in order to counter the natural human tendency to oppose correction. At the same time, discipline is presented as closely interwoven with doctrine, which is the essence of church order. The church must have a right state, which is defined according to the correct preaching of doctrine and is enabled by the application of discipline. Admonition and even excommunication are part of the structure of ecclesiastical discipline, but the most important aspect of discipline is its doctrinal core. Maintaining church discipline is not primarily a matter of rebuking sinful believers but rather of disseminating the right kind of doctrine in the church. Doctrine is therefore important for discipline not because it encapsulates a set of biblical truths but because it points to Christ as the Lord of the church as well as of all believers. Private and public discipline must be applied in accordance with the nature of the sins committed, which are essentially private and public, with the ultimate goal of restoring the life of the sinful so they follow Christ's teaching as exposed in Scripture.

DISCIPLINE AND ITS MAIN CHARACTERISTICS

A quick glance at Calvin's presentation of ecclesiastical discipline reveals the fact that order in the church is a requirement for the normality of spiritual life.[1] As order is a prerequisite of what our spiritual existence should be, it follows that the means whereby order is preserved become equally necessary.[2] It is now that Calvin's discussion of church discipline comes at issue with one of its primary characteristics, namely, that its compulsoriness is a reality that goes unquestioned. In other words, church discipline is absolutely compulsory because it is the very core of ecclesiastical life. The life of the church goes on as it unfolds through the individual lives of its members, but it is because of these very lives of believers that the enforcement as well as the application of church discipline becomes so important.[3] So the first characteristic of ecclesiastical discipline is its compulsory character.[4] Church discipline is a must, and there is no doubt about it should we want the church to lead a normal life from the standpoint of its spiritual quality.[5] It follows that every member of the church must know that discipline is a constant feature of the life of the church, which also means that it must become an equally constant characteristic of the member's own life.[6]

At this point, the first feature of traditional theology as presented in Calvin's thought is revealed. Thus, traditional theology is always alert when the idea of discipline and especially the necessity of its application are seen as abnormalities or even absurdities. Contemporary society, for instance, teaches us that we can do whatever we want for as long as we feel we are doing the right thing, so any limitations of our actions based on our own experience can only produce irritability and suspicion. Today's theology is no longer based on Scripture, as it was in Calvin's case, but on what we feel and experience; it is no wonder discipline is not an enjoyable issue. Calvin's doctrine—a true, genuine sample of traditional theology—teaches us that we need to come to terms with the normality of the church's life, which includes the idea of discipline. For traditional theology, a church without discipline is abnormal and absurd because it meets all sorts of criteria but it functions far from properly.

Having briefly presented the necessity of church discipline for the normality of ecclesiastical life, Calvin introduces a second feature of church discipline. Church discipline is indeed compulsory, but its compulsoriness must be applied to all the members of the church. At this point, Calvin explains how he sees the church from the perspective of its inner constitution with reference to its members. Within the church, there are two main categories of members: first, the clergy,[7] and second, the people.[8] Calvin realizes almost instantly that the word "clergy" may cause unease or even trouble for some more delicate ears; this is why he underlines that the word "clergy" is used only to highlight a point. Thus, although the word "clergy" itself is improper, he nevertheless decided to use it in order to point to those members of the church who have a church office and perform a public church ministry. The differentiation between clergy and laity in Calvin is not given by the spiritual nature of Christian ministry, because all Christians must work for the Gospel. It is, however, necessary to introduce two distinct categories of ministry, one of the clergy and one of the laity, especially due to the public nature of the former while the latter tends to be more restricted to one's individuality. This is why Calvin speaks of the clergy and the laity as different with respect to the public nature of the work of the clergy, and—given this distinction—a differentiation should also be introduced with reference to the types of ecclesiastical discipline.[9]

This presents us with the third characteristic of church discipline. After pointedly describing ecclesiastical discipline as, first, compulsory for the life of the church and, second, necessary for all members of the church, Calvin brings forward the third aspect of discipline, which pictures discipline as having a dual specificity. This means that, while compulsory for the church in its general membership and necessary for every individual believer, ecclesiastical discipline must be applied specifically to clergy and laity. In other words, church discipline should be exercised not only individually with reference to all the members of the church as individual persons but also specifically when it comes to the restoration of a certain member of the clergy. Calvin is convinced that the dichotomy of church discipline, which says there is a common discipline for all believers and a peculiar discipline for the clergy, is nothing but a sign of normality, even with reference to the world. Thus, he explains that discipline cannot be understood without comprehending the very nature of society. It is crucial to see that society in general—but also smaller components of society, such as the family—functions within a certain degree of normality, which Calvin describes by means of the notion of "right state."[10] The right state, however, can be easily disturbed so the balance of society or family is no longer there to make sure that the preservation of normality remains the norm for the regular life of society or family. When that happens and the right state is endangered, the need for discipline becomes more than merely evident. It is equally evident that Calvin makes a clear comparison between the family and the church; the church is presented as a family because if the right state of the family is restored by discipline, the same must happen in the church as embodiment of a better order. The family needs order and so does the church as both represent different degrees of order. The church, though, is, for Calvin, the encapsulation of the highest degree of order, so the necessity that discipline be enforced and applied within it becomes an obvious reality.[11]

This is actually the second characteristic of traditional theology as disclosed by Calvin's teaching. While it acknowledges the necessity of church discipline, traditional theology does not stop here. Mere acknowledgment is nothing without the practical implementation of ecclesiastical discipline, so traditional theology not only recognizes the necessity of church discipline but also acts toward its application in the daily life of the church. Today's church should come to terms with the reality of its own existence, which should be different from that of unchurched society. We tend no longer to see the church as separated from the world though still living in the world. The norm of today's people is anything but God, so the only other possibility is to guide one's life according to our human precepts. Contemporary society is highly experiential in the sense that human experience sets the ultimate standard for conduct, so anything that is not endorsed by human experience or anything that does not follow the urges of human experience should be dismissed as old and ineffective. This is why the frontier between the church and society gets increasingly blurred, so that there is no longer an acute awareness of what the church really is as compared to society or the world. The principles of the world invade the church, while the church succumbs to them without even trying to provide the feeblest opposition. While both society and the church should be guided by order—and in this they look similar—traditional theology teaches that the church is nevertheless different because, even as compared to society, it embodies a degree of order that is higher than what society has to offer. In traditional theology, a minimum degree of order is absolutely necessary in everything—and society makes no exception to this rule—so this is an extra reason for the church to strengthen its own life with the order provided by discipline.

DISCIPLINE AND THE GOSPEL OF CHRIST

Calvin knows for a fact that his defense of church discipline as necessary as well as beneficial for the life of the Christian community comes from nature, so the presentation of the "right state" of the church based on the argument of order needs to be supplemented by an explanation that also provides us with spiritual insight.[12] The interweaving between natural and spiritual elements in presenting ecclesiastical discipline is a *sine qua non* because nature itself can only provide limited arguments. Calvin is aware that some people manifest aversion toward discipline, so the natural explanation of why discipline is necessary will not appeal to them. Consequently, the spiritual reasoning behind supporting church discipline must go beyond what is naturally logical or beneficial into what is spiritually compulsory. In other words, church discipline cannot be properly explained without reference to the teachings of the church, in fact the very teaching or doctrine of Jesus Christ, the Lord of the church, which is actually his Gospel.[13]

This is where the third feature of traditional theology as taught by Calvin is seen plainly because, in traditional theology, ecclesiastical discipline is nothing without doctrine. Furthermore, it has no value whatsoever unless supported by the teachings of Jesus Christ. Our biggest problem today is the waning of Christ's importance both in the church and in the lives of ordinary believers. Christ is no longer seen as the Lord of the church, the risen and living God who constantly supports the church as it goes through history. Christ is present as a mere man, who is dead, and only his teachings bear a certain degree of relevance for the church, but they can also be interpreted in such a way that they fit our contemporary expectations. The immediate consequence is that discipline, which is based on and explained by doctrine, is not worth applying any longer. On the other hand, Calvin's teaching—and traditional theology for that matter—tell us to stick to the purity of doctrine as preached by Jesus Christ, the only source of benefit for all believers.

By making reference to Christ in connection with ecclesiastical discipline, Calvin puts together Christology and ecclesiology in his attempt to draft the spiritual aspects of his perspective on church discipline. The normality of the church or, more exactly, the normality of the everyday life of the church is totally dependent on Christ and especially on the doctrine of Christ.[14] Calvin shows no signs of doubt when he writes that the doctrine of Christ is the very life of the church, which means that the morrow of the church's life is in fact Christ himself.[15] There is no church without Christ, and there is no life of the church without the teaching of Christ. The church cannot exist apart from Christ, and it is equally true that the vitality of the church has nothing to do with teachings that exclude Christ. A healthy church is always closely tied to Christ and his teaching, as Calvin poignantly shows in his presentation of church discipline. Having established that the very life of the church has to do with the doctrine of Christ, Calvin moves forward in making it clear that the discipline of the church is just as important as the doctrine of Christ because it provides the church with the very means to support its life, which is Christian life in general.[16] This is why he writes that while the teaching of Christ is the life of the church, ecclesiastical discipline is the power of the church or the reality whereby the church can find the power to exist.[17] Calvin explains why ecclesiastical discipline supports the life of the church by saying that the various members of the church, or ordinary believers, can stay together in the body of the church and can also function properly as part of the same organism due to the fact that church discipline can hold them together. The lack of ecclesiastical discipline leads to the disintegration of the church, and Calvin knows this a tough lesson to learn. He is aware that opposition to the enforcement or reinstatement of ecclesiastical discipline is sadly a reality within the church;[18] this is why he warns that actions such as these can only lead to what he calls the total destruction of the church.[19]

Calvin's underlining of the person of Christ in connection with the doctrine of ecclesiastical discipline shows the fourth characteristic of traditional theology, namely, the compulsory link between discipline and Christ. No one can correctly apply church discipline in the life of the Christian community without reference to Christ, to his person, work, and teachings; any attempt to have a disciplined church will be just another human endeavor to enforce order in a community that is not merely human but also divine. Traditional theology, however, is convinced that Christ is the head of the church, so the church must follow his rule no matter what. This is why, when problems occur, the solution should come from the head, not from those who caused the problems. It is only logical—let alone that it is also spiritual—to act in accordance with the teachings of Christ, the head of the church, whenever an attempt is made for the application of discipline within the church. So in traditional theology, discipline comes from "above," namely, from the teachings of Christ, and its purpose is to help believers always keep their eyes on Christ.

Calvin seems to have lived in a society that bore a great resemblance to ours. Church discipline has never been eagerly accepted, let alone applied, because it works against the most fundamental instincts of the human nature. Man does not like to be rebuked or corrected, but it is exactly rebuke and correction that ecclesiastical discipline is meant to instill within the members of the *ecclesia*. What we have to understand from Calvin's doctrine—and this is the fifth characteristic of traditional theology according to his works—is that a church without discipline is a church without life, which is on the path to disintegration. At the same time, for traditional theology opposition to discipline is a permanent attitude in and outside the church, so the application of discipline has never been, is not, and shall never be an easy task.

It is at this point that the necessity of ecclesiastical discipline acquires a new facet. Discipline is a must in the church because the church is no man's land, so no matter what we say or do we do not own the church in any way. The church is not our property—let alone our private property—so the way we should behave in the church should be dictated by regulations that are not our own. Believers may not behave in churches as they please because no one is allowed to do in the church whatever he or she wants. In the church we must do only what we are required to do. Should anyone have any sort of doubts concerning what should be done in the church, Calvin plainly states that it is the preaching of the Gospel that must occupy the believers' minds and actions.[20] The preaching of the Gospel, however, cannot be done smoothly because believers are human and humanity means trouble. It is for this reason that

Calvin adds a compact list of actions that should accompany the preaching of the Gospel.[21] The list includes private admonition and correction as methods devised to maintain doctrine.[22] It is crucial to notice here that, in Calvin, private admonition and correction are not meant to preserve church discipline but church doctrine. This is quite illuminating because it reveals Calvin's perspective on the relationship between doctrine and discipline, namely, that discipline is maintained provided doctrine is kept pure. In other words, if doctrine is preserved correctly, then the church will be characterized by discipline; if doctrine is twisted, it is clear that disaster shall eventually strike the church. To be sure, if we want to have discipline in the church, some actions must be taken extremely seriously: first, preach the Gospel correctly, then give private admonition and correction with view to the preservation of correct doctrine. When these actions become a reality in the daily life of the church, discipline should not be counted among the problems of the church.[23]

If we have second thoughts about the necessity of discipline or we fear what might happen if and when we enforce it, we should probably be concerned with a totally different aspect, namely, the necessity to preach the Gospel correctly, which is the sixth feature of traditional theology based on Calvin's teaching. The first step toward discipline is surprisingly not rebuke or correction, but the preaching of the Gospel. The Gospel, however, must be preached correctly, and in today's world this presents us with the challenge to preach the Gospel in such a way that it becomes an ongoing preoccupation for all believers. When people in the church do anything but listen to the Gospel, then we have a case that requires church discipline. Therefore, according to traditional theology, the very first step toward the application of discipline is making sure that the Gospel is properly preached before admonition and correction are practically administered to believers.

Calvin seems utterly convinced that the key to ecclesiastical discipline is correct doctrine because private admonition and correction must be performed lest doctrine become lethargic. Lethargic doctrine spells trouble and dissipates order, so we must keep the doctrine full of life in order to have a church that lives in accordance with spiritual discipline. It is clear therefore that, in Calvin, the connection between doctrine and discipline is unbreakable, but this relationship becomes even clearer when he points out that discipline is a way to stop those who fight against the doctrine of Christ.[24] So it works both ways: from doctrine to discipline, in the sense that the preaching of correct doctrine should lead to discipline, but also from discipline to doctrine, if the preaching of correct doctrine is jeopardized in the church. In case the latter situation unfolds, Calvin finds a threefold function of church discipline: first, discipline is a means to stop false doctrine;[25] second, discipline is a method to stop indifference;[26] and third, discipline is a way to stop disobedience.[27] Calvin's threefold function of ecclesiastical discipline actually discloses three types of church members: first, those who fight against the correct preaching of the Gospel; second, those who are totally indifferent when it comes to the correctness of the preaching of the Gospel; and third, those who committed grave sins because of their dismissal of the correct preaching of the Gospel. In each case, however, doctrine is interwoven with discipline, and there is no way to separate the two realities of the church's daily life.[28]

DISCIPLINE AND THE LIFE OF THE CHURCH

The life of the church is the life of its members; to be more precise, it is the sum of the individual lives of all believers. Calvin does not lose sight of the fact that believers are human beings and human beings need to be managed. Church discipline presents itself as a necessity especially because believers are human beings in need of careful management. Calvin resorts to the situation of his own days when he notices that the church then experienced serious plight concerning the way people behaved and led their lives as part of the ecclesiastical body. Thus, Calvin points out that the church is at the brink of disaster, and this situation can be easily noticed because people management is deficient. Although he does not offer a detailed presentation of what he means by people management, Calvin nevertheless highlights two aspects that should characterize the life of the church but that were absent from the church of his time, as he himself notes. According to Calvin, people management in the church is faulty when care—meaning pastoral care[29]—and methodology—more likely a reference to the application of pastoral care[30]—seem to be among the aspects that no longer feature in the normality of the church's life. In other words, when pastoral care and the practice thereof are not part of the church's daily existence, the church finds itself in a serious situation that requires immediate action for a proper remedy. It is clear for Calvin that pastoral care and the application of pastoral care are closely connected to sound doctrine, and it is equally significant to understand—based on his previous explanation—that sound doctrine leads to pastoral care as well as to its application in the church. Likewise, when doctrine is no longer preached in a sound manner, the immediate consequence is the disparagement of pastoral care, which is no longer applied in the church, with consequences that throw the church into a whirl of problems requiring the application of ecclesiastical discipline. When pastoral care and its application in the church are lacking in the church's life, it indicates doctrine is also damaged, so the situation of the church is characterized by the *necessity* that discipline be enforced. Even though Calvin does not use this wording, it can be said that such a situation in the church is conspicuous because "necessity itself cries aloud that there is need of a remedy."[31]

The remedy envisioned by Calvin is ecclesiastical discipline and its application in the church. To be sure, discipline and its application in the church are totally tied to pastoral care and its application in the church. This means that the very essence of pastoral care is ecclesiastical discipline, while the application of pastoral care cannot be done without the application of ecclesiastical discipline. Resuming the distinction between clergy and laity, it can be argued based on Calvin's position so far that clergy can show they are concerned about the spiritual welfare of the laity only when they manifest and apply pastoral care. This inevitably means that the clergy's interest in laity can never exclude ecclesiastical discipline and its application in the church.[32] In other words, the constant spiritual as well as ecclesiastical relationship between the ministers of the church and the body of believers will always be characterized by discipline and its application. Consequently, the logical conclusion—which Calvin does not explicitly draw—is that the normality of the church's life presents the constant characteristic of ecclesiastical discipline. Even if this conclusion is not so clear in Calvin, what is clear indeed has to do with the fact that ecclesiastical discipline needs to be applied in the church. With respect to this issue, Calvin identifies two ways of applying church discipline, which are dependent on the two types of sins that afflict church members. Regardless of the specific manifestation of particular sins, the typology of sins in Calvin is dichotomic. Thus, there are private or secret sins[33] and public or open sins.[34] In plain language, believers can commit sins known only to themselves, or they can commit sins that are known to other people as well.[35]

It is vital to notice here—and this is the seventh feature of traditional theology—that Calvin does not seem surprised at all by the presence of sin among believers in the church. He does not lament the fact that believers sin; he knows that sin is a permanent reality in the believer's life so there is no point in weeping over something inherently part of human nature. What he does criticize in fact—and traditional theology should be doing this constantly—is the lack of counteraction in dealing with sin, or the nonexisting desire to fight against sin.[36] Sin may well be a reality in the church—and this is unfortunately an unpleasant sign of ecclesiastical normality—but the lack of discipline aimed at correcting or restricting sin in the believers' lives should not be a constant reality in the church. In other words, traditional theology teaches us that the reality of sin can and should be accepted in the church—very much like our own human nature, which nurtures sin—but the lack of disciplinary actions taken against sin must never be accepted in the church. So sin is there in every believer and this is why discipline must also be present in the church. The reality of sin points to the reality of discipline or, to use Calvin's reasoning, the fact that sin exists shows the necessity for discipline.[37] According to sound traditional theology, the more we realize sin is a constant trouble in the church, the more we have to understand that church discipline is not an option but a compulsory action that must be applied daily. Believers commit sins every day, and this is the very reason why ecclesiastical discipline must also be a daily preoccupation as part of church ministry.[38]

DISCIPLINE AND ITS APPLICATION IN THE CHURCH

When it comes to the application of church discipline, Calvin differentiates between private discipline, or private admonition,[39] as he calls it, and public discipline, or solemn correction,[40] as he puts it. These two kinds of discipline should be enforced in the church because of the dichotomy of sin's manifestation, which is private, public, or both. Private sins should be dealt with privately and public sins should be corrected publicly. It should be noted here that both private and public discipline must be understood as being the duty of every single Christian believer. Calvin is convinced that all believers must exercise their duty to apply ecclesiastical discipline, both private and public, for the welfare of the church in general as well as the profit of individual Christians. The application of discipline, however, is not an easy job, as Calvin also realizes. This is why he writes that believers "must study" how to admonish their brothers and sisters.[41] So the application of discipline requires discipline, in the sense that it takes quite some time before believers learn how to put discipline into practice. Having explained that the practice of church discipline is the result of diligent study and should be applied indiscriminately by all believers to all believers, Calvin proceeds with a brief description of each kind of discipline.[42]

This is crucially important because our society dislikes the idea of discipline to such a degree that the mere idea of subjecting someone to the "coercion" of discipline seems preposterous, let alone dedicating a certain amount of time to studying how to apply discipline. Reversing this conviction—so dear to contemporary society—is a discipline in itself, but the church has a lot to learn from it. For instance, we must understand that not only does discipline take time, but also learning how to apply it requires a huge chunk of our time resources. This is because discipline involves dealing with people, and dealing with people is anything but easy. Consequently, we must learn what discipline is and how it should be applied according to the typology of sins committed. Calvin is very supportive in this respect because he details the two kinds of discipline and the way they should be put into practice.

Private discipline, which is performed when the sins committed by believers were done without reaching public awareness, requires first of all a high degree of vigilance.[43] All believers must train themselves to be watchful over the spiritual welfare of their brothers and sisters, but the special duty of administering ecclesiastical discipline rests with the ministers of the church, with pastors and presbyters.[44] At this point, Calvin builds on one of his previous arguments, which says that doctrine and discipline are closely connected. As doctrine cannot exist without discipline and vice versa, the duty of the minister is also dichotomic. Thus, in addition to preaching the word of God and disseminating the right doctrine in the church, the minister must also carefully and watchfully apply discipline to all those who deserve it. In order to prove his point, Calvin resorts to Scripture and especially to Acts 20:20, 26, and 27. Although these verses do not refer specifically to the application of church discipline, they nevertheless mention Paul's active preaching of the Gospel for the benefit of all believers, as well as the fact that he taught them both publicly and from house to house, or privately. The verses also show that Paul's preaching discloses God's entire will or plan and, in doing so, he is innocent "of the blood of all men"; in other words, preaching the word of God in its fullness preserves ministers—and all Christians for that matter—from being guilty when it comes to the sins committed by others. It is clear that, in Calvin, preaching and teaching include ecclesiastical discipline and its application; this is why, in his theology, the duty of the minister resides not only in preaching and teaching but also in applying discipline whenever that is required. This proves to be highly important for Calvin because what is at stake here is not only the state of the believer who committed a certain sin but also the reality of the Gospel itself. Calvin is convinced that the Gospel is truly important because it has power and authority. Moreover, the power and authority of the Gospel do not and should not manifest themselves only through preaching and teaching but also through the application of discipline every single time that it is necessary.[45] In other words, the Gospel has power and authority not only in presenting true doctrine but also in correcting the deviation from true doctrine.[46]

Public discipline is not only the necessary measure to be taken against public sins but also the consequence of rejecting private discipline.[47] Calvin uses Scripture again to show that private discipline can turn into public discipline when private admonition is shunned. The reasons for such an option are irrelevant; what matters is the fact that the rebuked believer persists in his fault, which is a sign of disobedience.[48] Thus, based on Matthew 18:15 and 17, Calvin says that what was initially intended as private discipline must become less private. When private discipline no longer works, public discipline must be applied in four distinct stages, if the believer does not give up his resentful attitude. Thus, when private discipline is not enough, the four steps to be taken as part of public discipline stipulate that admonition is performed first before witnesses; second, before the elders or presbyters; third, before the church itself; and fourth, the believer is excluded from the fellowship of the church and he is consequently no longer considered a believer. After he carefully explains what should happen when private discipline turns into public discipline because individual admonition as a result of a private sin did not work, Calvin offers a brief presentation of public discipline as applied for public sins. He turns again to the text of Scripture and he uses two distinct passages: Galatians 2:14 and 1 Timothy 5:20. The first text is used to show what the apostle means by public sin, while the second displays the manner of as well as the reasons for public discipline. Thus, when Peter publicly committed the sin of hypocrisy by siding with Jews to the detriment of Gentiles, Paul corrected Peter's sinful attitude by rebuking him in public, which is the context of the sin itself. Public discipline must be administered in order that all believers should be made aware that sin is not to be taken lightly. The Gospel must be taken seriously not only as teaching but also as living, so any deviation from the right teaching, living, or both as exposed in the Gospel must be corrected privately, publicly, or both, in accordance with the nature of the sin that triggered ecclesiastical discipline. Discipline, however, regardless of whether it is private or public, should not be administered exclusively for the spiritual welfare of the sinful believer but also because it is commanded by Jesus Christ, the Lord of the church.[49] Calvin does not insist on this aspect here, but his doctrine of ecclesiastical discipline cannot be separated from his Christology, which pictures the reality of Christ's presence in the church as permanently indwelling. Christ himself is present in the church, and this is primarily why discipline must be enforced—as a sign of our obedience to the teachings of his Gospel.[50]

Calvin's lesson about discipline is not a course on how to implement ecclesiastical coercion in order to annoy believers at all costs; it is rather an invitation to know Jesus Christ and his church, which is also the essence of traditional theology as well as its eighth characteristic as revealed by Calvin's thought. In traditional theology, discipline is not needed because we have to comply with certain doctrines; discipline is needed because it is the only way to teach us who we really are and how we should behave in and outside the church. Church discipline teaches us that our lives must be sincere, not because certain dogmas tell us so, but because Christ tells us so. We need to follow Christ no matter what, and whenever this attitude gets off the right track discipline is available for correction. This is why church discipline is not something that should be seen as producing opposition to Christ but as a reality that brings us closer to him. But, as traditional theology teaches us, this can happen only in the church, not beyond its borders, which also teaches us that the church is not the world, so the church must not conform itself to the standards of the world. Christianity, Christian spirituality, and Christian life are not compulsory for the world, but neither are the standards of the world for the church. So, if discipline is necessary for Christian life—and it is according to traditional theology—then the world has nothing to say about it. It is only Christ who has anything to say about his church and its discipline, but he has already said what he had to say in Scripture, which is persistently used by Calvin to draft his theology of ecclesiastical discipline.

CHAPTER 3

TRADITIONAL CHRISTIAN
THOUGHT IN POSTMODERNITY

ION BRIA AND PASTORAL ECCLESIOLOGY
IN THE TWENTIETH CENTURY

INTRODUCTION

Historically, the twentieth century can barely be connected to traditional Christianity if one thinks of the dramatic changes produced by Protestant liberalism in the second half of the nineteenth century throughout Western Christianity. As it dawned, the twentieth century seemed an easy prey for theological liberalism, which continued to spread despite the shattering of the liberal conviction that the progress of humanity by science—also applied to theology—would eventually lead to the eradication of war. The ravages of the First World War proved the liberals wrong, but this did not mean the end of the movement. On the contrary, Western Christianity witnessed a resurgence of liberal preoccupations that affected not only Protestant denominations but also the Catholic church as it turned to the Second Vatican Council. Eastern Christianity, however, underwent a significantly different development. Largely affected by Communist propaganda, Eastern Europe found itself politically imprisoned almost immediately following the end of the Second World War. Thus, the churches in Eastern Europe—Protestant, Catholic, and the dominant Eastern Orthodox Church—clung to the traditional values of Christianity in an age of severe political persecution and social penury. This resulted in an increasingly evident preoccupation with the church and its practical life, as can be seen in the works of the reputed Orthodox scholar Ion Bria (1929–2002).

A well-known ecumenist in the West and executive secretary for Orthodox Mission Studies and Relationships for the World Council of Churches in Geneva until his death in 2002, Bria provides us with a series of extremely important issues that affect today's church, and he treats them from a pastoral as well as a missionary perspective. Thus, having briefly presented the reality of today's society, which does not have a thorough knowledge of the essence of Christianity, Bria comes up with some methods and models of mission within the larger context of the church's necessity to evangelize today's society in order to spread the knowledge of Jesus Christ to all human beings. Consequently, he underlines the extraordinary importance of the people's priesthood (the universal or, as he puts it, common priesthood), a reality as well as an evangelical teaching that should mobilize all parishes through a missionary and evangelizing spirit. The involvement of lay people within the pastoral problems of the church can only have a positive outcome, which will eventually shape the future of theology as well as the concrete, historical existence of the church itself. This desire, however, cannot be achieved without the promotion of an earnest morality and discipline among priests who address society in general because it is this society that is practically served by priests as well as by the lay people. Bria concludes his excursus about the problems of today's church with a brief analysis of the concept of political neutrality, which, besides the detachment of the church and its ministers from the official issues of state politics, presents their active involvement within the polis, namely, the fundamental problems (social, economic, cultural, intellectual) of our contemporary society.

Ion Bria develops an ecclesiology that attempts to adapt Orthodox Christianity to the new issues and the acute problems that became an integrant part of the constitution of today's society. He makes constant reference to the new situation of Romania following the dramatic events of December 1989, with the clear intention to educate both the clergy and the laity in connection with the brand-new realities of the post-Communist society. It is within this particular context that he uses—to a very large extent—the concept of the liturgy after the liturgy,[1] which means that the church[2] should continue to pursue its pastoral and missionary endeavors on a regular basis beyond the spiritual services of the church.[3] Bria is very keen to underline that the church's mission to implement the program of the liturgy after the liturgy is thoroughly based on the confession of Christ to the contemporary society.[4] This is why he makes it clear—again with reference to the post-Communist Romanian society, but it can be extended to the entire Western social context—that we are presented with a new situation, which is both utterly complex and different from what we had in the past, a situation that confronts us with new possibilities and critical issues.[5] Bria knows for a fact that the assessment of the new situation cannot be done without a correct understanding of the old society. Regardless, however, of how the old society was and functioned decades ago, it is of paramount importance to realize that the new society must be evaluated correctly by the church. The church should be aware of what happens here and now; it should build an image of the contemporary society in such a way that the church itself should prepare to reach the men and women of today's world. Although Bria does not insist too much on detailing the format of the old society, he nevertheless explains that the difference between the old and the new situation must be sensibly perceived as well as approached by the church. In order for the church to make this assessment, it needs a new vision.[6] The church cannot approach the new society with its complex issues without being fully aware of the need to reorient itself in such a way that it becomes internally fit for such a task. This makes it quite clear why Bria highlights the necessity that the church should not only devise new programs and projects for today's society but also change itself from within. In other words, Bria writes in plain words that in order for the church to be able to address the new and pressing issues of today's society, the church itself has a deep need for reform and renewal.[7] What the church needs today, in Bria's view, is a thorough reformation in order to train itself for the new task of addressing contemporary society.[8]

As peculiar as it may sound, Bria's call for a reformation of the Orthodox church's perspective on its own theology and development gives us the first feature of traditional theology as it surfaces from his works: while constantly aware of the rectitude of its doctrinal tradition, traditional theology must be open to contemporary realities in order to be able to address the issues that trouble the people living in a certain historical context. In doing so, traditional theology must be permanently willing to reform itself in order to face the challenges of contemporary times. So a distinguishing property of traditional theology is its disposition toward reformation in all respects for as long as the integrity of doctrine is kept intact.

For Bria, the assessment of the new post-Communist situation of contemporary Romania, which tends to become a reference to today's Western society, should begin with the correct evaluation of what happened during the Communist regime. Such an evaluation, however, which tackles a period spanning more than forty years, is not an easy task, so the attempts made in the early 1990s by various individuals or groups within the church to reconcile the church with its own past during the Communist regime were utterly fruitless. These attempts varied from acid criticism of the church for its submissive attitude before Communist authorities and the vehement reactions of parish priests who resisted Communism to the drafting of an awareness that involved the necessity of moral invigoration for the laity. Unfortunately, this led to the demise of the much-needed ecclesiastical renewal[9] because of those who understood renewal as a return to the old privileges of the church, seen as *the* national church.[10] None of these seem highly important for Bria because in his view the traditional mission of the church, which was exercised during Communism to greater or lesser degrees with view to the application of the social apostolate in society, does not totally match the present situation of post-Communist society. Bria makes it explicitly clear that the mandate of the church can no longer be confined to the preservation of an inalterable tradition as well as a collective memory. As the new situation is totally different from the old, what the church must do these days is to perform explicit mission.[11] By the concept of explicit mission Bria understands the preaching of the Gospel and the teaching of Christian doctrine to everybody.[12] He also details what he means by "everybody": "everybody" refers to all those who have forgotten, lost, or ignored the Christian confession of faith. Basically, what he says is that the Gospel should be preached and the Christian doctrine should be taught to every man and woman who is part of today's society. The new situation presents us with two fundamental realities: first, there are new frontiers of church mission, which the church should take advantage of, and second, the Orthodox Church no longer can perceive itself as correlative to the Romanian people. In other words, there is a gap, an ever-growing dissociation between the Romanian Orthodox Church and the Romanian people. This is because—by means of this association between the Romanian Orthodox Church and the Romanian people—the old way of the church was based on institutional as well as political conformity. Within the present society, this old way is no longer an option. The church must understand that the new challenges of post-Communist society present us with brand-new possibilities, and the new generation of believers (priests and lay people) must walk on what Bria calls the "mystical-liturgical path."[13] This particular choice excludes the old "social-cultural path," which resulted in political and institutional conformity. Hopefully, the new mystical-liturgical path should lead to personal freedom of belief and practice. This explains why Bria introduces the idea of conversion[14] with reference to every believer. Thus, both priests and believers must undergo a true conversion, which must result in a deep structural reform in order for the church to successfully face the realities as well as the challenges of the new, pressing issues of contemporary society.[15]

These details take us closer to the second feature of traditional theology as revealed by Bria's work, and this is the necessity of conversion. There is no true Christianity and no genuine believer without conversion. This is crucial because conversion links the believer to God through faith and, at the same time, it connects him to his fellow men through morality. So conversion is important both to faith and to ethics because it lays the basis for a community that professes a distinct morality. The necessity of conversion therefore calls for the necessity of a particular type of morality, which is not optional for believers in particular and for the church in general. It is actually morality that testifies about the reality of conversion, so traditional theology will always defend both: conversion in man's relationship with God and morality in his relationship to fellow human beings.

Ignorance toward Christianity

The first pressing issue the church has to face today is that the essence of Christianity is no longer known to the majority of our contemporary society, who are virtually ignorant when it comes to defining the basics of Christian life and message. The Communist regime turned society into a space severely restricted in terms of religion. Thus, according to Bria, the liturgy was kept but due to the constant interest of the Communist authorities in quenching the people's desire to attend the church and to participate in religious life in general, those who eventually remained closer to the church clung to the external ritual of the liturgy while they almost totally missed its inner meaning as well as its eucharistic dimension. The huge urban development turned the cities into mission fields, but the church did not live up to its perpetual duty to evangelize.[16] Parishes were established within cities, but they lacked a parochial system as well as a missionary plan. The almost immediate result was, as far as Bria is concerned, the loss of the meaning of faith.[17] Bria is aware that every believer must confess his or her own faith, but it was actually the very content of faith that became a problem for believers. This was the legacy of the Communist regime, which the church of the early 1990s, and also the church of today, had to face and still has to provide with an adequate solution.[18] One issue of concern for Bria is the fact that the church tended to define itself in terms of the conflict between revelation and modernity, which can also be translated in terms of the difference between Orthodoxy and heresy. Bria suggests that such an approach turned the church to the unfortunate situation of preserving the strictness of tradition according to the old canons. A second issue of concern, also in connection with the solution the church must find for today's lack of knowledge about the essence of Christianity, has to do with the detachment of *lex orandi* (law of prayer) from the *lex credendi* (law of belief). In Bria's exposition, a widely held and influential view is that which confines *lex orandi* to the liturgical ritual. Thus, both clergy and laity mistakenly grew to understand the life of the church as adherence to the liturgy or, more exactly, to the details of the liturgy, while unfortunately forgetting the necessity of preserving the *lex credendi*. The ritual of the liturgy is therefore empty without inner faith; this also resulted in a liturgy characterized by extreme luxury and ritualism.[19] This was only part of the problem; the remaining problem consisted of the fact that the people took part in the liturgy as mere spectators who needed no faith. Actually, Bria emphasizes that personal faith and its confession[20] were almost entirely lost as people became increasingly preoccupied with the externals of the liturgical ritual. The third issue of concern is, for Bria, the fact that Christianity became less and less known not only among simple believers but also within the university setting. Thus, the younger generation was no longer exposed to the religious culture of the church, so the history and the doctrines of Christianity were deliberately ignored as part of a curriculum that could have treated them as belonging to Christianity itself. Instead, the history and the doctrines of Christianity were perceived as mere religious issues, which were dealt with in history of religion courses.[21]

This third issue was not entirely disastrous because, while it pushed simple people away from the essence of Christianity, it nevertheless provided intellectuals with a bridge between religion, seen as philosophy, and Christianity, seen as a religion. Thus, the dialogue between philosophy and Christianity was encouraged somehow unexpectedly. Bria seems very pleased with this new possibility for explaining the essentials of human existence by resorting to the philosophy of Christianity. The church must grasp the opportunity to make use of its doctrines to explain existentialist philosophy, the philosophy of life, and the methodology of the knowledge of reality through the mediation of Christian doctrines and history.[22] According to Bria, the first categories of people who must seize this new possibility consist of theologians, priests, and missionaries, namely, the ministers of the church. They must realize that the church exists within a pluri-religious as well as a multireligious setting. This awareness is crucial, as they need to understand that the church will eventually be confronted by other religions, and the church must always be prepared to foster a proper answer. The ministers of the church must also become vitally aware of the fact that each age—including ours—has its own way of dealing with religious issues. Following a brief reference to Kant, Hegel, and Schleiermacher, who studied the philosophy of religion with the intention to know the absolute, and then to Lenin and Marx, who rejected religion on antisocial grounds, Bria tries to make us aware that our own time is concerned with issues such as truth, absolute values, and religion in terms that force us to come up with an answer. For Bria, however, the answer does not lie in the method provided by the history of religion school. Religion may deal with various issues, within or beyond the boundaries of the university system, but this is clearly not enough. Bria makes it clear at this point that the only valid path toward the true knowledge of Christianity, as well as to the adequate answer that discloses the reality of truth, absolute values, and religion, is connected to the person and the work of Jesus Christ.[23] When it comes to Christ, however, he must not be seen in just any way; in order for us to grasp the very essence of Christianity we must see Jesus Christ as the one who opens for us the book of truth and makes truth known to us.[24] In other words, we cannot have a full understanding of Christianity unless we perceive Jesus Christ as revealed in Scripture but also as the revealer of truth. At the end of the day, Christianity can be fully grasped only when we see Jesus Christ as the Lord of history and the Savior of the world. It is a pity that Bria does not insist here on the subjective dimension of Christianity, although this can be inferred based on his general perspective on Christ. In Bria, Jesus Christ is presented not only as the Lord of history but also as the Lord of the individual believer, the same Christianity that drafts Jesus Christ not only as the Savior of the world but also as the Savior—the personal Savior—of each man and woman who trusts him.[25]

Having presented Bria's understanding of Jesus Christ, we see the third characteristic of traditional theology according to Bria's doctrine: the centrality of Jesus Christ, preached and witnessed as the Savior of humanity. Traditional theology cannot exist without the saving work of Jesus Christ because what he did for humanity is the essence of truth for Christian believers. It is because of this truth that traditional theology also preaches the fundamental importance of trust when it comes to presenting Christ as Savior. So, in traditional theology, there is an indestructible connection between salvation, truth, and trust, because they all depend on belief in Jesus Christ as revealed in Scripture.

MISSIOLOGICAL METHODOLOGY

The second pressing issue for the church these days concerns the methods and the models for mission. What we really have to understand today is that the church does have a mission, and its mission has to do with the reality of man's salvation by God.[26] No matter how weird this may sound, the church must do its mission whilenever losing sight of the fact that its mission cannot be separated in any way from God's decision to save humanity. Bria underlines once again the reality of today's church as utterly different from its more or less recent past, primarily because society itself has changed dramatically. The challenges the church is presented with will definitely be new as well as very demanding. Regardless, though, of how demanding and difficult these new challenges can be, the church must relentlessly preach God's salvation of humanity. Bria is aware that the church today uses phrases that seem to have been long gone, such as "Romanian Orthodoxy" or "our national church," phrases that do not help the advancement of the church's mission. Romantic as these phrases may be—and this is actually the label Bria stuck on them—they do not help the church in either pressing forward with its mission or in presenting itself as it really is. For instance, such phrases can lead to the blaming of priests—which Bria does not endorse—while the real essence and the mission of the church remain unknown to most people. Bria insists that the church present itself to the world in a correct manner. Thus, the church is God's people, consecrated through the sacred alliance of the New Covenant.[27] Defined as the people of God who were put aside due to the New Covenant, the church must preach the history of salvation. For Bria, the preaching of the history of salvation is the practical exposition of what God did in the past, does in the present, and will do in the future for the entire humanity, which he loves so much that he sacrificed himself for it. The church is a community that functions like an organism, an organism Bria defines as both historical and social. This historical-social organism has a human face because it is a place where people die and rise from the dead together with Jesus Christ.

The reality of the church as being closely connected to the person and work of Jesus Christ does not exempt it from problems. Thus, the church is not holy in the absolute sense of the word, so it is not made exclusively of saints.[28] The human element of the church is the one that always causes trouble, and Bria is aware of this. When he says that the church is not exclusively composed of saints, he actually says two things: first, that the church also has sinners within it (which may or may not refer to the Protestant *simul/ semper justus et peccator*, or the fact that believers are both simultaneously saved and sinners),[29] and second, that the church is indeed made of saints, which means that every redeemed person is a saint.[30] The understanding of the church in this particular way is crucial because it involves a mixture of realities that, as Bria says, are "non-cosubstantial by nature" though "convivial by grace." The church is a conglomerate of institutions and traditions that shape themselves without disappearing, transform themselves without changing, and share the basic characteristics of faith and morality as well as thirst for God. Bria explains once more that the church must be understood according to this definition if the ministers of the church are indeed willing to heal its historical crises.[31]

Nevertheless, the understanding of the church as Bria defines it is far from being enough. It is not sufficient for the minister of the church to understand the church as it really exists in the world as connected to the person and work of Jesus Christ as well as inspired by the Spirit to preach the salvation of humanity. The minister of the church must also realize that the church undergoes a natural process of aging, which should lead to a dramatic reformulation of the church's missionary perspective. It is not enough for the church to understand itself properly; having realized that, the church must do missionary work in the most practical way possible. For Bria, this means that the missionary strategy of the church, which suffers from pastoral approximations and missionary improvisations, must be drastically redefined with specific reference to pastoral, missionary, and educational principles and methods. The church must never forget that when the actual liturgy ends within the walls of the church, another liturgy begins beyond the walls of the church.[32] Both liturgies must constantly target the orientation of today's society, so the

redefinition as well as the reformation of church mission becomes
a perpetual necessity. Parish churches must never fear the novelty
of mission but rather boldly engage in changing what needs to be
changed in order for the ministers, theologians, and ordinary believers to be real partakers in the mission of the church.[33] For Bria, the
old way, meaning the old violent apologetics as well as the spirit
of strife in defending the church, no longer serves the church or
its mission. Internal defense does not work any longer because it
does not prove to be sufficient means to advance the mission of the
church. What the church really needs instead is a new spirit as well
as a new exegesis. For Bria, the new spirit and the new exegesis that
the church so badly needs these days should be deeply rooted in
the biblical principle that the church is the salt of the earth. This is
actually a new awareness, which should awaken the ministers of the
church from their lethargy and routine, but it should also produce a
powerful impact on ordinary believers. If and when ordinary believers understand that they make up the church, which is the salt of the
earth, they will automatically realize that it is absolutely necessary
for them to be the salt of the earth. This awareness, now rooted
deep within ordinary believers, will turn them into missionaries and
preachers.[34] Bria knows for a fact that the Orthodox Church has
been frequently accused of being very shallow in terms of missions,
but such a realization—namely, that all believers should become
missionaries and preachers—will rapidly exempt Orthodoxy from
this particular accusation. This should also lead to a reorganization
of parishes both throughout the countryside and within cities. Without a conscious living and practical application of the liturgy on a
daily basis, believers will eventually become "wandering individuals," with incalculable damages for the church's life.[35]

Having defined the necessity of the church to reform its missionary strategy, Bria proceeds with the practical solution for the
implementation of the program. In order for the church to renew
its missions but also to redefine its attempts to foster an explicit
evangelization methodology, the church must pay increased attention to biblical exegesis and biblical studies. The constant use of
the Bible is the necessary condition for the dramatic reformation of
the church's missionary and pastoral agenda.[36] The church must use
the Bible because the church should not preach itself or for itself;
the church must always preach Jesus Christ as well as the mission of
Jesus Christ in full accordance with the teachings of the New Testament.[37] In order to make it clear that the Bible should be a never-
ending preoccupation of the church, Bria resorts to the patristic

tradition, which presented the Bible as a collection of letters sent to us by God or as God's invitation to come closer to him, to ask for and then receive his gift—evidently, the gift of his salvation or his saving grace.[38] The Bible is important, as Bria plainly notes, because Jesus Christ addresses the church through the Bible, which means that Jesus Christ makes himself heard and seen through the Bible. There is simply no other way through which Jesus Christ can be revealed to us apart from the Bible. Bria is fully convinced of this reality, and this is why he further insists that God feeds his people through the Holy Sacraments, which are deeply rooted in the Bible. It is the Bible that discloses God's plan for the church following the resurrection of Jesus Christ as explicitly written down in the Gospels.[39] Therefore, Bria underlines that the church is tied to "the Lord's Scriptures." The Bible must be understood both historically and spiritually but, even more important, the Bible must be read in the church. This is vital for the church as well as for believers because they listen to God's personal word in and through the written and proclaimed words of Scripture. Bria writes that the Bible must produce a powerful and lasting impact in the believer's heart. This is why the Bible must be read, explained or preached, and interpreted. When the Bible is read, proclaimed, and interpreted for all believers (and nonbelievers), the immediate result should be personal confession of one's faith.[40] Jesus Christ must be personally present within believers, and this cannot happen without the personal faith that stems from the reading, preaching, and interpreting of the Bible.[41] Bria also insists that personal faith must always (or as often as possible) be accompanied by the confession of sin.[42] Actually, the normal life of a believer should be constantly characterized by the following: the reading of the Bible, the listening to the Gospel, the prayer for the forgiveness of sins (the confession of one's sins), the intercession for brothers and sisters (the members of the church), the embrace of peace, and mutual forgiveness. The church must preach the Gospel outside its walls for the benefit of the entire society, in the city or, as Bria writes, the very place where good and evil exist within the human condition.[43] It is in society, in the very midst of good and evil, that the church must establish what Bria calls a "moral community." This moral community should be characterized by catechetical, educational, and social works, all of which are meant to support the people in need.[44] Bria also explains that such a moral community cannot be built without personal faith as well as personal confession of one's sins. Thus, believers must practically apply the values of the Gospel in order to help civil society.[45] The ministers of the church should be continually preoccupied with the growth of the personal faith of their believers but also with the clear identification of the content of the Christian faith. In practical terms, this means the priest's detachment from liturgical ritualism and his adherence to the exposition of the Gospel in all its richness.[46]

The fourth characteristic of traditional theology as disclosed based on Bria's thought is the necessity that faith—the believers' and the church's faith—must grow constantly as a result of the preaching of the Gospel. This is a proof that Gospel preaching must be done with a great deal of responsibility because it should result in the confession of sins. This in turn is followed by a particular sense of morality as all those who confess their sins did so because they had been convicted by the Gospel. The new morality of the people is built on faith and, as faith grows, morality is also expected to grow. So, for traditional theology, the link between the growth of faith and the preaching of the Gospel, which results in a new morality for all true believers, can never be underestimated.

UNIVERSAL PRIESTHOOD

As far as the third pressing issue for the church nowadays is concerned, Bria lists the return of what he calls "common priesthood," as well as the missionary mobilization of parishes. Common priesthood is just another reference to what Protestants mean by universal priesthood, or the priesthood of all believers, because Bria does not refrain from plainly stating that our new church reality implies the necessity that lay people should get involved in the mission field. Thus, ordinary believers should be willing to spread or cultivate the seeds of Christianity—Bria says Orthodoxy—within the current situation of our society. Having said that, Bria seems convinced that the most important trend that takes shape these days—at least within the Romanian Church or, more exactly, the Romanian Orthodox Church—is the reawakening of the *laos*, which for Bria is a reference to the people of God.[47] The next step for Bria is to define this particular *laos*.[48] Those who are part of the people of God share at least four main characteristics. First, the people of God is made up of men and women who read the Bible. Second, they not only read the Bible—as if in a mechanical way—but also meditate upon the Bible. Third, they are very eager to go to church each Sunday, and fourth, they long to be closer to the altar in order to receive the Holy Sacraments. It is actually at this point that Bria explains the essence of common priesthood. All those who share these four features, the reading of and the meditation upon the Bible, church attendance, and the reception of sacraments, are actually those who explain what common priesthood is all about. At the same time it is Bria himself who writes that common priesthood is the priesthood of all Christians or, in Protestant language, the priesthood of all believers. In addition, the priesthood of all believers is nothing but the willingness of the laity to be partakers of the priesthood as well as the mission of the church.[49] Bria highlights that common priesthood, namely, the participation of ordinary believers in the mission and priesthood of the church, should be not only formally recognized but also supported, as well as carefully developed in three distinct directions.[50]

The first direction in which the priesthood of all believers should be helped to develop itself into active missionary endeavors is the reconciliation of contrary views. Bria notes that both priests and lay people undergo a serious process of polarization. As far as Bria is concerned, polarization is damaging for the church because it produces views that tend to develop in totally different, and oftentimes quite opposed, directions that will eventually result in irreconcilable perspectives. This unfortunate situation should be avoided at all costs because it can and will deeply affect the visible unity of the church. Bria criticizes the founding of various associations, and specifically religious associations, that promote the strict observance of ancient traditions and customs as if they were the core of true Christianity. For Bria, such an attempt is nothing but an overglorification of our ancestors—like an ancestry cult—which can lead to dangerous schism. On the other hand, there is an opposing or at least a very different tendency that, instead of looking back to the ancient tradition of the church, dares speak of church renewal in a rather courageous attempt to look ahead to the future of the church. This specific tendency is furthered by theologians, priests, and believers who want to see the church in a renewed state based on evangelization and ecumenism, namely, on an enlarged perspective on the church.[51] Bria is convinced that this particular trend should be supported in order to find an authentic path as well as a viable process of church renewal. What those concerned with church renewal practically have to do— at least as far as Bria is concerned—is give theological and spiritual instruction to ordinary believers through systematic catechization and theological formation.[52] This presupposes a consistently broader approach of the reality of the parish church and also of the parish church seen as a dormant or latent field in which the seeds of the Gospel grow unseen. In Bria, this particular category includes

Christians who, despite not observing church attendance or fasting, nevertheless love the church of Christ.[53]

The second direction that concerns the development of the priesthood of all believers has to do with the active involvement of higher ecclesiastical structures in church mission and parish support. It is interesting to note that while Bria does not discard the official attempts of the church's hierarchy to support its own development through the establishment of new bishoprics throughout the country, he nevertheless insists on the fundamental importance of the parish churches. This is why he warns that the vitality of Christianity—he actually writes about the vitality of the Orthodox Church— is totally dependent upon the zeal and the mission of the parishes. Bria is sure that the newly established bishoprics have absolutely no chance to promote the essence of Christianity without a thorough reformation of the parochial system. If parish churches do not work properly, bishoprics are practically doomed. Bria is particularly concerned about the parishes within cities that seem to have been seriously affected by the spiritual crisis of our contemporary society. This is also because active pastoral work is almost nonexistent within these urban parishes. Bria issues an earnest warning when he writes that the parish system is literally archaic, and the fact that it is so old makes it function inadequately. The outcome can have disastrous consequences because most of the people who live at the outskirts of cities are almost completely untouched by the Gospel. At the same time, Bria is very concerned by what he calls the "interests of greater parishes," which tend to ignore the reality of smaller city churches that need to work more closely with people. What Bria actually infers here is that smaller parishes need all the support they can get from bigger parishes, which, having understood the new situation of today's society, should actively support the missionary as well as the pastoral efforts of smaller churches. In other words, bigger parishes—which are considered risk free—should no longer enjoy undeserved privileges as in the past; on the contrary, smaller churches should be actively supported with view to the development of church mission and pastoral work.[54]

The third direction connected to the support of the priesthood of all believers consists of the integration of lay people into the mission and pastoral work of the church.[55] Bria makes it clear that the marginalization of laity is not only a serious ecclesiological error but also a canonical failure. Modernity—as well as postmodernity— presents us with serious challenges that the church needs to face, oftentimes to the point of open confrontation. This duty, however, cannot be accomplished unless laity is fully integrated within all parish churches. Bria underlines that all believers must be integrated in parishes, urban and rural, because the missionary mobilization of parishes is nothing but a sign of true pastoral care.[56] In Bria, it is more than clear that pastoral care translates as the rediscovery of church mission.[57] There is no mission without pastoral care and there is no pastoral care without mission. This theological principle is crucial for Bria because he insists that the parish church is a multifaceted structure of communion. Believers must realize that they belong to a community that has a task and a mission. This means that they themselves must share in the same task and mission. Believers will therefore understand that they belong to this community, and then they will get involved actively in the pastoral work and the mission of that community. Church belonging is crucial both for pastoral work and for the church's mission. For Bria, there is no true Christianity without church belonging. In other words, one cannot be a genuine Christian without going to church. Being a Christian is not only attendance at collective rituals and events such as baptisms, marriages, and funeral services. This actually means that one's participation at baptisms, marriages, and funeral services does not automatically turn him or her into a true Christian. As a matter of fact, it does not. Believers must participate in the entire life of the church as a way of recognizing their belonging to a community that has a pastoral task as well as an evangelizing mission.[58] Bria goes so far as to give some examples of people who consider themselves true Christians while they show utter indifference toward the life of the parish church. Thus, he writes that some schoolteachers and principals, mayors and public clerks within cities and villages are mainly nominal members of parish churches. While Bria may or may not be fair in identifying these social categories as nominal members of the church, he is definitely right in saying that indifferent people are in fact only nominal members of the church, which in turn means that they are not true Christians. Thus, it seems that for Bria one's capacity as a nominal member of the church does not equal a claim to genuine Christianity.[59]

This is actually the fifth feature of traditional theology according to Bria: one's membership in a church does not equal the inner reality of his or her faith. In other words, if someone says he is a member of the church, this does not mean that he is a true believer. So in traditional theology, it is not church membership that secures one's faith but rather faith must lead to church membership.

THE STATE OF THEOLOGY

A fourth pressing issue for the church today is the state of its theology but also the state of its actual life in the future, both near and remote. Bria is aware that a full evaluation, as well as an objective assessment of the theology of the church nowadays, is very hard to make.[60] The reason for this lies in the very small number of theological works produced by contemporary theologians. Bria even drops the bitter remark that there are theologians all over the place but many of them have no written works whatsoever.[61] The sad reality, according to Bria, is that the theological market has only works that were written before the Second World War, as well as papers published by theologians who were recently converted to faith or show affinities for Slavonic culture. It is quite clear for Bria—although he does not say this explicitly—that today's theology of the church should look not exclusively to Russia or the East for that matter but also to Western culture if ecumenism has any significance whatsoever.[62] He then launches a more or less veiled criticism against the faculties of theology, which seem to be rather cramped because they only prolong what he calls conventional methods that lack perspective and orientation. Bria also criticizes the inclusion of theological faculties within state universities, which, despite the fact that they can offer a wider apprehension of as well as access to theological learning to a larger number of believers and even to women, is devoid of any realistic perspectives. For Bria, this means that, once part of state universities, theological faculties will eventually fall prey to secular thought rather than become centers of ecclesiastical learning and spirituality. Bria is not afraid to say that academic competence is a problem within theological faculties with reference both to professors and to students, which presents us with the fact that today's theology fell not only behind the theology of twenty years ago but also behind that which preceded the Second World War. This is a huge setback, which may lead to causes as grave as the failure to integrate students in the life and mission of the church. Bishoprics do not encourage students to get involved actively in church ministry, nor do they offer vacant parishes to young graduates. This means that the future of contemporary theology is very somber if there is no connection between theological faculties and parish churches. As far as Bria is concerned, theology—and he means Orthodox theology—does not have a future unless theology itself is popularized and stylized. Priests must do church mission, but in order to do that they must be fully aware of the current state of church affairs. They also need to master a theology that is not only at hand and simple but also transparent and open to everybody. He realizes, however, that such a theology is not easy to achieve given the fine balance that must be kept between the apophatic discourse on the one hand, and apologetics on the other.[63]

The church must realize that its theology is not just a bunch of teachings that must be enforced among believers. Theology must be done in such a way that believers understand it, appropriate it, and then live it. Thus, Bria writes that theology must recapture its peda-gogical orientation because theology is in itself doctrine or teaching. Theology must teach, but teaching itself has a target, an objective. This is why theology must teach and train a wide range of believers from parish priests and theologians to teachers and missionaries. All these categories of believers must be trained in such a way that the reality of the church presents itself as appealing. Bria actually writes that they must open wide the gates of the church and also inculcate the moral rectitude of believers. This means that the church should be willing to accept everybody, but this acceptance must not be per-formed lightly or at any costs. Priests, theologians, teachers, and missionaries should be trained extremely well, so that their compe-tence presents Christianity as appealing. There is, however, a price attached to this: following the believers' decision to enter the gates of the church or become active members in the church, the reality of a new life[64] is no longer an option. Once someone enters the church, the quality of his or her life must change dramatically. There is no ecclesiastical membership without moral transformation, and Bria is fully aware of this when he warns that the church must stay away from a variety of surrounding realities that have nothing to do with the teaching and morality of Christianity.[65] Bria mentions briefly but precisely the necessity that the church should not take the path of syncretism or the position of integrism. Christian doctrine is a sum of teachings that originate in the Holy Scripture as presented by the Gospel. Syncretism has nothing to do with Christianity for the simple reason that the church does not need anything more than the Gospel presented in Scripture. Moreover, the church must not guide itself in accordance with anything that goes beyond the limits of the Gospel.[66] With reference to the specific context of the Roma-nian Orthodox Church, Bria issues a crucial warning expressing his concern that Christian virtues could be mixed with what he calls "Romanian popular and religious flaws." If popular beliefs promote certain values, it does not mean that they are necessarily correct. Furthermore, if popular beliefs uphold certain religious teachings, it does not automatically entail that they are authentic. Bria makes it clear that the church should not guide itself according to popular thinking. The church has only one guide and this is the Gospel; anything else lies beyond the true validity of the teachings of the Gospel. Church parishes should never accept the guidance of popular belief, not even when elements of the Gospel are present. The Gospel should not be altered by anything, as this is why the mixture of the Gospel and popular teachings is most damaging for the church. Likewise, putting together the holy with the profane or the secular as well as religion and ideology can only lead to results that are far from beneficial for the church's life. Theology is teaching but not just any kind of teaching. Theology is the teaching of the Gospel, so the minister of the church must broaden his apprehension of theology by accepting the principles of the Gospel, not archaic dogmatism or exclusivist confessionalism.[67]

The next step for Bria is to criticize some beliefs that, in his opinion, hinder the church from achieving its full capacity to work according to the Gospel.[68] The first belief criticized by Bria has to do with the reading of the Bible. Some in the church are convinced that the Bible contains some very complicated texts, and this is why not all people can understand and interpret Scripture. In other words, the church should not encourage the reading of Scripture by all believers but only by the clergy who were trained for this task. The same belief says that the interpretation of Scripture is reserved only for those who have this vocation and were ordained within the apostolic succession, namely, those who have the gift of Orthodox teaching. It is more than evident that the reference is to the ordained clergy, the ministers of the church, while lay people are automatically excluded. The only duty of the laity is—as a logical consequence—obedience to the Gospel although, as only the clergy can read and interpret the Gospel, it turns out that lay people should be obedient not to the Gospel but to the clergy or, in the best possible situation, to the Gospel as taught by the clergy. Bria knows for a fact—and he writes as if priests were also fully aware of this—that believers who do not read the Bible for themselves fall prey to all kinds of erroneous teachings and this often happens much too easily. For Bria, reading and interpretation of the Bible is not the exclusive duty of ordained ministers or of those who display what he calls exegetical erudition; on the contrary, all believers have the duty to read and interpret Scripture for themselves and their own spiritual growth. Bria points out that among laity there are believers who are called by the Holy Spirit (or the charismatics), so they have a duty to be partakers of the church's spiritual edification.[69] These charismatic believers are called to wield the sword of the Spirit, which is the word of God. All these lay people and, by extension, all believers receive words of wisdom from above in order to proclaim—through the power of God—the salvation of his church.[70]

The second belief Bria does not hesitate to criticize is the interdiction of the laity's access, and especially of women, to theological education and to church mission. Bria highlights once more that the mission of the church is both liturgical and catechetical, which means that the church must proclaim the Gospel no matter what. This belief, which is clearly wrong at least in Bria's perspective, deprives parish priests of valuable co-workers who could easily help them perform the mission of the church as needed. With reference to women, Bria insists that the ordination of deaconesses should be seriously reconsidered within the church because women can be ordained as part of the clergy should they be elected for the ministry of deaconship.[71] He does not insist on pushing women toward priesthood, but the restoration of female deaconship would be a recognition of the tradition of the primary church, as well as the acceptance of the dignity of women as equal contributors to the ministry of the church. With reference to the biblical command that the woman should be silent in the church, Bria explains that this interdiction does not bar women from their didactic or pedagogical responsibility *and* mission.[72] Women could and should teach Christian doctrines within parishes, public schools, and religious institutions, as well as theological seminaries and faculties.[73]

The third belief Bria opposes is concerned with the election of priests and bishops.[74] According to this belief, the laity should not be part of the election of priests, and neither should priests have anything to do with the election of bishops. It is a pity that Bria does not elaborate on this issue at all, but it seems that the exclusion of laity from the most important decisions related to the life of the church is neither beneficial nor biblical. Bria's criticism reflects his conviction that priests must be elected by ordinary believers, or by the communion that makes up the parish church, while bishops should be put into office by their fellow ministers whom they should serve.[75]

These three beliefs, which for Bria are utterly wrong, depend on the poor quality of the theological education.[76] Bria is convinced that theological education today does not reflect the mission of the church and especially the new demands that must be met by the church through its mission. The faith and the liturgy of the church

must be explained to what Bria calls a "new public," the larger mass
of all those who live within the new society of our times. This is
why the church must find a way to improve theological education
in universities, public schools, and the media (television, radio, and
newspapers). This task, however, can never be completed unless
ordinary believers are well trained theologically but also in fields
such as humanistic studies, pedagogy, and didactic methodology. At
the same time, the minister of the church or the priest, whose duty is
to implement theological education in the minds and souls of ordinary believers, must be trained in many respects in order to be able
to accomplish his mission. Thus, the priest must be ready to com-
prehensively explain theology to intellectuals and competently speak
about sexual morality to youngsters and their parents, as well as disseminate religious literature among children and young adults.[77]

Consequently, the sixth characteristic of traditional theology
becomes almost self-evident as we read through Bria's exposition:
the ministers of the church must be solidly trained in all respects,
but the excellence of training must be accompanied by a specific way
of life. In traditional theology, ministers cannot exert their duties
unless their training is attached to a morality lived in the midst of
the community of believers. So traditional theology teaches us that
while solid training is crucial for church ministers, this can be rendered useless if not followed by a profound desire to wholeheartedly
serve the community of faith.

THE MORALITY OF CHURCH MINISTERS

The fifth pressing issue for today's church is the morality and discipline associated with the ministers of the church. While praising the
majority of parish priests who lived during Communism and, through
great personal suffering, carried on their spiritual duties toward the
church, Bria is not so sympathetic with many of the priests who pastor their flocks today. Once personal freedom was reinstated after
the fall of Communism, Bria notices that many priests saw a great
opportunity in stressing the value of public worship and the right to
teach theology in public schools, as well as the chance to reorganize
the general mission of the church. This suddenly led to the drafting of new programs, so many churches began to face economic
and financial pressure. As most of the church's ministers believed or
were led to believe that their biggest problem was the lack of church
buildings or fundamental parochial institutions, most of them started
ambitious building projects. Countless material resources and moral

energies were invested in church building, as Bria suggests, which entailed not only the actual building of churches or monasteries but also land acquisition, art restoration, and parochial reorganization. This whole new situation soon became a real problem for the church in general because, as Bria writes, many priests created a "maximalist perspective" on their parishes, which started to support the building of monasteries, hospitals, orphanages, asylums for elderly people, and many other costly financial projects.[78] Bria seems to be particularly dissatisfied with what he calls "grandiose cathedral building projects" in cities and villages, where—in too many cases—the sheer poverty of the local population is not only general but also public.[79]

Some of the priests, however, grew to realize that church building or the building of church institutions is not the biggest problem their parishes have to face these days. Thus, they reached the conclusion that the real issue for their parishes has almost nothing in common with economic and financial pressures; on the contrary, what their parishes suffered from was in fact the knowledge of faith and liturgy among the members of their churches. Bria believes that because of the lack of faith and liturgy knowledge, the social life of believers reached a poorer state, but eventually the parish itself went through a crisis concerning its identity and moral unity. Our society is chaotic, if we are to believe Bria, but this must not necessarily influence the church in such a way that the parish itself becomes a similar reality. The church is indeed undecided or even insecure, at least sometimes, but despite these social issues of serious gravity, the parish must recognize and reconcile with itself. The biggest issue within this particular context is no longer the parish itself and its problems—chaotic life and the loss of morality, identity, and unity—but rather the spiritual formation as well as the spiritual life of church ministers.[80] In contemporary society it may well be the case that believers act hectically, like sheep without a shepherd, but the real issue is when priests begin to act in a similar manner. When he tackles the problems of the priests themselves, Bria begins his discourse with the careful observation that the mission, the pastorship, and the morality of priests is a battlefield. What he means is that the entire life of the pastor is a spiritual battlefield where both victories and failures are a daily reality. The priest is not exempted from spiritual difficulties, but the real problem begins when he is subject to a serious spiritual crisis. Such grave spiritual crises are really problematic not only for the life of the priest but also for the life of the parish because they are a sign that his priestly mission is no longer fueled by his faithfulness to Christ.[81] Bria underlines that every priest is chosen and sent by Christ—through the prayer and the laying on of hands of the bishop—to lead the spiritual lives of his flock in the parish church or elsewhere. When the priest's mission undergoes an intense spiritual crisis, then it is clear that his faithfulness to Christ is also problematic. For Bria, the priest's faithfulness to Christ must be total, and the spiritual crisis begins when the priest is no longer willing to be subject to Christ with his entire life. When his dedication to Christ is not total, it is only a matter of time before spiritual crises erupt into serious problems that affect the life of the entire church. The priest must have Christ in his heart and life, Bria underlines quite emphatically, so he must be a *christophoros* in his parish church—he has to bear Christ in his entire life. When the priest does not have Christ in his heart and life, he is nothing but a false minister. Bria's language is even tougher when he says that such a priest is not only a false minister but also an impostor. The life and ministry of such false ministers is to be decried because they are themselves pastoral cases.[82]

Bria goes even further in describing the portrait of the false ministers because of his conviction that this is a real issue for today's church. Thus, the false minister cannot integrate himself into the life of his parish, so he lives in a parallel reality. Bria lists a significant range of words that draft the image of the false minister as a stranger, a tourist, a Sunday visitor, or even a commuter who does not have the slightest clue about what field pastorship really means. He does not know his own parish, and neither does he know who is spiritually as well as socially active in his church. On top of it, he does not have any idea about what Bria calls the hidden face of the parish, which consists of the poor, the elderly, the handicapped, and the orphans among many other gravely afflicted social categories.[83] This is why the false minister or the false priest mistakes priesthood for the ecclesiastical ritual and pastorship with "popular religious psychoanalysis." This does not mean anything but the mere fact that the false priest is not concerned about his parish at all; what he does for his parish is only to perform the external ritual of the liturgy and give counsel in accordance with what people generally believe to be true. At this point, Bria is even harsher when he says that such ministry is actually "television pastorship." In other words, the priest who has serious moral issues can only do two things for his parish: perform the external ritual of the spiritual service of the church and give advice according to what he sees on TV. If so, he does not differentiate himself from any other ordinary citizen whose life revolves around his daily job, which he does almost mechanically, and watching TV for most of his spare time. He is fatally biased in approaching the members of his parish; he favors some to the detriment of others; and he does not explain his authoritarian and bewildering decisions. An even worse situation is when the false minister runs a personal business and entertains a net of personal relationships that help his business. Such a minister has a paternalistic approach when it comes to dealing with his parish members; unfortunately, as Bria openly writes, he is nothing but a person who becomes isolated, frustrated, and estranged because he cannot relate to his flock. This minister can and actually must be dismissed, and his parish has every right to withdraw its trust in him. He broke his vow for the parish he engaged with through ordination, so the parish is totally entitled to send him away.[84]

There are other issues that cause trouble to the minister of the church. Sometimes it is his own family that sees his profession as mediocre, so they denigrate his ministry as inferior to other professions. In other instances, the priest may have problems because some people mistake the parish for a public or state institution, so they ask the priest to perform "political projects" that are totally opposed to his mission. It is quite unfortunate that Bria does not give any examples of such projects that prove to be incompatible with the priest's spiritual duties, but he tackles nevertheless what he calls the most tragic situation that afflicts both the priest and his parish. This is when the priest, or rather the false minister, tries to conceal his weaknesses and immorality with theological motivations. This is a sort of cover-up attempt when the priest says that he can perform the liturgy despite his spiritual state. In other words, the church suffers the most when false ministers offer theological arguments in favor of the teaching that the reality and the efficiency of the liturgy does not depend on his moral virtues. Bria reiterates the traditional doctrine of the church with reference to the liturgy and especially to the Eucharist,[85] which says that whatever the priest does in this respect is spiritually effective because Christ himself is present there through the working power of the Holy Spirit, while the minister himself is only the human instrument whereby the liturgy is performed.[86] Thus, Bria underlines once more that the priest must be a *christophoros*, a bearer of Christ and particularly of Christ's image before the people who partake at the liturgy. For Bria, Christ's words addressed to Peter, "Do you love me?" (John 21:15–17) must be a constant as well as utterly serious warning for the minister because the question itself is frightening.[87] The minister must be converted to Christ; he must be willing and able—in the Spirit—to accept Christ in his heart. There must be a special place for Christ in the heart of the minister; otherwise he is bound to failure and disappointment. If accepting Christ is a problem for the priest, he should confess the hardening of his heart to the bishop for spiritual counsel and guidance.

Bria insists that the priest is connected to his parish church, to which he is actually sent with a mission, in the special capacity of pastor. The priest is not an ecclesiastical clerk who performs religious services based on specific orders. His duty is to fortify and edify his flock, the members of his parish, as a moral and liturgical community. The parish is the Lord's flock, not the priest's, so it is at this point that Bria restates his conviction that the priesthood and pastorship are not some form of popular religious psychoanalysis. The priest must not lead the flock in accordance with human traditions, by force or by threat. His personal opinions have no value unless based on the commandments of the Lord himself, whose flock he must take to green pastures. This is why the morality of the priest is absolutely necessary for his ministry. He must acknowledge his own human limitations in order to live a holy, sanctified life.[88] Bria explains that priesthood means giving up the things of the world in order to embrace the things of heaven. To give a few practical examples, the priest must give up opulence and compromise, violence and money, barbaric words and false godliness. Bria is well aware that many of today's priests have nothing in common with true spiritual ministry, and they must be disciplined in accordance with the demands of the Gospel. Before discipline is enforced, however, it is better if the priest himself confesses his sins before God in order that his own soul, as well as his parish church, should be healed.[89]

Thus, in traditional theology, a central role is played by the acknowledgment of the reality of sin, which is also the seventh feature of traditional theology as identified following Bria's pastoral reasoning. There is no proper Christian life without the confession of sin and, at the same time, the conscious realization that sin is reality encompassing man's entire existence. Traditional theology teaches us that sin must always be dealt with in close connection with one's awareness of God; in other words, there is no sin if sin itself is not compared to the existence of God because sin is always directed against God and then against other human beings. Once sin is acknowledged for what it really is, the path to a new life and a new morality is made possible. The acknowledgment and the subsequent confession of sin, which eventually leads to a changed morality, is compulsory for each Christian believer and especially for the ministers of the church, whose duty is to care for the spiritual welfare of the entire church.

POLITICAL AUTONOMY AND POLITICAL NEUTRALITY

The sixth and the last pressing issue for the contemporary church in Bria's ecclesiology is concerned with the church's perspective on politics and society.[90] Before drafting his own view on politics and society as part of the church's assessment of today's world, Bria mentions that the Orthodox Churches have had various political attitudes in dealing with civil authorities.[91] Thus, he mentions symphony—or actually Constantinian symphony—which is based on the cooperation between the church and the state, between the patriarch and the emperor, with the sole purpose of the people's common good. It is in this context that Bria mentions—in very general terms—that the chief of particular states ordered the mass baptism of his subjects or that the state entered a political alliance with the church with the result that the church itself became a state church as happened in Greece. Bria also makes reference to what Emperor Theodosius the Great did in the late fourth century when he inserted Christianity within the political structure of the Roman Empire in order to preserve the Christian religion as well as to keep it safe from persecution. Without offering key details that would have helped us better grasp his entire perspective on the political involvement of the church, Bria only says that the church fought for political autonomy and sometimes even for total political independence as happened with the church of Constantinople during the period of the iconoclastic emperors.[92]

In order to protect the church from harsh criticism for its political engagement at various instances during its long history, Bria advises us not to judge the church because its purpose in dealing with the state the way it did—sometimes in close cooperation with political authorities—was to promote its pastoral and missionary interests in a certain social context. It is here that Bria resorts to a pneumatological perspective when he says that charismatic Christians, or those who have the Holy Spirit of God, are able to discern the proper methods for spreading the Gospel within a certain setting. Thus, for Bria, political engagement is somehow permitted, and even expected, if the main reason behind it is the very advance of the Gospel itself within a given political and social context.[93] When it comes to politics, and especially to church politics, Bria introduces the concept of political autonomy, which he sees in connection with the church's relationship with political parties, not with the state or with the national state in Romania's particular case. Thus, the church should be politically autonomous with reference to political parties but not necessarily so with the state. Bria is a bit optimistic about the state's perception of the church when he writes that the state seems to have understood the church's role in the nation's moral resurgence. Following this glimpse of optimism, Bria takes a more realistic step in defining the church's political involvement because, in his view, the church—with reference to the Romanian Orthodox Church—did not get thoroughly into some fundamental social issues that should have been implemented in society following the fall of Communism. Thus he mentions serious social aspects such as the family, political power, death, violence, corruption, and the national state, all of which should have been approached by the church in order to offer an effective teaching about them for the entire society. As the church did not do it, the unfortunate result was a lack of earnest theological studies in some of the most crucial social and political issues of today's context. Bria's exposition of the lack of serious theological response in crucial social and political issues becomes dramatic when he writes that some capital sins got specific names, and he lists violence, sexual abuse, rape, luxury, injustice, tyranny, despotism, and torture.[94] It is unfortunate that Bria does not elaborate on how the church should offer particular responses to each of these capital sins, as he himself calls them, but he is clearly distressed by the present situation of the church as well as of the society's development. He laments society's moral decay while the church seems to be utterly incapable of fostering reliable answers to these critical problems. Bria warns that old methods, such as lists of sins, moralist canons, and paternalist advice, do not work any longer so something else must be done rapidly. This is why he insists that the relationship between the church and the state should be conceived in therapeutic terms or, with reference to theology, in soteriological terms.[95]

Bria is convinced that the church should help society in order to offer salvation to its members. Though he does not insist on what this really means theologically and socially, Bria nevertheless issues a crucial thesis within the contemporary ecclesiological setting. Thus, he writes that the church should seriously consider the issue of separation from the state should that be absolutely necessary. The separation between church and state should no longer be a taboo, a subject banned or forbidden based on who knows what grounds; it must be given serious consideration because it could become necessary today. This is why he insists that the church must exercise its moral freedom in assessing its relationship with the state and, if necessary, separate itself from the state.[96] In other words, the church must distinguish between its faithfulness to God on the one hand, and its national, specifically ethnic, loyalty on the other. It is at this point that Bria's notion of political autonomy becomes clearer. The church must enforce its political autonomy toward the state lest it betray the gift of the Holy Spirit. This attitude of the church can be seen in various respects such as the church's capacity to supervise the relationship between Christian faith and national culture, as well as the church's duty to free itself of the constraints of the state in order to enter a serious dialogue with civil society. In other words, the church must be actively involved in society in order to implement the light of the Gospel among its members. Thus, the church must build up a morality, which should take precedence over politics as well as over individual and collective habits; the church must therefore be socially active and politically engaged in order to change people's mentality in accordance with the Gospel. The church must also be open to the European agenda with the same concern for spreading the light of the Gospel to all people. In all these aspects, the church must maintain as well as affirm its political autonomy seen as part of the church's *politeia*, or discipline, as Bria puts it. The church's political autonomy, however, must be continuously reassessed and elaborated within a stricter ecclesiology. The church must not serve the state, so the church must not be conformed to politics; what the church should do is stay autonomous in order to promote its spiritual mission. The church must refuse to be the political instrument of the state or, more specifically, of any national state. The church must serve the kingdom of God, not the kingdom of the world or the state.[97] What is interesting is Bria's reluctance to completely give up the traditional doctrine of the symphony when he says that the Romanian patriarchy can still work from the perspective of the church-nation-state relationship, but this must be done in order to promote the Christian mission based on ecclesiological faithfulness, not on political conformity. Thus, the church must elaborate on what Bria calls a new social apostolate, which openly criticizes the failures of the church as well as the problems of the state. He also underlines that this social apostolate, which is clearly fueled by a deep social and political awareness, must defend religious freedom, human rights,[98] and social justice[99] for each member of today's society.[100]

Bria's notion of political autonomy goes hand in hand with another concept, that of political neutrality. It is a bit difficult to define in clear terms what Bria means by political neutrality because he himself does not offer an affirmative definition of the term but rather a negative assessment of what political neutrality is not. From the very start, Bria makes it clear that there is no such thing as strict political neutrality because the church cannot simply isolate itself from the society in which it actively lives and works. The church must pursue its Christian morality within today's society, it must express its perspective on various social issues, it must consolidate its theology within public schools and universities, and—the last but certainly not the least important—it must be deeply concerned with offering pertinent advice to the younger generation. Thus, the church's political neutrality, as defined by Bria, is not conservatism or lack of trust in the present or in the future. Likewise, it is not giving up those who face serious social problems, such as the poor, marginalized women or youngsters, the unemployed, or anybody who lives a tough daily life. The church is called to show the relevance of the Gospel message in today's society in order to reject the cultural values of today's secularization.[101] Political neutrality is active social engagement with a view to the promotion of the Gospel throughout all the strata of our contemporary society, which must be done irrespective of the formal policy of the state.[102]

Therefore, the eighth characteristic of traditional theology based on Bria's pastoral ecclesiology is the preaching of the Gospel to everyone, at all times and all costs. The Gospel should not get entangled in the webs of politics if we want it to be effective against the powerful influence of secularization. So, in traditional theology, the Gospel is always opposed to secularization because the values of God stand in sharp contrast to the values of the world. God is not the world, which also means that the church is not to be mistaken for the world, so traditional theology is that which promotes the irreconcilable opposition between the morality of God and the morality—or rather immorality—of the world.

To conclude, the six issues presented by Bria as compelling for the state of today's church bring forward a consistent variety of themes that the church should seriously take into diligent consideration. Thus, beside the fundamental realization that the church itself lives in a brand-new society with brand-new concerns and challenges, the church must critically reflect on its current situation as well as on the things that should be done. Bria does not refrain from openly defending the necessity of church reform and renewal, which should be based on the church's apprehension of the Gospel. In doing so, the church should return to the content of the Gospel itself, namely, to the New Testament and the Bible in general as the fundamental means whereby our Lord, Jesus Christ, was revealed to us. The acceptance of Jesus Christ by the church, based on the constant reading of the Bible, should have a powerful and visible impact throughout the members of the church but also on its ministers. Thus, personal and community holiness and sanctification should emerge as critical for the life of the church, with reference both to the ministers of the church and to the ordinary believers as its members. Having accepted Christ in their hearts, the ministers and the members of the church should begin to practically apply the mission of the church to take the Gospel to everyone. This should impact society in order to transform it in accordance with the light of the Gospel. As the church does its mission on a daily basis, it should maintain its moral freedom from the state through a carefully observed political autonomy as well as political neutrality.

CHAPTER 4

RADICAL CHRISTIAN THOUGHT
IN EARLY POSTMODERNITY

ERICH FROMM AND PSYCHOANALYTICAL CHRISTOLOGY IN THE FIRST HALF OF THE TWENTIETH CENTURY

INTRODUCTION

Heavily influenced by classical liberalism and especially by Adolf von Harnack in theological matters, Erich Fromm (1900–80)—who acquired fame after his association with the Frankfurt School of critical theory as he joined the Frankfurt Institute for Social Research in 1930—produced a series of works that, in addition to sharply opposing traditional theology, took theological liberalism a step further than his equally famous predecessors. While von Harnack was interested in finding the true Christian message by detaching the Jesus of the Gospels from the Christ of Paul's epistles primarily on cultural grounds, Fromm approached Christianity and especially Jesus Christ from a psychoanalytical perspective. Thus, his interest in the idea of Christ stems from his conviction that this particular religious notion ignited collective fantasies that later became more complex with the unfolding of early Christian history. Christ is seen as an image that should be tackled as dealing with social psychology but must be understood in terms of psychoanalysis. Thus, as a science concerned with experience and the influence of experience on human emotional development—both individual and collective—psychoanalysis reveals that early Christianity saw the historical person named Jesus as being elevated to the level of God. This was the only way Jesus could have been perceived by a group of uneducated poor Jews, who only nurtured hatred toward the government as well as hopes for a better world. This adoptionist perspective changed gradually as Christianity grew to include wealthy non-Jews, so the historical Jesus now became the Christ who was no longer a mere man but a God-man. This is why Christianity gave up the early expectation of a future and better world, and focused on the need for salvation in the present time. Therefore, for Fromm, this historical development of theological ideas has to do with the way social classes perceived the world they lived in: from the early proletarian view of a poor man ascending to heaven as God and who could give humanity a better hope for the future, to the later and obviously more complex doctrine of a God-man who deals with the needs of our daily experience in the present moment, promoted by the ruling class. This way, the notion of Christ can be adapted virtually to any particular social context with a view to fitting it into social and individual human experience.

PSYCHOANALYSIS, SOCIAL PSYCHOLOGY, AND RELIGION

Before initiating his discussion of the dogma of Christ, Fromm's first step is to lay out the methodology he uses as well as the social-psychological function of religion. These two aspects show from the very start that Fromm's approach does not intend to follow closely the tenets or the method of traditional theology. It is clear that his methodology is revealed to deal with psychoanalysis, while his discussion of Christ is included in the notion of religion, not of theology.[1]

With respect to his methodology, which is interwoven with psychoanalysis, Fromm points out that one must be aware of one of the greatest achievement of psychoanalysis,[2] which is, in his view, the disavowal of the distinction between social and individual psychology.[3] Fromm is convinced that such a distinction is false because the individual human being cannot exist outside its social realm. He indicates that he draws heavily on Freud and especially on his conviction that while one can identify the individual man's desire to look for satisfaction in order to fulfill his instincts, there is no such thing as a social instinct because it lacks the features of origin and elementary character. This is why, for psychoanalysis, the object of study is the individual man and the groups of people to the very same degree. The individual begins to develop his psyche in a group, which is his family.[4] There is no qualitative difference between individual and social psychology; should there be a difference at all, it is merely quantitative in the sense that the object of study is both or either singular or multiple.[5]

Fromm's intention is therefore to show that the method of social psychology in attempting to investigate the psychic structure of a group is basically the same as the method used by psychoanalysis to search the individual's psychology. It is important thus to realize that psychoanalysis proceeds from what can be seen in the individual's behavior, which can be normal or neurotic; in either case, however, a series of underlying causes based on previous experiences—which include the essential component of sexuality—plays a crucial role in the development of the individual's psyche.[6] Beyond these experiences, past and present, Fromm is ready to accept the existence of the constitutional element of the individual's psychic structure, which must also be taken into consideration although it remains outside any possibility of investigation. In other words, psychoanalysis admits the existence of a psychological core of the individual's psychic constitution, but it can only investigate the impact of experiences upon it, which result in further experiences. Thus, for psychoanalysis, what is important resides in concepts such as experience, life pattern, and emotional development, which can be investigated beyond the unreachable psychological marrow of the individual's inner constitution.[7]

It is clear therefore that, in Fromm, the methodology of psychoanalysis coincides with that of social psychology, but a difference still exists between the two. According to Fromm, while psychoanalysis focuses on the investigation of neurotic individuals, social psychology aims at doing research on groups of people defined by psychological normality. Psychoanalysis searches the inner depths of a person who cannot adjust himself to the reality of his social context, and it is because of this incapacity for self-adaptation that he or she becomes neurotic. On the other hand, social psychology deals with the psychological attitudes of normal people—taken into consideration as a group—and the way they relate to their life experiences. With reference to the dogma of Christ, Fromm explains that he uses social psychology, which means that he attempts to tackle the reasons for the development of the dogma of Christ throughout history.[8] For him, this development is an issue of social psychology because religious ideas are connected to the reality of social life; thus, if the dogma of Christ changed as time passed, one should investigate the people's conditions of life, which must have had an important psychological impact on their religious experiences. It basically works like this: people live in certain social contexts that influence both their psychology and their experiences; the impact of the social conditions of life on individual/social psychology and experiences also results in the alteration of religious concepts, such as the dogma of Christ.[9]

Fromm's considerations lead us to the formulation of the first feature of radical theology, as revealed by his analysis, which works with the presupposition that every religious notion is subject to change and therefore correction. It must be stressed, however, that in radical theology the alteration of religious concepts must happen whenever the religious experiences of people impose such a change. In other words, for radical theology it is clear that it is human experiences that change religious concepts, not vice versa. Applied to the Bible, this means that human experience modifies the way we should interpret the Bible, not that the Bible changes the way we should understand our own experience, as in traditional theology.

Resuming the idea of alteration of religious notions, which include the dogma of Christ, it seems equally true for Fromm that social psychology cannot do without psychoanalysis, which searches the impulses of the individual human being. The individual has both sexual and ego impulses, which are regulated by the social context in which the person lives. Sexual impulses can be given up in favor of ego impulses; for instance, libidinous desires can be quenched but thirst, hunger, or the need for sleep cannot. At the same time, the degree to which sexual or ego impulses are satisfied can vary, in the sense that the repression of some sexual impulses can be compensated by the gratification of some ego impulses. This compensation, though, is controlled by social reality, so society both satisfies and frustrates the individual. The experience of the individual, which begins with his childhood, includes a wide variety of repressed and gratified impulses, so the individual learns how to control his inner drives by facing certain social realities.[10] Fromm is convinced that childhood experiences shape the psyche of the adult individual in connection with both satisfaction and frustration. This is why the adult transfers his love and fear, originating in his childhood, to what Fromm calls a fantasy figure, such as God. The concept of God, however, is supplemented by the social reality of the ruling class, which always has authority over the individual. Thus, the individual nurtures love and fear both for God and for the ruling class to the extent that the two become coincidental. Fromm is convinced that the ruling class tries to control the psychology of the masses by imposing on them the image of God, which actually represents the people's infantile psychological dependence on a father figure, so vitally important for the experience of each individual's childhood psyche.[11]

The actual way whereby the ruling class imposes the image of God as father figure on the psychology of the masses is religion.[12] The ruling class does not want the masses to develop their ego impulses, such as better food or improved social life; what they want is to turn the attention of the masses toward the satisfaction of their sexual impulses by means of religion. In this context, satisfaction can also mean control or even resignation because the function of religion is to help the masses cope with their accumulated frustrations, which social reality cannot satisfy. If sexual impulses cannot be satisfied by social reality, it means that they must be satisfied by fantasies. Consequently, religion functions as a means whereby the sexual impulses of the masses are controlled through collective fantasies in close connection with the idea of God.[13] The teachings of religion—the dogmas of Christianity included—are illusions and fantasies that offer satisfaction for mankind's most urgent impulses. In Fromm, religion has three main functions with reference to mankind in general, to the vast majority of people, and also to the ruling class. Thus, for mankind in general, religion is a way to find consolation for the problems of life; for the vast majority of people, it is a way to come to terms emotionally with their "class situation,"[14] while for the ruling class, religion offers the possibility to rid themselves of guilt caused by the fact that they oppress the exploited classes.[15]

Fromm's intention in dealing with the dogma of Christ now becomes clearer, disclosing the second characteristic of radical theology: the definition of Christ in total opposition to traditional theology. So Christ is definitely not seen in terms of the preexistence of the Logos or the Son of God as in traditional theology, which ascribes him an ontological status; on the contrary, in Fromm's radical approach he is a mere dogma, which—as part of a religious system—is meant to deal with the psychology of social classes, both ruling and oppressed. Thus, Christ is not a person but an image with a certain significance for all those who live in particular social contexts. The image of Christ is bound to change depending on which social class makes use of it; for the ruling class, the image of Christ is meant to offer a certain kind of psychological significance; for the exploited masses, the same image of Christ will provide a totally different type of psychological impact.

THE IMAGE OF CHRIST AND THE IDEA OF JESUS AS MAN MADE GOD

Fromm begins his discussion of the image of Christ from the idea of Jesus, but in order to present what he means by this, he initiates a presentation of the Jewish society in the first century AD. He argues that, other than Rome, Jerusalem probably had the largest mass of people gathered within the same geographical and social area. Unlike Rome, however, Jerusalem did not enjoy any Roman privileges, so the basic needs of its people were not counted among the preoccupations of the Roman emperor. Fromm quickly presents Jewish society and its three main social classes: the Sadducees, who were the upper class; the Pharisees, who constituted the middle class; and the proletariat, which was composed of beggars, unskilled workers, and peasants. In Fromm's presentation, the Sadducees and the Pharisees are sharply distinguished from the land folk, the lowest social class in Jewish society, who hated the upper classes and were in turn hated by them. Even the middle class of the Pharisees was somehow divided into the intellectual elite and the urban as well as rural proletariat. The idea is that Jewish society was clearly divided into social classes so opposed to one another that revolutionary movements—almost always religious in nature—became a permanent feature of everyday life. It is within this troubled social context that messianic movements appeared, and Christianity was only one of them. In addition to this specificity of Jewish society, the problems increased as the upper classes began to oppress the lower classes not only through their own means but also with the support of Roman authorities.[16] Fromm also insists on what happened on the eve of Jesus' birth, especially the rebellions of the Zealots and the movement of John the Baptist, who succeeded in capturing the attention of the exploited masses.[17]

This presents us with the third characteristic of radical theology as revealed by Fromm's approach, which teaches that Christianity is a mere religion that is not different from any other religion in the world. Thus, the beginning of Christianity follows the pattern of any other world religion, while its origin is not divine and metaphysical but human and historical. This means that Christianity as a religion is the product of the masses, and it is because of this particular fact that its notions and teachings can be altered whenever the experience of the people changes in any way whatsoever.

As far as Fromm is concerned, decoding Christianity as a religious movement must start with the movement of John the Baptist, which had some basic characteristics such as the preaching of the kingdom of heaven, the coming of judgment, deliverance for the good, and the destruction of evil. This particular type of preaching attracted the most despised classes of Jewish society, which became the people who reportedly supported Christianity in its early phase of development.[18] Thus, according to Fromm, at the very beginning Christianity was a religion of the exploited masses who longed for social justice and began to nurture an expectation for the improvement of their lives in future. The uneducated lower classes adhered to the teachings of early Christianity almost instantly, so Christianity can be defined as a "significant historical messianic-revolutionary movement."[19]

It is very important for Fromm to offer a psychological analysis of the masses who accepted the early teachings of Christianity because it proves his initial theory, according to which psychoanalysis and social psychology have a crucial role in the investigation of religion in general and of Christianity as a religion in particular. Christianity is a religion of the poor, of the oppressed masses, who had a cluster of psychological characteristics: they nurtured hope for the dramatic change of their life conditions as well as hate for their oppressors. From the perspective of psychoanalysis, the hope that their lives can be changed means that they also believed in a good father who could help them, which is an obvious reference to God. Then, their hate for those who oppressed them translates into their collective fantasies about the Judgment Day, when all their oppressors—the rich in general, the Roman emperor, the Pharisees—will be rightfully judged by God, their good father. When Jesus came, he continued the work of John the Baptist, but he managed to captivate the masses by persuading them to accept his work as the beginning of the kingdom of heaven. This is why the eschatological expectation of the fulfillment of the kingdom of heaven in future—for some, a very near future—was instrumental for the entire activity of Jesus.[20] Fromm also highlights that Jesus began to preach his teachings to his disciples, who were asked to conform themselves to a set of rules: a dramatic alteration of one's mental perspective, the renunciation of the pleasures of the world, the denial of one's self, the willingness to have one's soul saved, the belief in God's grace manifested as support for the poor and the oppressed, and the belief in Jesus as the Messiah who was called by God to enact his kingdom on earth. All these prove, according to Fromm, that Christianity had in the beginning a very limited purpose in focusing exclusively on the oppressed classes of Jewish society.[21] Thus, Christianity was reactionary and revolutionary because the only expectation of the masses was an improvement of their social status and of their life conditions based on their sheer hatred of those in power.[22]

The image of Jesus is crucial at this point because it defines the image of Christ. In Fromm, Christ must be seen first of all through the image of Jesus, who was a historical character. The masses, however, developed the adoptionist belief that Jesus, a mere man, was God's messiah raised from the dead by God himself.[23] Jesus was therefore adopted by God in virtue of his resurrection, taken to heaven at the right hand of God, and meant to return to earth in order to enforce his rightful judgment over the wicked. Fromm explains that such an adoptionist belief presupposed that Jesus was not messiah from the beginning; he was born as a mere man but later on he was adopted by God as an act of God's will. In other words, Jesus is an image created by the uneducated Jewish class in order to fit the expectations of their daily experiences. This is why, in Fromm, the image of Jesus is a fantasy that was meant to substitute for the crude reality of oppressed people.[24] Jesus is the image of a man who can become God by being adopted by God. For Fromm, this is a fantasy that captured the imagination of the oppressed class despite the fact that it did not improve the conditions of life. Jesus could not help the oppressed gain the upper hand; people were not able to overturn the rich and they knew it. So they decided to accept the image of Jesus as a fantasy that helped them transfer the satisfaction of their needs from reality into fiction. Fromm is convinced that the Jews unconsciously hated the idea of God, but consciously they did not dare express this particular hatred; in turn, however, they hated all the rich by accepting the image of Jesus with its promise of a better future and of a rightful judgment. Thus, the first aspect of the image of Christ is the idea of Jesus, which was devised to satisfy in fantasy the boiling feelings of hate accumulated by the lowest and oppressed Jewish classes against the ruling classes that exploited them on a daily basis. Thus, through the idea of Jesus, the image of Christ is meant to offer psychological satisfaction by turning the harsh realities of life into religious fantasies. The bottom line is that the image of Christ can change man's life experience into psychological satisfaction through the acceptance of the idea of Jesus.[25]

Consequently, the fourth feature of radical theology emerges because—as we can clearly see in Fromm—the image of Christ is distinct from the idea of Jesus. The idea of Jesus is based on a historical figure while the image of Christ is a theoretical reality that changes constantly according to various modifications of collective human experience. For radical theology, Christology is dichotomic in the sense that Jesus is separated from Christ. The hypostatic union of traditional theology, which recognizes the full divinity and humanity of Jesus Christ, is dismissed by radical theological thought, which accepts the reality of Jesus's historical existence only as detached from the subsequent image—or images—of Christ.

THE IMAGE OF CHRIST AND THE IDEA OF JESUS AS PREEXISTENT GOD

Fromm is convinced that after the end of the first century, the dogma of Christ acquired a new facet. The initial adoptionist doctrine of the idea of Jesus, the man who was adopted by God, turned into something completely different. It has been shown that the idea of Jesus begins with the historical reality of a man who began to preach about the kingdom of God and the apocalyptic expectation that judgment will come upon all the rich and the powerful. Following his death at the hands of the wicked, Jesus was believed to have been raised from the dead, and in this was also raised beyond the boundaries of historical reality into the transcendent reality of God. So what was initially a mere man is now a man become God. The man of history becomes the God of metahistory, a belief that took deep root in the minds of the uneducated Jewish lower classes of the first century. In the centuries to follow, however, a dramatic change happened because Jesus was no longer seen as the man who became God but as a figure who has always been God.[26] In other words, the shift is from a man living in history and ending up in metahistory to a God who lives in metahistory, comes to history by incarnation, and then returns to metahistory. Fromm seems to be convinced that the underlying reason for such a dramatic change of perception is the changing of the social context, which also involved a psychological change in the mind of certain social classes. This means that this change bears with it a social-psychological meaning, which can be discerned only through a thorough study of the people who nurtured the belief. Fromm notices that the shift from the adoptionist image of Jesus, the man who became God, to the more elaborated image of Jesus the Son of Man who has always been God, happened when Christianity went beyond the boundaries of Jewish society. The vast majority of believers were still part of the lower classes, but with the missionary efforts of the apostle Paul, Christianity also began to infiltrate the ruling classes, the educated, and the wealthy.[27] Paul himself had a different social status as he was a Roman citizen and part of those who administered political and legal power. So Christianity began to establish itself outside Palestine as a religion not only of the poor and uneducated but also of those in power, whose degree of education and financial status were well above those of the lower social classes. Christianity did not stop here but went as far as to reach the emperor's household, so it is clear for Fromm that the mindset of the new believers was totally different from that of the early Christians. It is equally important to realize that the shift from Jesus the man who became God to Jesus the God who became man happened not only at the level of social classes—namely, from lower to upper classes—but also at the level of nationality. Once Christianity went beyond Palestine, it is clear that it was not only the Jews who accepted the dogma of Christ but also people from all the nations that made up the Roman Empire.[28]

At this point, the fifth characteristic of radical theology based on Fromm's approach is the belief that Christian doctrines changed as the teaching about Jesus moved from one geographical context to another. So, for radical theology, it is not only history that plays a crucial role in altering the content of doctrine but also geography, which brings with it different social and cultural patterns. So the teaching of Christianity is not unitary as in traditional theology; on the contrary, there is no unique Christian teaching for radical theology but merely a range of different clusters of doctrine that change as time elapses and the social-cultural context changes. There is no single theological truth for radical theology; the only thing that is certain and may be considered truthful is the fact that the idea of truth is subject to change due to historical, social, cultural, and intellectual factors.

Going back to Fromm's argument, the shift from Palestinian to Roman Christianity was made possible because the structure of Roman society changed. When it became possible for aliens to acquire Roman citizenship, it was increasingly clear that the initial class stratification, which involved a clear distinction between the lower and upper classes, also changed. Roman society was no longer divided into the lower and upper classes of first-century Jewish society; the class differentiation surely remained, but Fromm notices that the economic development within the Roman Empire and the acceptance of aliens for citizenship produced what he calls a "progressive feudalization." The idea is that those who became Roman citizens were now part of the upper and middle classes, so other people of lower standing began to work for them. This means that work stratification got back eventually to the initial situation—very similar to first-century Jewish society—with its distinct social classes. Thus, those of lower condition who became Roman citizens had a chance for financial improvement and once achieving that status, they began to oppress those of even lower social standing, which marked the beginnings of the medieval order.[29] The social change brought about a dramatic doctrinal transformation. From the image of Jesus and his eschatological expectation of the kingdom of God that will bring justice for the oppressed, Christianity turned into a religion of the ruling classes with a deep conviction that the kingdom of God has already become a reality through the incarnation of Christ. Thus, Christians no longer looked forward to the future expecting the kingdom of God to come; they rather looked backward to the incarnation of Christ, which already marked the coming of the kingdom. The strict ethical demands of the first Jewish Christians loosened, and the church—now a community including the ruling class—began to work hand in hand with the state, especially in the fourth century. The church no longer looked like a totally different community from the world; it turned increasingly into a community that reflected the pattern of the Roman Empire with its absolute monarchy.[30] Christians were no longer preoccupied with living exemplary moral lives; what they wanted now was to find satisfaction for their conscience through the church's means of grace, or the sacraments. If the early Christians of first-century Jewish society hated all kinds of authority, the new Christians of the fourth century loved authority and especially that provided by the clergy.[31]

All these changes brought about a deep psychological transformation. Jesus was no longer seen as the man who became God but rather as the God who became man in order to suffer for humanity. Fromm explains that the fantasy, which is fundamental for religion, also changed from tendencies that were initially hostile to the father figure to passive submission and love toward the father figure. So the image changed from Jesus the man who became God to Christ the preexistent God of a realized eschatology. Satisfaction was no longer to be sought in the very near future but in the present because all that Christians could hope for was already at hand in Christ. It is important to understand that, in Fromm, the image of Christ the preexistent God had a twofold function: first, to provide a collective fantasy for the lower classes, which could still identify themselves with the suffering of Jesus, and second, to offer an equally crucial collective fantasy for the upper classes, which experienced psychological relief by accepting and professing the love of Christ. This psychological relief was necessary because the upper classes oppressed the lower classes, so the upper classes unconsciously accepted the image of Christ the preexistent God as a means to accept a higher authority toward which they could be submissive. For Fromm this is the final proof that the social function of religion, which is the preservation of social stability,[32] was achieved once more: the lower classes accepted the suffering of Christ because they could embrace them as their own condition, while the upper classes accepted the love of Christ because the preexistent God represented a higher authority that relieved them of the guilt resulting from their oppression of the lower classes. Dogmatically, Jesus was no longer the man become God but the preexistent God become man through incarnation, a doctrine that—unconsciously again—produced in the minds of fourth-century Christians a shift from the father figure to the mother figure. As Christ is both man and God, Fromm is convinced that the only human explanation that makes sense is that of a child in his mother's womb: they are at the same time two distinct individuals and yet one single being. Thus, the collective fantasy of the new Christians, from both lower and upper classes, shifted from the original father figure of the Jewish God to the maternal figure of Mary,[33] the "Great Mother" who mediates salvation through the church.[34]

It is evident that in Fromm the image of Christ is used to prove that it can fit different social contexts. The purpose of the image of Christ is always to prove the fulfillment of the social function of religion, which is to calm the masses in favor of the ruling class.[35] Religion is meant to offer social stability, and the image of Christ can do it in every social context. It did it in first-century Judaism, when the lower uneducated classes identified themselves with the sufferings of the man Jesus who taught them to wait for the full revelation of the kingdom of God in the very near future, and it also did it in the subsequent centuries, when even the upper classes were caught in this collective fantasy. The difference, though, was prominent because Jesus was no longer the man become God but the preexistent God become man through incarnation. From a mere man with authority only over the lower classes, Jesus became the preexistent God who exerted authority even over the ruling classes. Stability was achieved because both lower and ruling classes found satisfaction in the religious fantasy of the image of Christ as preexistent God: the lower classes understood his suffering on the cross for the benefit of all people, while the ruling classes found a higher authority to which they could submit themselves. At the same time, psychological satisfaction came not only from Jesus, the God incarnate, but also from Mary, the mother of God, who supplements as well as completes the figure of the father, so crucial for Fromm in psychoanalytically understanding the mindset of the lower and upper classes as both accepted the image of Christ. Fromm uses Christ to explain the experience of mankind in different social and economic contexts, with specific reference to the fact that the image of Christ can provide psychological satisfaction to every individual human experience, regardless of whether it belongs to the lower or the upper classes.

This is actually the sixth feature of radical theology as discovered in Fromm: the fact that the image of Christ can offer psychological satisfaction. While traditional theology speaks of salvation from sin, radical theology professes the possibility of relief from anguish. Consequently, in traditional theology the result of salvation from sin is peace with God; this, however, does not work in radical theology, which believes that the result of man's relief from his own inner fears is psychological satisfaction. It is evident then that in traditional theology peace has a metaphysical component as it is given and kept by God, who offers salvation, while for radical theology the psychological satisfaction is merely a human feeling that is produced as well as hopefully maintained by man.

THE IMAGE OF CHRIST AND THE IDEA OF JESUS AS SECULARIZED GOD

Following the idea of Jesus as man become God and then the idea of Jesus as preexistent God become man, Fromm investigates what he believes to be another development in the dogma of Christ, namely, the idea of Jesus as secularized God.[36] This particular interpretation of Jesus stems from the teachings of Gnosticism. The Gnostics were socially part of the Hellenistic middle class. Educated and comfortably wealthy, most Gnostics approached Christianity from a thoroughly secularized perspective. This is why their teachings identified neither with the first-century idea of Jesus the man who became God nor with the later idea of Jesus the God who existed before creation. For the Gnostics, Jesus was thought of in terms of the notion of aeon but there was a sharp distinction between the heavenly aeon, who is Christ, and the human manifestation of that aeon, or the Jesus who lived in Palestine. In believing so, the Gnostics dismissed both the idea of Jesus as man turned God and the idea of Jesus as God turned man because they rejected any real union between Christ, who has divine nature, and Jesus, who was just a human being. The resulting concept is that of Jesus seen as secularized God, in the sense that Jesus must be conceived as a man with special qualities that can be termed "divine" even if they are not of such nature. Fromm is clearly a fan of the Gnostic interpretation of Jesus as he writes that "the gnostic ideas of faith . . . correspond exactly with the expectations which we must have on the basis of our study of the social-psychological background of dogmatic development."[37] In other words, social psychology tells us that a man can only be assessed for what he is; so if we see Jesus and he is obviously a man, we must say that he is what he turns out to be: only a man. Any religious significance attached to Jesus, such as his claims to divinity, must be psycho-analytically and social-psychologically interpreted as inherently and essentially human because our historical experience does not prove the existence of a realm that can be conceived as divine. Jesus is divine only to the extent that we are willing to ascribe some special features to him, but these characteristics are essentially human. They can be called divine only based on their specificity, but we all know that they are in fact human.

Hence, Fromm unveils the seventh feature of radical theology, which is the necessity to redefine the divinity of Jesus. However, as only traditional theology believes in the actual divinity of Jesus, the only option for radical theology to continue to speak about Jesus in a relevant way for contemporary society is to drastically reassess the meaning of divinity. Radical theology is willing to talk about the divinity of Jesus for as long as divinity is not ascribed any metaphysical characteristics. Devoid of any metahistorical ontology, the idea of divinity is left with a significance that does not transcend the limits of time and history, so in radical theology divinity is only a special human quality that makes a person truly exceptional.

Resuming Fromm's idea of divinity, it has to be underlined that the Gnostic belief in Jesus as a special man or a man who can be seen as having a set of particular human characteristics—which are so special that we could call them "divine" (and it is because of these characteristics that Jesus was believed to be a secularized God)—also affected Gnostic anthropology and eschatology.[38] For the Gnostics, there was a sharp distinction between the supreme God and the lesser God who created the world.[39] This means that the world was bad from the beginning, so nothing can be done to make it right again. Evil existed from the beginning, so there is no real redemption of humanity as validated by the idea of Jesus as man turned God and by the idea of Jesus as God turned man. The Gnostics were convinced—and Fromm fully subscribes to this interpretation—that Jesus was a man who remained human for his entire life. Jesus, however, was a special human being, so special that some believed him to be divine. As for the Gnostics there was no such thing as redemption of humanity, and Gnosticism began to preach the individual's ideal of knowledge. The human being can attempt to reach a higher state in life through knowledge, so it was knowledge that showed one's true measure. This is why the Gnostics divided people into pneumatics, psychics, and hylics, with degrees of blessedness based on knowledge waning from the first category to the last.[40]

The idea of Jesus as secularized God, so dear to the Gnostics, met fierce opposition from the apologists who came forward with the so-called Logos Christology. Thus, unlike the Gnostics who believed that Jesus was a man throughout his entire life, the apologists pictured Jesus as the incarnation of God's divine Logos, which, from the standpoint of psychoanalysis, is an attempt to restore the authority of the father figure.[41] The Logos shares in God's divine nature and, although he originates in God's being as what Fromm believes to be a voluntary ejection by God of the Logos for the purpose of creation, the Logos is not separated from God. As far as Fromm is concerned, the Logos is a creation in relation to God, but he is not subordinated to God by nature; the Logos is subordinated to God only by origination. The Logos Christology of the apologists also fought monarchianism, which shared the Gnostic distinction between God and Jesus. In both its adoptionist and modalist manifestations, monarchianism tried to preserve the monarchy of God as distinct from the importance of Jesus. Thus, Jesus could be seen either as a man inspired by the spirit of God as in adoptionist monarchianism or as a manifestation of the Father as in modalist monarchianism; in either case, however, Jesus was thought to be totally different from God. From the standpoint of psychoanalysis, which Fromm favors, monarchianism and Gnosticism were religious movements that unconsciously attempted to react against the father figure as well as against God as father figure. While the Gnostics distinguished so sharply between Jesus and God that no connection could be made between humanity and God (the father figure was dismissed as being too remote from humanity), the monarchianists raised Jesus to the level of God's nature, so God is dethroned because he cannot exist on his own without reference to humanity (the father figure is displaced and identified with humanity).[42]

In Fromm, the last attempt to separate Jesus from God in lines with the Gnostic tradition was Arianism.[43] For Arius, Jesus or the Son of God was an independent being from the Father to the point that their essences or natures were utterly different. Jesus was not true God, so he did not have the qualities of divine nature; this is why he did not deserve the same honor as the Father and his knowledge was far from perfect. He was indeed created before the world but he was still a creation of God, which made him a different being in relation to God. By contrast, Athanasius highlighted the co-eternity and the co-essentiality of the Son with the Father, which psychoanalytically is an attempt to produce conformity to the image of the father or the image of God as father.[44] However, in both Arianism and Athanasius's established orthodoxy as encapsulated in the Nicene Creed, the image of Christ is congruent with the human expectations that result from man's daily experience. The lower classes could easily identify themselves with Arianism, which tried to separate human nature from divine nature or the expectations of the lower classes from those of the ruling class, while the upper classes found themselves willing to embrace Nicene Christianity, which is a sign that the ruling class was unconsciously willing to embrace the plight of the lower classes by identifying the image of Jesus with that of God the father.[45]

Fromm's discussion of the masses' unconscious willingness to accept theological doctrines displays the eighth feature of radical theology, which is that Christian doctrine is not accepted consciously but rather unconsciously. According to radical theology, people may believe that they have specific reasons for accepting certain doctrines, but what ultimately counts for the actual reception of Christianity—irrespective of its forms, orthodox or heretical—is the unconscious component of individual as well as collective psychology. It should be highlighted here that, for radical theology, this unconscious decision to choose certain forms of doctrine is historically conditioned because people make their choices based on a series of specific actions with concrete repercussions in time and space.

To conclude, in Fromm, the image of Christ is used to explain psychoanalytically the experience of the social classes, lower and ruling, based on the evolution of Christology in the first four centuries. The image of Christ can be deciphered through the idea of Jesus, which can fit different social contexts in order to provide psychological relief for a wide range of attitudes and experiences of the individuals who make up the lower and upper classes. Thus, the idea of Jesus—so central to Fromm's image of Christ—acquires threefold significance.

First, Jesus can be seen as the man who became God, and this particular image was famous among the lowest classes of first-century Jewish society. In Fromm, this attitude toward Jesus should be psychoanalytically interpreted as the unconscious desire of the oppressed masses to overthrow the father figure and particularly the father figure of God. The idea of Jesus as the man who became God bears with it the central imagery of human suffering with which the oppressed masses could easily identify on a regular basis. As they could not overthrow their oppressors in reality, they unconsciously used the religious image of Christ as Jesus turned God in order both to overthrow the father figure of God—which represents the authority of the ruling classes—and to find a reason for their constant suffering in the death of Jesus. The idea of Jesus the man turned God also contains a revolutionary element in its eschatology, because Jesus preached the coming of the kingdom of God, which brought with it the final judgment of the wicked. As Jesus was believed to return from heaven to enforce the judgment, the masses used the image of Christ to unconsciously explain the experience of their constant suffering through their repressed desire to overthrow the father figure of God, who is also and simultaneously identified with the ruling, oppressing class. God is overthrown because the man Jesus is made God, so God is no longer the only divine monarch; in the very same way, at a different level, the ruling classes are unconsciously overthrown because their authority and power will be eventually challenged when God's final judgment is dramatically enforced on earth. This is how the image of Christ as Jesus turned God is used to explain the attitudes and experiences of the lowest Jewish class in first-century Jewish society. Thus, the image of Christ is used specifically to make sense of the daily experiences of oppressed people in the specific context of first-century Judaism.

Second, the image of Christ is presented by means of the idea of Jesus as the preexistent God. This second idea of Jesus represents for Fromm a significant dogmatic development, which discloses a dramatic change in the inner structure of the people who accepted Christianity. If the first idea of Jesus as the man turned God found wide acceptance among the lowest and most oppressed classes of first-century Jewish society, the second idea of Jesus, now as the preexistent God, is a clear indication that the members of the Christian church no longer come exclusively from the lowest social strata. Through the missionary endeavors of the apostle Paul, himself a middle-class educated fellow, Christianity began to reach the upper classes of non-Jewish people to the point that even the Roman emperor's household was caught by his teachings. This time, however, as Christianity began to make sense not only to the oppressed classes but also to the exploiting ones, the image of Christ needed a drastic reinterpretation, which for Fromm is an evident dogmatic evolution from the idea of Jesus the man turned God to the idea of Jesus the God turned man or the preexistent God. Jesus was no longer seen as the man whose exemplary life made him so special that God himself raised him from the dead in order to adopt him as his Son. The ruling classes could not accept such an image of Christ because they could not accept—not even unconsciously—the fact that their authority could be overthrown in any way. What they could accept was a confirmation of their authority, which was strengthened by the image of Christ as the Jesus seen as preexistent God. Jesus no longer has to live like a man and suffer in order to acquire a higher status; Jesus is now the preexistent God who accepted incarnation in order to save humanity. This means that Jesus has always had full authority as God, which is the ruling classes' unconscious attempt to reconfirm their authority over the lower classes. At the same time, however, Fromm indicates that the ruling classes experienced—again unconsciously—a deep feeling of guilt toward those they oppressed, so Jesus is not only the preexistent God but also the God who decided to take human form in order to redeem those in need. This is why the preexistent God, who had full authority over everything, decided to suffer for the salvation of the entire humanity. So the image of Christ as the Jesus seen as preexistent God helped the ruling classes of non-Jewish ancestry—wealthy educated Greeks and Romans—to reconfirm their authority as well as offer relief for the sorrow they experienced as a result of oppressing the poor. At the same time, however, the image of Christ as the Jesus who became man despite being God from the beginning was still appealing to the lower classes due to the fact that he suffered and died on the cross. The father figure and particularly the father figure of God no longer needs to be overthrown because Jesus was always God. A particular development of this image of Christ as the Jesus seen as preexistent God is the rise of Mariology, when Mary is believed to be the mother of God who sheltered and protected Jesus. But as Jesus is both God and man, this is again a confirmation that the upper classes found satisfaction in two ways: first by reconfirming their authority through the image of Jesus as preexistent God or as a figure who has always had full authority, and second by finding a way to compensate the suffering of the oppressed masses through the idea of Mary who accepts Jesus in her womb. Either way, the image of Christ is used to explain the experiences of the social classes in the specific context of the pagan society of the second and third centuries.

The image of Christ underwent a third distinct development. Fromm makes it clear that from the idea of Jesus as the man turned God to the idea of Jesus as the God turned man or the preexistent God it was necessary that contexts should be changed. Different contexts meant different experiences and, as experiences needed to find a proper significance, the dogmatic evolution of Christology was nothing but a normal development. Fromm identifies though a third image of Christ, to which he finds himself quite attached, and this is the idea of Jesus as the secularized God. Nurtured particularly by the Gnostics, this image pictures Jesus as a man who has always been a man and will always be a man. The Gnostics believed that there is a sharp distinction between the realm of God and the realm of humanity and in that belief they performed a radical shift in anthropology and cosmology. Thus, they said that the world was not created by the supreme God but only by a lesser God, and this is why the world has always been evil. Because the world is evil from the beginning there is nothing that can be done to redeem it. No one can redeem the world, not even Jesus, the man of exquisite human qualities. The Gnostics believed that the man Jesus corresponded to the heavenly aeon of Christ but the two, Jesus and Christ, could never be identified with each other in reality. There is no real or hypostatic union between Jesus and Christ or between humanity and divinity, so the only way to put together the idea of Jesus as man and the image of Christ as God is to say that Jesus was a man of tremendous qualities that were so special they could be considered "divine." It is in this that Jesus can be seen as the secularized God: he is a man, but he is such a special man that he can seen as having divine qualities. He is not divine, but his exemplary life was believed to have been similar to that of a divine figure. Psychoanalytically, this is again an attempt to overthrow the father figure of God because he is seen to be so remote from humanity that human beings cannot even attempt to come closer to him. Consequently, the Gnostics did not focus on the idea of redemption but rather on the ideal of knowledge. Fromm explains that this type of Christological imagery was taken over by adoptionist and modalist monarchianism as well as by Arianism, all of which attempted to picture Jesus as distinct in nature and essence from God the Father. To be sure, the image of Christ as the Jesus who can be seen as a secularized God was another attempt to psychoanalytically explain the unconscious desire of some religious communities to make sense of their daily experiences by overthrowing the father figure—particularly the father figure of God—in contexts imbued with the oppressing authority of the ruling classes.

CHAPTER 5

RADICAL CHRISTIAN THOUGHT IN MID POSTMODERNITY

PAUL RICOEUR AND THE FALLIBILITY THEORY IN THE SECOND HALF OF THE TWENTIETH CENTURY

INTRODUCTION

As a Protestant writing in the second half of the twentieth century in western Europe, Paul Ricoeur (1913–2005) could not ignore the recent legacy of theological liberalism despite his predominant philosophical interests. Although he did not share the "classical" liberal interest in Christology, Ricoeur was intensely concerned with the problematics of anthropology, hermeneutics, and hence biblical interpretation. These are all closely related to his notion of fallibility as the possibility of the existence of moral evil in the constitution of humanity, in close connection with some fundamental issues such as myth, symbolism, symbolism of evil, human reality, freedom, and transcendence. The significance of Ricoeur's idea of fallibility is presented mainly in connection with contemporary radical Catholicism and especially with reference to the works of Edward Schillebeeckx. Ricoeur's concept of fallibility and its satellite notions—myth, symbolism of evil, human reality, freedom, and transcendence—are analyzed in close relationship to Schillebeeckx's anthropological idea of humble humanism. Then Ricoeur's notion of fallibility is compared to Don Cupitt's philosophical nonrealism, which posits the existence of God as merely a conceptual reality embedded in man's consciousness.

The notion of fallibility in Ricoeur is presented by means of the idea of fault.[1] In describing fault, Ricoeur resorts to the introduction of two fundamental aspects that depict the nature of fault, namely, opaqueness and absurdity. Therefore, the very nature of fault is opaque and absurd, so it escapes pure description. In other words, there is no possibility of a pure imagery of fault that can be presented in unmediated terms. Fault cannot be presented in a purely theoretical manner because it goes beyond the reasonableness of pure rationality.[2] In order to understand the nature of fault, one has to break the barriers of fundamental ontology[3] and pure description.[4] Thus, for Ricoeur, fault is somehow external to man's ontological constitution.[5]

In speaking about fault—and it is evident that fault has to do with the human being itself—Ricoeur places his philosophy against Christian theology, understood in traditional terms. It is quite clear that he does not want to enter any dispute with Christian theology, but the mere presentation of fault as part of the human being's constitution—regardless of whether fault is external or internal to man—begs for a comparison. One can speak of both similarities and dissimilarities between Ricoeur and Christian theology. The similarity resides in the fact that both Ricoeur and Christian theology see the nature of fault as opaque and absurd. Christian theology presents human fault in terms leaving no doubt that fault is a human reality that pushes human beings to act in unreasonable ways. The dissimilarity has to do with the possibility of describing fault. If for Ricoeur fault escapes pure description, Christian theology has no problem in identifying fault as a reality closely connected to what the human being actually is in the world or how it can be presented in a purely theological way.

FAULT AND MYTH

Why cannot Ricoeur present fault in a direct way? Because his conviction that fault is external to man's ontological constitution requires a certain mediation in presenting the idea of fault.[6] For Ricoeur, fault can be properly described only if we make use of mediating concepts. This is because while the inner constitution of man, which does not contain the reality of fault, can be presented by pure description, the idea of fault, which is external to the inner constitution of man, needs a more practical or empirical presentation, and this cannot be done unless we use concepts that mediate the state of man as inner constitution and the state of man as external reality.

It is clear that Ricoeur's anthropology is dualistic when it comes to the representation of the human being: there is first the reality of man's inner constitution, which can be thought of in terms of pure description, and then there is the reality of man's external manifestation, which is triggered by action of passions over the will.[7] This is important because the concept of will seems to be the actual connection between what can be called the theoretical image of man, which has nothing to do with fault, and the practical/empirical image of man, which is characterized by fault. This connection introduces the mediating concepts that put Ricoeur's theoretical and empirical man together, and these concepts are myths,[8] or what Ricoeur calls "concrete mythics."[9]

It is crucial once again to underline Ricoeur's stand as compared to traditional Christian theology, and in this respect one can only identify a thorough dissimilarity between Ricoeur's thought and Christian anthropology. Human fault is seen in Ricoeur as being properly mediated as well as described by means of the idea of myth, which calls for a symbolic, even supernatural, presentation of a natural reality. In Christian theology, however, there is no such thing as myth in presenting human fault. Christian theology has a very concrete image of fault as ontological reality because it is fault that breaks the connection between God and man. In Ricoeur, the idea of myth automatically annuls what traditional Christian theology sees as ontologically real. In other words, the notion of myth makes reference to supernatural realities that must be understood in terms of natural realities, while in Christian theology supernatural realities are understood as having ontological existence. But why is myth so important for Ricoeur? Because it presents the practical reality of the human being as affected by passions that result in the empirical reality of fault, and fault cannot be adequately presented unless introduced into philosophical reflection. In other words, if one really needs to know how the reality of human fault should be understood, then he or she must resort to philosophical discourse, which is capable of presenting the issue of fault provided fault is understood in mythological terms.

Myths belong to religion, but as far as Ricoeur is concerned religion cannot help philosophy because religious myths exist in an "unrefined state."[10] This can mean that religion in itself is unable to offer a relevant and meaningful explanation[11] of what the human being is in its fundamental ontology unless accompanied by the philosophical discourse that informs both the theoretical and the practical existence of man. Ricoeur's plan is to refine the myths of religion—and theology—in order to provide a relevant account of man's existence in the world. Therefore, he perceives myth as the shell of language. Myth is the image of language or, as Ricoeur puts it, a secondary development of a primary language.[12] This particular sort of language is the "language of avowal,"[13] which, in Ricoeur, presents the idea of fault. It is crucial to note here that for Ricoeur it is this primary language that presents fundamental importance as compared to the myth. This is because the fundamental language behind the myth addresses philosophy, while the myth itself can only speak to religion and theology. The language behind myth is to be approached by the philosopher, and it is the philosopher who can eventually decipher as well as refine the idea behind the religious and theological myths.[14]

In other words, any direct reference to myth will lead to discussions of sin and guilt, both of which are irrelevant for today's people and philosophically crude in the sense that philosophy just cannot accept them unless refined by means of philosophical discourse. If Ricoeur's ideas are applied to Christian theology, it means that traditional Christianity is religiously irrelevant for the men and women of today's world, as well as philosophically inadequate for those involved in the quest for truth. To give just one example, the traditional idea of sin as presenting traditional Christianity is totally irrelevant without being refined through the idea of fault as extracted from the mythological image of religious sin.

Therefore, the first characteristic of radical theology emerges from Ricoeur's approach, and this is the reassessment of major traditional doctrines through the idea of myth. For radical theology, which is fundamentally rational and thus accepts only the proofs that can be accepted by reason and senses, any traditional doctrine that implies supernatural elements is automatically discarded. The example of the doctrine of sin, which is included among supernaturally informed teachings because sin can only be perceived as such if connected in some way to God, is not singular. Any other traditional doctrine that makes reference to supernatural realities—Christ's preexistence, his incarnation, the virgin birth, his resurrection and ascension, our salvation from sin, eternal life, Christ's return, and the final judgment—are all reinterpreted in such a way that their supernatural elements are canceled in favor of explanations that satisfy the rationally oriented experience of contemporary people.

From Myth to Symbol

What Ricoeur proposes is to advance a philosophical discourse that reinterprets the direct language of religious myths in order to present them as indirect and metaphorical concepts that inform our image of humanity. Thus, the idea of sin as a direct and proper term must be turned into an indirect and figurative term if we want it to be philosophically relevant. In Ricoeur, this transition from direct meaning to indirect significance and from mythology to symbolism is called the "exegesis of the symbol."[15] To put it in simple terms, the exegesis of the symbol is actually hermeneutics, so in order to refine mythology Ricoeur resorts to hermeneutics. The application of hermeneutics to religious mythology results in philosophical symbolism. With direct reference to the idea of fault, the application of hermeneutics to the traditional religious and theological mythology of sin leads to the symbolism of evil.[16] It should be stressed here that Ricoeur's symbolism of evil is the philosophical translation of what he calls the mythics, or the mythology of "bad will."[17] This seems to be the practical application of his understanding of man as external reality because it can be investigated by means of the concept of fault. Thus, fault must be understood symbolically by deciphering and refining fundamental myths—such as original sin—as symbols of the conflict between order and chaos. To take the practical example of traditional Christian theology, the myth of Adam's fall, for instance, should be understood as the symbol of sin. It is clear therefore that, in Ricoeur, hermeneutics moves from myth to symbol and then from knowledge to philosophy.[18]

It is not enough for Ricoeur to understand and apply the dynamics of hermeneutics from mythology to symbolism; this would be to go only halfway. After the refinement of myths and their subsequent understanding as symbols, it is absolutely necessary that symbols should be drawn closer to man's knowledge of himself. Actually, following the transformation of myths into symbols, one must perform the insertion of symbols into man's knowledge of himself.[19] With reference to the concept of fault, Ricoeur leads us to believe that the myth of Adam's fall cannot be properly understood if taken on its own or in its original religious and theological setting. In order for the myth of Adam's fall to be accurately presented today, we must apply the hermeneutics of the symbolism of evil to this myth, and this is how we shall expose it as the symbol of sin (or of original sin). Once here, we have to understand that symbolism must also be deciphered by means of language—in Ricoeur's case, the language of avowal, which expresses the ideas of fault and evil in philosophical terms. This particular language, however, is a matter of self-consciousness, and self-consciousness is a matter of one's will since the symbolism of evil is based on deciphering the mythology of bad will.

So fault and evil have to do with bad will, and we know this because we translated the myth of Adam's fall into the symbol of original sin, and we reached the conclusion that the idea of fault or evil is an issue with a direct connection with the individual will. This does not mean we have automatically discovered the locus of evil in human will;[20] this would be too simple. Having established the way hermeneutics functions from mythology to symbolism, or from the mythology of bad will to the symbolism of evil with reference to the idea of fault, Ricoeur still asks himself which is the locus of evil.[21] If human reality is affected by evil, how and where did evil manage to get within it? What actually makes evil possible in human reality?[22] For Ricoeur, finding an answer to this question is unveiling the essence of fallibility.[23]

To Ricoeur, this means that man is fallible and evil is part of his existence, but the actual way evil grew to affect human existence is what concerns him.[24] It is absolutely essential to stress here that Ricoeur notices a crucial fact, namely, that it is possible to admit that evil came into the world through man. At this point—at least at the level of basic linguistics—Ricoeur concurs with traditional Christian theology because both admit that evil came into the world through man. The problem begins, however, when we attempt to see what the coming of evil into the world through man means for Ricoeur and what it means for traditional Christianity.

The explanation is pretty straightforward with traditional Christianity. Sin is not understood as a symbol because Adam's fall is not considered a myth. Adam's fall is a historical fact, therefore original sin, and sin in general, is an ontological reality that places the human being in direct opposition to God—and God is neither myth nor symbol but a person who has an ontological status. In other words, traditional Christianity promotes a dual ontological reality: the metaphysical reality of God and the physical reality of man. Sin is performed by man and caused by man, so the locus of sin is the human being. Traditional Christianity also allows for the difference between sin and evil, as the sin of man is the manifestation of an evil that exists beyond man.

For Ricoeur, though, things are a bit more complicated. Sin is a symbol because Adam's fall is a myth, not a historical fact; therefore, original sin and sin in general are mere symbols of human reality as characterized by evil. Ricoeur's presentation of Adam's fall as a myth leads not only to the explicit transformation of sin into a symbol but also to the implicit annulment of traditional Christianity's dual ontological reality. Thus, in Ricoeur, God can be either a myth or a symbol because sin itself is a symbol. There is no ontological status attached to sin in Ricoeur, so if sin does not exist as ontological reality, why should God? There can be a metaphysical reality of God in Ricoeur, but this does not necessarily have to be ontological; it can be mythical or symbolic or even conceptual, but it does not seem to be ontological. Therefore, in Ricoeur, God seems to be present only as a concept that symbolically explains the fundamental nature of religious and theological mythology.

The second feature of radical theology now becomes clear in Ricoeur: the traditional doctrine of God, which ascribes to him ontological status and therefore a genuine, real existence beyond the boundaries of physical reality, is given up. God is no longer the God who lives outside nature; God is now the God who lives within nature. This is an indication of the fact that God cannot be a being in the true sense of the word; he can only be a concept, a myth, or a symbol that helps us decipher the intricacies of our own experience.

FINITUDE AND INFINITUDE
BETWEEN FREEDOM AND EVIL

Ricoeur's philosophy of fallibility cannot be understood unless the fundamentals of his understanding of man are unveiled. For him, man is a dual being in the sense that he is ontologically confronted with the disproportion between the polarities of finitude and infinitude.[25] Man must be understood in terms of the mediation between human finitude and infinitude because it is this mediation that explains man's fallibility.[26] Thus, the translation of myths into symbols and their subsequent insertion in man's knowledge of himself lay the basis of a philosophical discourse that paves the way to the idea of the possibility of evil,[27] and this is fallibility.[28] In other words, fallibility is the possibility of evil because fault and evil realities resulted from the translation of myths, such as Adam's fall, into symbols, such as original sin. Nevertheless, both myths and symbols must be inserted in man's knowledge of himself, so sin—understood as symbol—teaches man about himself, not about something beyond him. But this is not enough for Ricoeur. Translating myths into symbols and then inserting symbols into man's knowledge of himself is not sufficient. What we have to do from now on is apply a certain type of hermeneutics to symbols. Thus, symbols must be understood against the text, but Ricoeur's hermeneutics reads the text by working not only behind the symbol but from the symbol.[29] This means that the symbols we find in the text can lead to new meanings that inform man's knowledge of himself.[30]

It seems that Ricoeur's theory of fallibility based on his hermeneutics that works from the symbol makes sure that his anthropology benefits from some sort of ongoing relevance.[31] If the symbol is the starting point of hermeneutics, the meaning of the symbol undergoes a constant process of change, which is aimed at offering an understanding of humanity that presents constant relevance throughout history. Thus, Ricoeur's philosophy is historically conditioned to such a high extent that it can offer a relevant image of humanity at any given historical stage. The symbols of religious and theological texts can therefore be permanently translated from myths into new images of humanity that explain why the possibility of evil is present within man's existence. It is interesting that Ricoeur prefers to talk about fallibility in terms of the possibility of evil, not in terms of the actuality of evil. This does not of course cancel his recognition of the actuality of evil; on the contrary, he seems to attempt to provide an explanation of why evil is constantly present in human life, and fallibility described as possibility makes evil an immanent reality of man's existence. In fact, it is the possibility of evil that explains the actuality of evil as manifestation of human fallibility, and in this respect Ricoeur resorts to psychoanalysis[32] and political philosophy.[33] He is convinced that in order for us to understand fallibility properly, we have to go beyond religion and theology into the realm of psychoanalysis and political philosophy. Human fallibility is so vividly confirmed by the historical reality of evil that Ricoeur cannot conceive human fallibility without the problem of power. Resorting to psychoanalysis and political philosophy does not mean breaking up with religion and theology—it is actually the other way around: psychoanalysis and political philosophy continue what religion and theology initiated by symbolically presenting the reality of human alienation.[34] In other words, Ricoeur acknowledges that the human being has a fundamental problem, which can be described in terms of the possibility of evil or fallibility. This is because fallibility is present in everyday reality to such an extent that from mythological religion and theology to scientific psychoanalysis and political philosophy, man has abundantly proved his utter inability to know himself. Ricoeur is convinced that the symbolism of evil is always followed or accompanied by the empiricism of the will; fallibility is not only a philosophical-theoretical issue but also a historical-practical problem. Man has a serious problem that can be understood only if he accepts the reality of his will as being a slave-will,[35] a "free will that is bound and always finds itself already bound."[36] So man's fallibility must be perceived by means of the tension between his free will and the realities that constantly bind his will.

Even if man's will is bound, Ricoeur still speaks of freedom in connection with evil.[37] He cautions us to be very careful when we link freedom to evil because such a discussion does not solve the problem of the origin of evil. The idea of freedom shows only the place of the manifestation of evil but not its origin. Ricoeur realizes that the introduction of freedom within the discussion of evil may direct our attention to the idea that evil may be a reality stemming from outside the human being. In other words, the human being itself may happen not to be what Ricoeur calls "the radical source of evil."[38] This also entails that man proves not to be "the absolute evil doer."[39]

At this point, Ricoeur's vision appears to come much closer to traditional Christian theology where evil is indeed an external reality to the human being. Man is certainly not the source of evil; the source of evil must be searched beyond the possibilities and frontiers of man's existence in what the primary sources of Christianity call "Satan," seen as a creation of God who chose to use his freedom in an utterly faulty way. Therefore, in traditional Christianity, evil even has an ontological status in the sense that it exists as a reality that manifests itself actively. Moreover, evil is even a personal reality because the originating being of evil can relate itself to the created reality of God's universe, including the human being. It is true that Ricoeur does not seem ready to admit that evil has an ontological status as in traditional Christianity; he nevertheless acknowledges the possibility of ascribing to evil an external dimension or an otherness with a real existence beyond the human being.

This is obvious when Ricoeur says that evil affects human existence. It is indeed very difficult to perceive evil on its own in the sense of pointing one's finger to a reality—personal or impersonal—that can be called evil. What can be seen, however, is that human reality—to which evil may be external—is categorically affected by evil, and it is in this particular way that evil can be seen as manifest. In other words, we can identify evil by noticing the way it manifests within human existence. Evil is manifest when it affects human existence, so it is from this empirical observation that we can trace evil back to its—probably external—origin beyond the human being. It is important to see at this point the very way Ricoeur describes the mechanism of evil. The human being is affected by evil—and this is pretty much the only way we can see and understand the existence of evil—but we gather from this that evil can exist beyond us. If this is true, then evil does exist apart from us and beyond us but, at the same time, evil affects us in such a way that we are contaminated by it. So, in Ricoeur, the manifestation of evil within the human being is realized by contamination.[40] This means that the origin or the source of evil is totally inaccessible to us directly; man can have access to evil only by the mediation offered through its relationship to us, namely, through what Ricoeur calls "the state of temptation, aberration or blindness."[41] Thus, evil is mediated to the human being, who in turn is contaminated by it.[42]

Such a presentation of evil can lead to some sort of an objectivized perspective on evil in the sense that evil is a reality that can affect us in a way that excludes our subjective contribution. Evil is out there, beyond the reality of our own being, and it affects us without any subjective contribution from us. We are affected by evil because evil manifests itself within us in a way rather implacably impressed upon us. Ricoeur realizes such a danger, so he continues to portray evil as a reality that not only affects us but also is committed by us. The concept of responsibility as attached to freedom[43] is crucial here because freedom must take upon itself a double role: that of accepting evil as committed and that of seeing evil as not committed. This apparently leads to the conclusion that evil is manifest and thereby committed by man through his own freedom. Therefore, freedom is both the manifestation and the author of evil as far as the human being is concerned. Man can equally manifest evil and author evil. This does not mean that freedom is the origin of evil but only that it can manifest itself as the author of evil within the human being. The bottom line for Ricoeur is that evil can be set within the realm of human freedom, which eventually places man in a position of relationship with the origin of evil.[44]

Ricoeur is again quite close to the traditional side of Christianity because the manifestation of evil is evident in Scripture, and it is related to man's acts, personality, and nature, as well as to Satan as the very source of evil. Where Ricoeur departs from the Christian tradition is his theory of human freedom as connected to evil because God is excluded from the picture. There is no explanation of the relationship between evil, man, and God in Ricoeur. Evil may come from outside the human being—and Ricoeur is pretty clear about this—but nothing is said about why evil is so persistently attached to humanity. Of course, the supernatural dimension of evil, which involves the ontological status of evil, is not present in Ricoeur's theory. In traditional Christianity, on the other hand, man is anything but a free being. Evil affects him in such a way that life can better be described as being choked by the reality of evil; man is utterly sinful because this is his very nature. Man cannot exert his freedom in connection with evil; what man can do is refrain from certain manifestations of evil in his life, but this does not mean he enjoys total freedom in living, assessing, and manifesting himself in relationship to the reality of evil. In other words, man cannot avoid evil because evil is linked to his very nature. Whatever man is in his natural state generates evil even if man can—to a certain and very limited degree—avoid some manifestations of evil; he cannot, however, avoid evil because he is evil. Thus, traditional Christianity may accept Ricoeur's theory of contamination when it comes to presenting the way evil affects the human being, but this must be supplemented by the observation that man is not only contaminated by evil and chooses to act in an evil way; man even likes to act evil and cannot live without being and acting evil.

The third characteristic of radical theology is thus unfolded based on Ricoeur's anthropology: while evil may be ascribed an external dimension by comparison with man, so that man could be considered evil because evil exists outside him, there is no indication that evil has an ontological source as in traditional theology. Quite the contrary, in radical theology man is seen as evil but not because he was influenced by an ontological evil that affected man's created nature, but because the variegated conditions of man's natural environment turn out to produce a general context that can be described as evil. This also has implications in connection with the way radical theology perceives human freedom. Thus, in radical theology, man can act freely despite the evil conditions within which he lives. He cannot eradicate evil, but he can strive to turn the world into a better place. In clear opposition to traditional theology, which does not believe in the possibility that man could change the world by his own power and inner qualities, radical theology is very optimistic about man's capacity to act against evil.

THE PRIMORDIAL SELF BETWEEN THE CONSCIOUSNESS OF FAULT AND THE CONSCIOUSNESS OF EVIL

A certain apprehension of this necessity can be detected in Ricoeur when he acknowledges the fact that he does not want to commit certain evil acts but he nevertheless does them. The realization of this dilemma, which places the human being between the rock and the hard place in relation to his own self, is defined by Ricoeur as the "consciousness of fault."[45] When we commit evil acts, we actually see who we really are. Ricoeur even says that we are "contracted and bounded"[46] in an act that displays our inner selves. The mechanism or even the mechanics of evil presuppose a causality of evil that pushes the human being to act evil despite his desire not to commit evil. This means there is something beyond our will but still within ourselves that forces us to commit evil acts despite our desire to oppose such manifestation. The phrase used by Ricoeur to introduce this entity beyond our will but still within ourselves is "primordial self."[47] The primordial self cannot be directly accessed by us; what we can do in relationship to it is see and perceive its specific acts, which trigger within us the consciousness of evil. In this sense, the consciousness of evil makes us resort to the primordial self or, in Ricoeur's words, "this consciousness is a recourse to the primordial self beyond its acts."[48]

The consciousness of evil cannot exist, however, without an awareness that allows the human being to realize its fallibility. This particular awareness, which permits us to see our relationship with evil, is termed by Ricoeur "the consciousness of freedom."[49] We have to enjoy this freedom if we want to see ourselves as we really are, but at this point Ricoeur holds a divergent position in relation to traditional Christianity. It is true that Christianity admits the reality of sin cannot be fully apprehended without freedom. Man, however, does not possess freedom in his natural state affected by sin; man is free only after God intervenes in his life and makes him aware of his condition. So, in traditional Christianity, man reaches the state of freedom despite his natural sinful constitution, which makes him a slave to sin and blind to the consequences of sin. Man can indeed see both his sinful condition and the results of his sin following the external intervention of God upon his natural condition, which results in freedom. Unlike traditional Christianity, which presents the reality of human freedom as an external and divine intervention despite man's natural state, Ricoeur posits the reality of freedom within the natural constitution of humanity. Man is free in his natural state even if his dual anthropology makes him aware that his will is bounded and constrained by the reality of the primordial self. Moreover, unlike traditional Christianity, which allows the consciousness of evil and the consciousness of freedom only in man's regenerated state—namely, following God's external intervention in man's life—Ricoeur presents both the consciousness of evil and the consciousness of freedom as realities of man's natural constitution.

This hermeneutics is possible because man is capable of handling the significance of religious mythology. For Ricoeur, the world of myths is broken[50]—a rather vague statement but one that could be interpreted in the sense that the world of myths is deciphered. If this is true, then it follows that myths have already been translated into symbols, so we now have to grapple with the significance of symbols. As Ricoeur's hermeneutics is based on his conviction that we must not work behind the symbol but from the symbol, it means that we must wrestle not only with the current significance we attribute to symbols but also with what the symbol can acquire in future. With reference to fallibility, we shall have to recapture the symbolism of evil as presented by the myth of the fall. Ricoeur's translation of the myth of the fall into the symbolism of evil presupposes at least the recognition that the myth of the fall is not all encompassing.[51] To be sure, in Ricoeur, the myth of the fall does not include other equally crucial myths.[52]

At this point, Ricoeur distances himself again from traditional Christianity, which makes the fall responsible for chaos, spiritual blinding, and a restless soul.[53] At this point, it should be reaffirmed that traditional Christianity does not place the fall, as well as the resulting chaos, spiritual blinding, and restless soul, within the category of myths. The fall is the willful acceptance of sin and also the committing of sin, so it is a reality that can be seen as deeply rooted in man's existence. Sin is a human reality and the way from total freedom to total sinfulness is not a myth that requires symbolic hermeneutics—or man's intervention upon himself in order to refine the myth of the fall with view to producing the symbolism of evil. The fall is a human reality that requires God's intervention from outside the human being in order to restore man's existence with view to producing a new reality: personal, spiritual/physical, historical, existential, and so on. To draw the line, traditional Christianity—unlike Ricoeur—tackles the issues of man's fall, chaos, spiritual blinding, and the restless soul from the perspective of human reality and causality as historical events with ongoing historical consequences. Ricoeur breaks the fall apart from the rest and insists that the fall is a myth that presents us with a symbolism of evil. One possible conclusion is that the fall—as a myth, of course—cannot be held responsible for the reality of evil in the world. The fall is just a myth that talks about the reality of evil, but it is not in itself the very cause of evil. This is why in Ricoeur freedom can exist "after" the fall; there is actually no "after" moment following the fall because the fall itself is not a historical event but only a myth. As a myth, the fall cannot be followed—in a chain of causality—either by chaos or by spiritual blinding and the restless soul. They are all myths presenting the reality of human evil in a form that can be refined symbolically. Myths are important for Ricoeur because they display not only our fallibility—and also our fault—but also the fact that we can relate to our fallibility in freedom. It is due to myths that we can fully realize the consciousness of fault as well as the consciousness of freedom. Myths are therefore ways that help us cope with our own existence by explaining to us that our faults not only belong to ourselves but also can be understood by freedom. In other words, the myth—which is essentially part of the past—supports our understanding of ourselves in the present, so it is only logical to claim that myths connect the past to the present and the present to the past. This is because by understanding, deciphering, and refining the myth—the fall, for instance—we affirm our awareness of fault, so we manifest our consciousness of fault, which, for Ricoeur, is the condition of the consciousness of freedom.[54]

It is here that we are presented with the fourth characteristic of radical theology promoted by Ricoeur, which is the insistence on the specific redefinition of fall as myth. If in traditional theology the fall is seen as a historical event because man is believed to have sinned against God and therefore brought sin in the world, in radical theology the fall does not exist as a historical event. The fall did not happen in history as any other event; it is just a myth or even a figure of speech that tells us evil is in the world and therefore we should act responsibly against it and against its devastating consequences. So, in radical theology, we are not free from evil, but we can try to counter its influence because the myth of the fall makes us aware of its presence among us.

THE PRIMORDIAL SELF AS THE ADVERSARY AND THE OTHER

The myth of the fall is crucial for Ricoeur because it can be treated independently from other myths, which means that, on its own, the myth of the fall is subject to colorful symbolism.[55] Ricoeur can trace at least two aspects that flow directly from the myth of the fall. The first is the coming of evil into the world[56] by means of man's positing of it,[57] and the second is man's positing of evil as the result of man's yielding to the adversary.[58] It is quite clear that Ricoeur's understanding of the myth of the fall is based on an exegetical hermeneutics that stresses the idea of evil; what is less clear—or actually rather unclear—resides in Ricoeur's use of the concept of "adversary." Ricoeur's "adversary" is essential at this point provided we understand the mechanism of evil as extracted from the symbolism of evil based on the myth of the fall. Evil exists in the world because it came into the world, and it came into the world because man affirmed or postulated it.[59] Evil may well exist beyond the human being itself, but this means that evil exists also beyond the world of man. Evil, however, entered the world of man as soon as man postulated it or acknowledged it. One could speculate on the meaning of Ricoeur's idea of positing evil unless he had said that man posited evil because he yielded to the adversary. So the coming of evil into the world is directly linked—through man's positing of it—to the fact that man surrendered to the adversary.[60]

Who or what is the adversary? It is very difficult to say who or what the adversary is given that Ricoeur does not elaborate on the idea of the adversary. Even without a clear definition of the adversary, it is quite logical to see the connection between evil and the adversary as well as the fact that man seems to be in the middle—namely, between the reality of evil and the reality of the adversary. The difficulty of identifying the adversary resides in Ricoeur's—probably deliberate—decision not to name the adversary. Some observations can nevertheless be made: first, the adversary is somehow beyond man's will because man yielded to him or it; second, the adversary is—at least to a certain degree—connected to the reality of evil as either the source or a cause of evil; and third, the adversary is not necessarily external to man even if it affects his will. These three characteristics lack a clear referent, but they do remind us of Ricoeur's definition of the primordial self. The primordial self lies within man and acts beyond man's will, and the consciousness of fault—and implicitly the reality of evil—is manifested in its specific acts. But why is the primordial self the "adversary"? Probably because it cannot be directly accessible to man, so man has no power or capacity to control the evil mediated through his specific acts.[61] Man acknowledges the reality of evil, he can even realize that there is something in him that binds his will, but he cannot refrain from doing the wrong deeds he hates to perform. This particular awareness of man triggers his consciousness of fault, but the consciousness of fault is available to man only through and due to the consciousness of freedom. In other words, man is aware of the reality of evil because he is a free being despite the binding nature of his primordial self. This interpretation seems to be confirmed by Ricoeur's conclusion that by means of affirming evil, freedom finds itself in an odd position, and this is the position of the victim.[62] For Ricoeur, the position of the victim, which is clearly applied to man, and consequently to his freedom, must be judged in relationship to what he calls the Other.[63]

Of course it is not freedom that posits evil; as a free being, man himself is capable of positing evil and therefore of placing himself in the position of a victim. Man is his own victim if the primordial self transcends only his will but not his being. Freedom, however, brings about responsibility, and responsibility in connection with evil and especially the performance of evil acts produces guilt.[64] This is why, in Ricoeur, man's status as a victim is doubled by his state of guilt based on the responsible application of freedom with reference to the reality of evil.[65]

These observations provided by Ricoeur are very important because they reveal the fifth characteristic of radical theology, namely, its "linguistic" resemblance to traditional theology. In other words, the language used by radical theology is oftentimes almost identical to the language of traditional theology, so it is not always easy to distinguish between them. Quite obviously, words like freedom, responsibility, evil, and guilt are all part of the language of traditional theology and anthropology, and at the same time we can see them extensively used in the radical discourse. The only possibility for differentiating between the language of radical theology and that of traditional theology when the resemblance appears so obvious is the awareness that radical theology sees the supernatural events of traditional theology as myths and symbols. Thus, realities, which in traditional theology are believed to be historical, in radical theology are considered mere concepts, as we can see in the next section.

From Myth to Noncoincidence and Disproportion

Ricoeur is utterly concerned with showing that fallibility can be discussed primarily as a concept.[66] The best possibility he finds for this task is the appeal to pure reflection, which he defines as a "way of understanding and being understood," which is not attainable by means of "image, symbol or myth." This approach is crucial for Ricoeur because without the mediation of imagery, symbolism, and mythology, pure reflection discloses a reality that belongs to the essential constitution of the human being. In this sense, fallibility is not a mere concept but also a reality that presents the fragility of the human being as well as its characteristic of being subject to commit erroneous actions in all respects. In attaching fallibility as a concept to the possibility of pure reflection, Ricoeur wants to make sure that the sum of the human being's most fundamental features includes fallibility as one of man's essential characteristics. This is Ricoeur's explanation of fallibility as a concept.[67]

In this particular way of approaching fallibility as a prominent part of man's structure, Ricoeur comes closer to traditional Christianity, which presents man's fallibility—concretized by means of the idea of sin—as an innate distinctive of human nature. Man is born fallible and will definitely stay fallible for the rest of his life. There is no doubt that in this very specific sense Ricoeur's philosophy could agree with traditional Christian theology. There is, however, a fundamental difference between traditional Chrsitianity and Ricoeur's apprehension of fallibility, which is given by the particular perspective on fallibility adopted by traditional Christianity on the one hand and Ricoeur on the other. While Ricoeur sees fallibility as an essential characteristic of man's human being in its natural state, traditional Christian theology approaches fallibility as part of man's inner constitution after the event of Adam's fall. When it comes to the fall, Ricoeur parts ways with traditional Christianity for which the fall was an actual and historical event. This means that man's natural constitution had certain characteristics prior to the fall and other characteristics after the fall. The fall functions as a rupture in man's natural constitution, which is totally changed after the event of the fall. It is evident that Ricoeur cannot accept such a breach in man's natural structure, and his conviction is informed by his perception of the fall as a nonevent. If the fall is a nonevent, it transcends the biological level of man's existence in the sense that it does not disrupt man's life within history as some sort of cataclysmic interruption of his natural state. There is no point in history when man was different from what he is in the present, so whatever the fall describes is categorically not a historical fact but something that goes beyond this particular level of man's life. Therefore, it is logical to presume that the fall should be approached in a totally different way, which is congruous with Ricoeur's conviction that man's nature has been constantly the same throughout history. This is why Ricoeur sees the fall as a myth, and the myth is structurally a nonevent. The myth may present a certain event followed by subsequent events that appear to be historical but are essentially nonhistorical, so they cannot be conceived as having been part of the actual development of history as an intricate web of events. Myth is part of history insofar as man, who conceives it, is part of history, but it also transcends history because its core structure is separated from the reality and possibility of historical events. So in Ricoeur the fall presents the reality of fallibility not only as a nonevent, but also as a concept available to pure reflection.

To be sure, fallibility is an ontological feature of humanity, so humanity cannot be conceived without the possibility as well as the reality of fallibility.[68] Likewise, fallibility cannot escape any discourse about humanity because it is contained by the reality of man's natural constitution. Fallibility, however, cannot be clearly presented unless it proves empirically that something is wrong with the human being. How can we know that something is wrong with the human being if the human being is characterized by fallibility as structurally embedded within itself? We know that something is wrong, and fallibility can be seen as an innate possibility of man's natural constitution if man is seen to exist in some sort of a "non-coincidence" with himself.[69] For Ricoeur, this noncoincidence of man with himself appears as a certain disproportion, which is the very reason or cause of fallibility.[70] Thus, fallibility shows that man's existence is characterized by disproportion or noncoincidence, which is, at the end of the day, an ontological constituent of man's natural state.[71] It follows that it is most natural for man to be fallible or characterized by fallibility, which presents man as a complex being,[72] a being that exists in such a way that he appears at the same time in a position of showing utter greatness but also fundamental nothingness.[73]

To make a clear case in favor of fallibility, Ricoeur is eager to explain what he means by disproportion.[74] It is important not to forget that disproportion proves fallibility, so fallibility is seen in disproportion.[75] When applied to human reality, it is crucial to know where disproportion can be sought and how it can be identified. Disproportion can be investigated by means of the Cartesian paradox of finite-infinite, but Ricoeur is not very happy with this approach to fallibility. The reason for his discontent is the fact that the paradox of finite-infinite can present fallibility as an ontological characteristic of man based on the concept of intermediacy.[76] If the disproportion of fallibility is assessed from the perspective of the intermediacy between finitude and infinitude,[77] then we need a reference point that is totally transcendent to humanity and even to its realm of existence. It is quite natural to understand the human being as characterized by finitude in the sense that it is finite and limited with respect to its own existence; the problem appears when we have to define human finitude by comparison to infinitude. If finitude is utterly human as man's core structural essence, infinitude is the reality that describes man in opposition to what he is in his natural state. Therefore, man should be seen as finite in opposition to a reality that exists beyond his finite realm of existence. In other words, human finitude should be described in opposition to a nonhuman reality, which cannot be other than the reality of God—understood as utterly transcendent to man and his existential as well as historical reality. If disproportion is understood by means of the intermediacy between man's finitude and God's infinitude, then—Ricoeur believes—we find ourselves in a totally misleading position.

Ricoeur's conclusion is vital at this point because it introduces the sixth feature of radical theology, namely, the reluctance to see man in opposition to an ontological reality beyond his natural existence. Even if man's finitude, easily accepted by radical theology, tends to be better defined by comparison with the idea of infinitude—which can only be conceived as existing outside the natural realm of man's historical existence as in traditional theology—radical theology is not willing to accept infinitude as having ontological status because this would automatically admit the ontological status of God's metaphysical and transcendent existence. What radical theology does in order to solve the problem between man's evident finitude in history and the idea of infinitude—which cannot be confined to history—is to redefine the notion of infinity by depriving it of any ontology. Any other possibility ascribing ontological status to infinity would be misleading for radical theology, as Ricoeur himself puts it.

FALLIBILITY AS INTERMEDIACY

Why is it misleading to judge fallibility by means of the disproportion between finitude and infinitude? Primarily because the dialectics between finitude and infinitude presuppose the idea of intermediacy between finitude and infinitude as well as the idea of finitude as totally opposed to infinitude. If man is finite, then his inner constitution and being is characterized by finitude; to be sure, man is finitude when it comes to defining his natural state. Conversely, the idea of infinitude presupposes the reverse of finitude and, as finitude is represented by means of the being of man, it follows that infinitude is also represented by means of the idea of being. This being, however, is not finite but infinite, so this is the classic argument for the existence of God. We have the finitude of man and the infinitude of God in a relationship of disproportion because man is finite not only in relationship to God but also in relationship to his realm of existence as created by God. Ricoeur is very uncomfortable with this approach because it introduces the idea of "ontological locality,"[78] which places man within a reality characterized by the concept of "between." Man is fallible because he can be understood based on the disproportion between his own finitude and God's infinitude.[79]

It seems that Ricoeur dismisses this perspective because the idea of "between" as applied to man's finitude in opposition to God's finitude confers an ontological status not only to the reality of man[80]—which is rather obvious—but also to the reality of God.[81] Therefore, Ricoeur appears to experience a certain feeling of unease because of the possibility of seeing God in ontological terms, which pushes man to a definition in opposition to an ontology of total transcendence. Ricoeur is not willing to define man as well as man's fallibility—and finitude—by means of its opposition to the total transcendence of God's infinitude.

Such an enterprise would cause his exegetical hermeneutics of the myth of the fall and the resulting symbolism of evil to break down completely because myth is the very element that disrupts the intermediacy between the finite ontology of humanity and the infinite, total, and absolute ontology of God.[82] Myth actually annuls the total transcendence of God and restricts the idea of transcendence to the finite reality of man. Ricoeur seeks to retain the idea of intermediacy as well as the accompanying concept of disproportion, not as applied to the opposition between man's finite reality and the ontology of God's total transcendence but between realities that belong to man's immanent reality, both internal and external. Therefore, man does not mediate between levels of reality that can exclude his own reality; he mediates between levels of reality that not only include his own reality but also define his own reality. To put it in plain words, man mediates between himself and other people but also between himself and his own self.

There seems to be another reason why Ricoeur resents the idea of intermediacy if applied to man's finite reality—which defines his fallibility—in opposition to the ontology of God's total transcendence and infinitude. If God is ontologically real, it means that man must be defined in opposition to God. Whatever God is, man is not, or whatever God is in his infinitude, man is in his finitude, which automatically presupposes a reversed definition. For instance, if God is immortal in his infinitude, man is immortal in his finitude, which automatically means that his immortality should be defined in terms of finitude; at the end of the day, man's immortality is nothing but mortality defined from the perspective of God's immortality.

Likewise, if God is infallible in his infinitude, man is infallible in his finitude, which actually means that he is fallible as opposed to God's totally transcendent infallibility. The idea of disproportion between the ontology of man and the ontology of God is evident, but what seems to concern Ricoeur is not as much the idea of disproportion but rather the concept of intermediacy. If God is totally transcendent, it follows that his ontology is utterly opposed to man's ontology. Thus, if the idea of intermediacy is applied to the opposing realities of God and man, man is totally incapable of functioning as intermediary between himself and God. The intermediacy is not between man and God because man cannot apply this intermediacy by himself because of his finitude, which cannot find access to God's infinitude; the intermediacy is rather between God and man, so it is God who applies the intermediacy between himself and man because his infinitude can always find access to man's finitude. In the best of cases, the idea of intermediacy as applied to man can only be passive because the active side of it belongs to God. Man's intermediacy is passive because he cannot have access to God's infinite ontology; only God can have access to man's finite ontology so, in the end, intermediacy is more an action of God than a state that defines man.

Ricoeur simply cannot accept such a conclusion, so his idea of intermediacy focuses exclusively on man's ontology as defined by means of translating myths into symbols that can develop different meanings in order to find relevant ways to explain humanity.[83] In this manner, he cancels the ontology of God and promotes the ontology of man, so the intermediacy—and the accompanying idea of disproportion—should be tackled exclusively from the perspective of man with view to realities that not only encompass man's own reality but also exist within man's own reality. Therefore, the idea of intermediacy can achieve the full measure of man's active involvement;[84] man in himself is the state of intermediacy between all levels of human existence—internal and external—so it is no longer God who actively mediates his relationship to man, but it is man who mediates his existence within the finitude of his immanent ontology.[85] In other words, Ricoeur admits the existence of various levels of reality within man and outside man, but all these levels of reality are mediated by man.[86] To be sure, the possibility of fallibility as defined by disproportion—and intermediacy—has nothing to do with the idea of God's ontology of total transcendence but only with man's finitude as given by his multifaceted historical existence and experience.[87]

This is in fact the seventh characteristic of radical theology seen in Ricoeur, that is to say the rejection of any reality that lies beyond man's historical existence. If in traditional theology, man is aware of a reality that exists beyond his own and that he can later identify as the reality of God, in radical theology such a possibility simply does not exist. Any reality beyond man's reality cannot have an ontological status; in other words, it cannot exist. Any concept pointing to a reality beyond our existence in history—such as the idea of infinitude—must be reinterpreted and redefined as a symbol, which is also what happened to the notion of transcendence in Ricoeur's philosophy.

REDEFINING TRANSCENDENCE

The notion of transcendence is crucial for Ricoeur when it comes to defining the intermediacy of man from the perspective of the disproportion between the finite and the infinite.[88] Finitude and infinitude should be linked to transcendence, but we must be very careful when we identify what we mean by transcendence.[89] As shown before, Ricoeur is more than willing to work with the idea of transcendence as long as transcendence has nothing to do with God's ontology. If we accept that God is ontologically real, so he has an existence of his own that is active beyond the realm of man's existence, then the idea of transcendence tends to define God rather than man. This equation is unacceptable as far as Ricoeur is concerned, so he carefully redefines the idea of transcendence by means of the refinement of mythology through symbolism. Therefore, if the idea of God is encapsulated within mythology, then the reality of God's ontology fades away in favor of man's ontology.[90] The idea of transcendence can be retained, but it no longer underlines the infinitude of God's ontology; it only highlights the reality of man's ontology. It is no longer God who is transcendent but man.[91] In other words, we should not conceive transcendence with reference to God who exists beyond the finitude of man but rather with reference to man who transcends his own finitude. This is clearly a point of contrast between Ricoeur and traditional Christianity because the total transcendence of God's ontology is the stronghold of traditional Christian theology. Thus, God is transcendent, infinite, and infallible, and it is this particular definition of God that subsequently informs the image of man. Whatever man is in his historical reality should be defined in accordance with God's absolute transcendence. This results in a sort of reverse definition of man, which, while retaining the characteristics of God's absolute transcendence—infinitude, for instance—still posits them by contrast with God, so we can speak of man as being infinite but only in terms of his finite existence. In other words, man's transcendence—as presented by Ricoeur—is limited because man's nature is essentially finite.[92]

In contrast to traditional Christianity, Ricoeur attributes the idea of transcendence exclusively to the human being. Man is transcendent despite his finitude but also because of his finitude. This means that man is capable of nurturing feelings that seem to contradict his limited natural constitution; at the same time he displays these feelings as a result of his awareness of his limitations. For instance, as a limited being, man should be controlled by desires—which are not commendable by definition—but despite his finitude, man is still capable of exhibiting feelings of deep love. Man's love, as opposite to desire, is a proof of his transcendence because love rises above his instinctual cravings.[93] The human being manifests love in spite of what he is by nature, but also because he is fully aware of his finitude. This is why man purposefully shows love as an attempt to go beyond the limits of his own end in death.[94] It is very possible that—according to Ricoeur's understanding of human transcendence—man should perceive love as a means to continue his influence beyond the limits of his actual existence, or maybe he just enjoys the experience of transcending his own natural instincts during the actual span of his life. Whatever the explanation, Ricoeur is convinced that transcendence is an inner quality of the human being that—despite its restricted nature because of man's finitude—offers a positive definition of fallibility.[95]

It becomes evident therefore that fallibility must be discussed—according to Ricoeur—from the perspective of the human being alone. Fallibility may be a concept that presents a human reality, but we cannot investigate the reality of human fallibility by remaining stuck to its conceptual framework. Ricoeur's methodology of investigating fallibility is to acknowledge the concept but proceed from the reality of the human being and especially from its polarity between finitude and infinitude. Man is a being of utmost complexity, and his complexity cannot be properly assessed unless the totality of his humanity is both acknowledged and accepted. In order to understand human fallibility, Ricoeur suggests that we should promote a holistic view of man, a perspective that integrates the entire complexity of humanity in general as well as of the human being in particular. Thus, it is not sufficient to research the concept of fallibility as the possibility of evil seen as deeply embedded in our human nature;[96] what we should do is investigate man in his entirety, complexity, and existence, with particular attention to the intermediacy between his finitude and infinitude. It is the totality of humanity, which includes man's finitude and infinitude in relationship to himself and other humans, that should offer a comprehensive assessment of man's fallibility.[97]

It is important to realize that, for Ricoeur, this global perspective on the totality of humanity with view to a definition of fallibility can be achieved only by philosophy. The philosophical comprehension of fallibility, however, cannot be produced exclusively based on philosophical sources. Actually, Ricoeur admits that philosophy is, in a way, the second—though fundamental—step to be taken in order to define fallibility. The first step in assessing fallibility is not taken by philosophy but by nonphilosophy, which can be theology, religion, or both in general. With respect to fallibility, philosophy must offer comprehension, but this philosophical comprehension is based on a nonphilosophical—namely, theological, religious, or both—precomprehension.[98] Philosophy is reflection; nonphilosophy is an enterprise that precedes reflection.[99] In order to understand fallibility, we must seek the nonphilosophical precomprehension of humanity—given by theology and religion—and then, by means of reflection, achieve the philosophical comprehension that eventually illuminates man's reality as fallible being. At this point, the fundamental question is where can the nonphilosophical precomprehension actually be found? As far as Ricoeur is concerned, the nonphilosophical precomprehension of man's fallibility can and should be found in what he calls the pathos of misery (*pathétique de la misère*).[100] Ricoeur explains that this pathos is actually a precomprehension in itself because it makes man understand himself as miserable. In other words, the nonphilosophical precomprehension of fallibility is based on man's realization that his existence is characterized by misery.[101]

The bottom line for Ricoeur in assessing fallibility is the recognition of man's ontological characteristics based on the nonphilosophical precomprehension of fallibility, which presents man as a being that acknowledges its own misery. Although Ricoeur does not elaborate on this particular aspect, it should be stressed that the nonphilosophical precomprehension of fallibility can be given by theological and religious mythology. In other words, theology and religion produce myths that picture man as a being of utmost misery. From this point onward, theology and religion cease to explain human fallibility in a global way, so we must resort to philosophical discourse in order to obtain a philosophical comprehension of human fallibility. It is not philosophy that begins the task of unveiling the depths of man's fallibility; this resides in the prephilosophical endeavors of theology and religion. What philosophy does is not to begin but rather to begin again the assessment of human fallibility from the prephilosophical foundation offered by theology and religion. In other words, we need to pursue a genuinely philosophical anthropology, which globally takes into account man's complex disproportion and noncoincidence with himself due to the polarity of finitude and infinitude.[102] To conclude, the methodology to be followed with view to defining human fallibility includes prephilosophical and philosophical approaches to man's misery in order to portray a global perspective on his existence, which swings between finitude and infinitude, a perspective that necessarily goes all the way from pure reflection to total comprehension.

This is where the eighth feature of radical theology emerges from Ricoeur's thought: man's existence must be understood exclusively in terms of our historical reality. For radical theology, there is nothing beyond history as we see it. Our situation, finitude, and misery but also ideas that could connect us to realities beyond our own— such as infinitude, transcendence, and even God—must be seen in a way that matches only the experience of our natural lives. In other words, everything must be translated for the sake of relevance; if man's contemporary experience is dominated by reason, then all the fundamental concepts of traditional theology that explain the ontological existence of transcendent realities must undergo a process of radical interpretation in order to have them translated as culturally relevant myths and symbols.

SIMILARITIES BETWEEN PAUL RICOEUR'S CONCEPT OF FALLIBILITY AND THEOLOGICAL RADICALISM: EDWARD SCHILLEBEECKX

Theological radicalism is generally associated with figures such as Edward Schillebeeckx, who seeks to reinterpret traditional Christianity in terms of the experience of humanity.[103] Like Ricoeur, who begins his philosophical explanation of fallibility from the idea of fault and myth, Schillebeeckx explains that theology should be approached from the starting point of experience, which is subject to criticism and correction as an indication that the human being is confronted with the reality of fault. At the same time, experience is so fundamental to human life that it should prompt us to reinterpret everything through its lenses. Experience interprets and reinterprets culture, so if we want to find out what is relevant to us today we must return to the sources that explain how other people in the past lived out their own experiences. This is why we should read, interpret, and reinterpret cultural sources such as the Scriptures because they contain cultural experiences of particular human beings.[104] The content of the sources that present these experiences of the past, namely, the actual information we find in Scripture, must be interpreted and reinterpreted in such a way that it becomes relevant to us today. The reality of fault is embedded in every experience, past, present, and future, because every experience should be open to both reassessment and correction as well as to other experiences. Experience, however, is a speech event or an interpretative event, so it must be approached from the standpoint of hermeneutics. When hermeneutics is applied to past experiences, we realize that some of the past sources—the Old and New Testaments—use a language that must be actualized in such a way that it is relevant to us today. Schillebeeckx does not like the idea of myth very much because it could cast a negative light on the historical life of Jesus, but he does believe myth can be translated into theological or philosophical language.[105]

The interpretation of experiences, which actually means a reinterpretation of past experiences and sources, is crucial because man has an innate tendency to create symbols.[106] Symbols are important and necessary because they manage to convey realities difficult to render in ordinary words. Symbolism actually proves that experiences must be constantly reinterpreted so they fit the particular context of one's life, which must be made relevant based on the symbolism of past experiences.[107] We learn from the symbolism of past experiences, we correct them or we correct our own experiences; what matters is the fact that symbolism proves the finitude of human experiences as well as that of the human being.[108] The human being, however, does not easily accept its finitude so it tends to overcome its limitations, and this is clearly seen in religious life. Thus, we experience religious realities and try to understand their symbolism, which prompts us to have internal as well as external religious experiences.[109] This is, in fact, an attempt to go beyond our finite internal experiences to some sort of infinite external experiences, which become confessions of faith and liturgical manifestations or cults.[110] Therefore, human experience is a constant swing between internal experiences, or our personal, inner worship of God, and external liturgical, confessional experiences. Our inner worship of God is clearly finite because it ends with our personal existence, but the external confessional or cultic experiences continue long after our death. In other words, we move between the finitude of our internal, personal experiences and the infinitude of external, communitarian, and cultic experiences.

This balance between finitude and infinitude makes Schillebeeckx realize that human freedom is unfortunately being misused and even abused. When freedom is abused, the immediate consequence is a clear manifestation of evil, which he terms the "sin of the world."[111] The growth of human freedom leads to the growth of evil in the world, so human freedom must always be used with utmost responsibility.[112] This must be done is such a way that our understanding of ourselves and the world is drastically changed. This dramatic change, with particular reference to religion, cannot be done unless we understand that the past can only symbolically help us. The things of the past are not relevant for the things of the present, but we can use the symbolism of the past to interpret the things of the past in terms relevant to our present lives. Such a dramatic reinterpretation is possible only if we understand that human reality is actually the only reality that really exists. This automatically forces us to reconsider what was traditionally meant by transcendence. Thus, transcendence no longer points to an ontological reality that goes beyond our own world but to the reality of our own interiority. In other words, based on this radical reinterpretation of past symbols, such as God, we can now speak of immanent or interior transcendence, which is just another way of saying that man transcends himself and his own finitude. For Schillebeeckx, transcendence is the realization that one's finitude can be made relevant from the perspective of humanity's future, which is actually our God.[113] This means that transcendence is not absolute as a reality that totally goes beyond human existence but, on the contrary, it is historically conditioned as a reality that is completely human and exclusively confined by our experiences.

In Schillebeeckx, the immanence of transcendence makes our experiences relevant and also helps us understand the reality of what he calls "revelation." Revelation is clearly a reference to the past symbolism of traditional religion, which must be dramatically reinterpreted to fit our present experiences in a relevant way. Thus, when we realize that our transcendence is the swing between our finitude and the infinitude of our belief in God—which is our future—we actually understand the religious symbols that speak of God. God is no longer ontologically transcendent, but he rather becomes our own future as a manifestation of individual immanent "transcendencies"—or human lives—throughout the historical development of a continuously present actuality of the moment.[114] We have to undergo a process of liberation from old and irrelevant views to the acceptance of new and relevant realities. This can be performed by means of what Schillebeeckx calls the "experience of radical contrast" or just "the experience of contrast," which means saying no to the suffering and evil in the world. Good and evil, meaning and meaningless is a mixture that remains constantly enigmatic in the world, which is driven by the abuse of freedom. What we must do is to realize and fully understand the reality of evil and correct it through these experiences of contrast. They can help us fight evil and suffering once we comprehend the immanent transcendence of our own lives in light of our future. For Schillebeeckx, this means saying no to suffering and evil but also saying an "open yes" to a responsible use of freedom, which can provide us with "a better world with a human face."[115] To conclude, we have to accept that the symbolism of past experiences must be translated into new and relevant images, which help us understand our own finitude. Accepting this finitude implies the drastic reassessment of the traditional concept of transcendence, which should no longer be seen as ontological totality with reference to God but as finite immanence with reference to the human being. This should make us fight the abuse of freedom resulting in evil and suffering, and—at the same time— transform these experiences of contrast into an active openness to a better world as well as a better future.

SIMILARITIES BETWEEN PAUL RICOEUR'S CONCEPT OF FALLIBILITY AND PHILOSOPHICAL NONREALISM: DON CUPITT

An important step in Don Cupitt's establishment of nonrealism is the affirmation of fallibility as part of critical thinking. A parallel can be drawn between Cupitt's critical thinking and Ricoeur's philosophical comprehension, especially in the sense that Cupitt opposes critical thinking to precritical thinking—much like Ricoeur, who acknowledges that philosophical comprehension is preceded by nonphilosophical, namely, religious/theological precomprehension. Critical thinking is essentially nonrealist because it anchors human rationality in human existence.[116] Thus, critical thinking is confined to the limited and finite sphere of human thought and experience based on the conviction that there is nothing ontologically real beyond it. Fallibility is a fundamental feature of critical thinking as part of human experience. Due to the limited as well as provisional character of human knowledge, fallibility is the logical outcome of such a belief, which does not, however, stop Cupitt from positing the necessity that critical thinking should be essentially nonrealistic. Human reality is mediated by language, so hermeneutics is a condition of human existence because no human being can escape his own strictly confined personal reality. At the same time, human reality is hermeneutically conditioned due to the fact that man cannot step outside the reality of his own language. The immediate consequence is the positing of nonrealism as fundamental to critical thinking because man cannot imagine anything beyond what he perceives by means of his own body, which of course includes his feelings, senses, language, personality, and the like. As defined in connection with human reality, Cupitt's nonrealism is essentially realistic—powerfully and irrevocably sunk in the reality of the present moment—for the very simple reason that the world exists for us exclusively within the realm of what can be known in a human way.[117]

For Cupitt, myth is part of theology and religion and consequently part of precritical thinking. Therefore, critical thinking—which is characterized by nonrealism—must exclude myth from its intellectual pattern. A major change must occur that rids itself of myth because myth can no longer be seen as true in conveying significance and meaning. In nonrealistic critical thinking, myth is increasingly seen as untrue, so the need to leave it behind in hermeneutics is stringent. Thus, myth is gradually replaced by science as background for human knowledge.[118] Because myth does not convey the truth, Cupitt does not see any need to pass from myth to symbolism. Myth and symbolism are equated, in the sense that both convey a reality that does not fit the contemporary scientific perception of human society. One can conceive a realm of myth and symbolism, but that particular realm is utterly different as well as separated from the world of science and engineering. In other words, mythology is different and separated from mathematics.[119] In the best of cases, religious myth and language can explain how this world functions and what it should look like. One thing is sure, however: myth cannot speak about another world or a world that is ontologically real and transcendent to this world. This world is the only ontologically real domain, so myth can only make reference to this world, even though in utopian terms, which must be acknowledged as such. This means we should be aware of the finite character of our world and of our worldly existence; in this respect, the best myth can do for us is to make us understand that the infinitude of traditional theological realism should be understood in terms of the finitude of contemporary philosophical nonrealism. Another direct implication is connected to the fact that mythology must not be approached dogmatically, which results in theological realism, but pragmatically, which produces philosophical nonrealism as the only critical assessment of the world.[120]

We are finite human beings and this reality is disclosed by our critical thinking. We live in the world, which is limited, and we act in ways that are limited in themselves. We may make use of religious mythology, but we must be aware that fundamental religious concepts—like that of God—are mythological and must be retranslated. Our finitude must be considered in connection with the concept of God but not in the traditional precritical sense, which is characterized by the infinitude of theological realism; on the contrary, our finitude must be assessed against the critical evaluation of philosophical criticism, which is dominated by the rethinking of mythology in accordance with the claims of nonrealism. Thus, humanity moves between its own finitude and the infinitude of the idea of God, which is seen as an ideal standard of perfection or infinitude.[121]

Freedom is the result of critical freedom, while evil stems from a precritical understanding of the world.[122] As a matter of fact, freedom means having the courage to profess a nonrealistic approach to religious/theological thinking, which eventually kills the traditional God and disperses the divine throughout the entire world. Thus, God is no longer the standard of holiness; this world is. The concept of God and his traditional absolute transcendence must now be understood in terms of human, transient, and relative realities. Therefore, philosophical nonrealism is fundamentally postdogmatic as a manifestation of critical freedom, which fights the precritical attitude to evil. This is actually radical Christianity, as Cupitt dubs it, or theological radicalism, as seen in Schillebeeckx. To be sure, the foundation of radical Christianity or theological radicalism is the postdogmatic approach of critical thinking. This offers freedom that can be explained as religious freedom, provided humanity is freed from traditional religion.[123]

In Cupitt, freedom modifies the concept of transcendence as applied to God. Cupitt is willing to talk about the transcendence of God, but it is clear that God does not exist according to his critical thinking. Why then should the idea of transcendence be applied to the concept of God? Because transcendence makes God totally separate from the realm of humanity, and this is exactly what Cupitt has in mind. He presses the idea of divine transcendence to such an extent that God becomes gradually less visible by humans. Thus, I am free to conceive the idea of God as fundamentally transcendent in the sense that I cannot actually conceive or see God because he is far too distant from any human possibility to see him. Cupitt insists on transcendence to such an extent that God becomes utterly distant from humanity; he is actually so distant—so transcendent—that he becomes immanent. In other words, we realize that the concept of transcendence describes a reality totally different from our human existence; it is so distant that it cannot be accepted as ontologically real.[124] Thus, God is so transcendent that we cannot accept him as having an ontologically real existence. Consequently, God can only be a concept in my mind, which informs me on a standard that should be achieved in this world or within the immanent realities of human existence. In other words, transcendence becomes relativized as the idea of God is totally dependent on the historicity of human language and culture.[125] Everything is this world is dependent on the historicity of our existence, so even the notion of transcendence must be subject to this reality. Everything is local, limited, and fallible; transcendence makes no exception. It is actually enough that nothing is absolute in this world, so transcendence is not absolute either. Seen through the lenses of this particular definition of transcendence, God is only a linguistic reality that makes our present life meaningful in the sense that it can help us transcend some aspects of our lives. Transcendence—human transcendence—is our inner God, which gives us cultural identity in a world of constant changes.

CHAPTER 6

RADICAL CHRISTIAN THOUGHT
IN LATE POSTMODERNITY

VITO MANCUSO AND FAITH REASSESSMENT
IN THE TWENTY-FIRST CENTURY

INTRODUCTION

Vito Mancuso (b. 1962), one of Italy's younger theologians, whose lay affiliation succeeded in creating significant waves of both admiration and criticism, is one of the theological rising stars of today's academic agenda. A controversial figure perceived as a liberal within Vatican circles, Mancuso has recently stirred Italian traditional Catholicism by publishing a series of books that attempt to remake the faith of Christianity. An acquaintance of Cardinal Carlo Maria Martini, Mancuso launched a personal campaign directed against the dogmatism of classical Roman Catholicism in an attempt to offer a theology that matches the experience of contemporary people. Having published most of his books after the year 2000, Mancuso intends to reinterpret Christianity as a world religion, a mere human phenomenon, and in order to prove his point he resorts to the reality of man's historical existence. Following the empirical observation that Christianity exists as a religion among many others, Mancuso focuses on the concept of faith, which he dramatically reinterprets as man's awareness of the idea of good. At the same time, he explains that faith should not be understood in terms of obedience or as a gift of God, according to the pattern of traditional theology; on the contrary, faith should be reread as freedom in connection with man's capacity to evaluate his own experience as well as to produce a worldview. Thus, he relocates the concept of faith from its traditional *locus* in the reality of a metaphysical and transcendent God to the realm of human existence and experience as defined by love, truth, and freedom. Mancuso's reassessment of faith modifies the traditional doctrine of the Trinity and also the traditional Christian perspective on ethics and bioethics with special reference to the thorny issue of disability.

CHRISTIANITY AND OTHER RELIGIONS

Today's world is sufficient proof that religion is a global phenomenon posing various questions to the adherents of particular religions.[1] As globalization becomes more and more a daily reality, one acquires the rather disturbing realization that one's particular religion is not the only religion in the world and also that one's particular faith is not the only option for a spiritual life.[2] Christians today know that other world religions represent if not an outward threat at least a more or less viable possibility for inward spirituality.[3] Vito Mancuso writes his theology from the standpoint of a Catholic believer—or this is what he claims—who lives in today's world and asks, sometimes rather rhetorical questions, about human existence as we experience it these days.[4] Mancuso writes as if he were a mere Christian who becomes aware of what happens around him in the world.

The first aspect Mancuso notices as he inspects the world through the eyes of "the Christian" in connection with our contemporary perspective on religion as world phenomenon is the relationship between Christianity and other world religions.[5] It becomes clear from the start that, for Mancuso, Christianity is a religion that exists among other religions and, even if he does not say this from the start, the Christian religion should perceive itself as a phenomenon deeply rooted in the experience of humanity.[6] Resuming his approach from the perspective of an ordinary Christian believer, Mancuso explains that the first reaction of a regular Christian believer who faces the reality of world religions is a particular kind of personal awareness. Thus, the Christian believer knows his faith is different from the faith of other religious traditions. At the same time, the Christian knows the difference that exists between his faith and other faiths is somehow superior to the rest.[7] Such a reaction is triggered by the Christian's awareness that his faith represents *the* truth of man's existence, so his faith is the only *true* faith regardless of the countless other religions of the world. For the Christian, the equality of faith and truth is a presupposition that he cannot avoid as he contemplates the reality of world religions. Should he give up this conviction, his religion becomes just another religion, while the central character of his faith, Jesus Christ, turns into an exceptional religious man among other equally exceptional religious people such as Mohammed, Buddha, and Moses.[8] In other worlds, if the Christian no longer sees his faith as *the* truth, Christianity automatically transforms itself into a religion of equal standing with Islam, Buddhism, and Judaism. Mancuso is aware that such a renunciation on the part of the Christian leads inevitably to a radical reconsideration of Christian soteriology, in the sense that salvation should no longer be sought in Jesus Christ but also in other persons or just in something else.[9]

Although he does not say it explicitly, Mancuso does not seem to agree with this perspective, which is in fact traditional Christian theology. He is sympathetic to the ordinary Christian's reluctance to accept other religions as equally true to his, but, at the same time, he suggests that such an approach—that is, traditional Christian theology—is at the end of the day intolerant, sectarian, and closed. Again, he does not say it in plain words; what he does instead is to place himself in the shoes of the ordinary Christian who, while accepting traditional theology, cannot avoid seeing himself as intolerant, sectarian, and closed in relation to other world religions. At this point, Mancuso even uses a plastic image to illustrate the ordinary Christian's dilemma of clinging to his traditional theology but also realizing his intolerance as a result;[10] thus it is as if an enormous weight of past history oppressed his consciousness. It is clear that, for Mancuso, traditional Christian theology poses a serious threat to man's individual consciousness because it excludes from the start the individual experiences of other religious people. At the same time, the Christian understands that professing traditional Christian theology—which claims its superiority over other religions—leads to perilous dogmatism. To put it in a nutshell, the ordinary Christian reaches the point when he admits that he actually faces the dilemma of whether he should stick to his religion's claims of superiority or accept the equality of all world religions, Christianity included.[11]

Mancuso tries to investigate whether there is a way out of this dilemma but he quite rapidly concludes that traditional Christianity can only end up as a dogmatically intolerable approach to Christian religion.[12] In other words, there is no way out because traditional Christianity will never give up its conviction that the uniqueness and the absoluteness of Christ are *the* essence of its truthfulness. Traditional Christianity will always reject the dominant worldview, which admits—with reference to God's existence—that there is something above us, something that cannot be defined with absolute certainty.

There is no room in traditional Christianity for the plurality of world religions or for the relative character of its dogmatic claims.[13] The Bible is superior to any other religious writing, so traditional Christianity will always reject what seems to be the much more reasonable acceptance of a global spirituality based on the best precepts of all religions. In doing so, however, traditional Christianity will not put an end, once and for all, to all human divisions resulting in wars produced by the diversity of world religions. Nevertheless, in clinging to traditional theology, the ordinary Christian will eventually sense that something is wrong with such an approach.[14]

Mancuso avoids—at least at this point—a clear answer concerning whether Christianity, as a religion, is superior to other religions. On the other hand, what he does show is that traditional Christian theology is not the only approach to Christianity. He associates traditional Christian theology with a faith lived based on doctrine and truth, not on dedication and love. It is clear that Mancuso prefers the second option—namely, the faith of dedication and love—because this is the only option that can at the same time preserve the absoluteness of Christ and accept the plurality of other religions.[15] Thus, the absoluteness of Christ is valid as long as he embodies the dedication and love that can be seen in other religions as well. In other words, in embodying dedication and love, Christ is a symbol of the good that man must exert on his fellow human beings. So, for Mancuso, Christianity is superior to other religions because it manages to ascribe an absolutely decisive role to the idea and practice of the good.[16]

Two facts should be stressed here: first, even if Mancuso ascribes superiority to the Christian religion due to its capacity to understand and practice the good, what he understands by Christian religion is not traditional Christian theology but a modern inclusive approach to Christianity as religion;[17] and second, the superiority he attaches to the Christian religion is somehow relative because the idea of the good can be decisively understood and practiced in other religious traditions as well.

These explanations offer us a clue for the identification of the first feature of radical theology as presented by Mancuso, and this is the conviction that Christianity is just another religion among the various religions of the world. There is nothing special about Christianity in the sense that it is objectively revealed from a reality that transcends our historical existence. Christianity may or may not be superior to other religions due to some specific doctrines that could offer better explanations for man's actual situation, but as a religion originating in history—not as a dogmatic or even philosophical system—Christianity is like any other world religion.

THE MEANING OF CHRISTIANITY AS RELIGION

The second aspect brought forward by Mancuso in connection with how we should understand religion today is the origin as well as the meaning of Christianity as one religion among others. A normal approach to this particular problem should consist of the study of the Bible as the primary source of the Christian religion. Nevertheless, the selection of the Bible for such a study poses another problem, namely, whether the Bible itself is or should be considered superior to the primary sources of other world religions, such as the Koran.[18] Mancuso does not seem ready to concede the superiority of the Bible because his understanding of religion starts from below, from the realm of humanity, and there is no human, rational reason why a certain book or collection of books should be seen as superior to another one. This is clear from another set of rhetorical questions Mancuso asks as he prepares to unveil his perspective on the origin and meaning of Christianity as religion.[19]

The first question is whether we could find any meaning whatsoever in what we call faith in God. In a world populated by men and women, a species that has always entertained the idea that they are the full measure of all things, the meaning of faith and especially of faith in God needs clarification. The second question follows and it concerns the possibility of faith, namely, why some people believe and others do not. The third question, and this is probably the most rhetorical of all, is whether anyone still believes today in the doctrine of God's election, which Mancuso understands to convey the idea that believers are better than nonbelievers. Leaving aside the fact that the traditional doctrine of God's election has nothing to do with the incorrect assumption that believers are better than nonbelievers, it should be underlined here that Mancuso's questions are indeed reasonable if the religion of Christianity is approached wholly from an anthropological perspective.[20]

The next step for Mancuso is to present in a critical way the teachings of the Roman Catholic Church and especially of the *Filius Dei*, the dogmatic constitution of the First Vatican Council.[21] In short, Mancuso criticizes the idea that man should believe in God because he depends totally on him, but also the teaching that the natural light of reason can show us God.[22] Mancuso is absolutely right in saying that the light of reason, or the assistance of our natural abilities, cannot lead us to God for the simple fact that some people believe in God while others do not. Believers and nonbelievers use their reason and, even if both categories attempt to find a way to reach God, only believers can be said to have attained the knowledge of God. But, for Mancuso, if the use of reason was indeed exercised by both and only some reach faith, then something is wrong with the teaching that the natural light of reason is enough to show us the way to God.[23] A clarification is needed at this point, namely, that Mancuso seems to identify traditional Christian theology with the teachings of the Roman Catholic Church. While he does not dismiss other forms of traditional theology—such as the Protestant approaches to faith—as incorrect, he nevertheless does not say anything about them and his only reference to traditional theology is the criticism of traditional Roman Catholicism.

Another observation is crucial here. If while explaining the first aspect of how we should understand Christianity and especially its relationship to other world religions, Mancuso presented his case through the eyes of the ordinary Christian believer, he now slightly changes his perspective. Thus, in dealing with the origin and meaning of Christianity as a religion, he no longer approaches the current issue through the eyes of the Christian believer but through the experience of the self.[24] In other words, it is not only the Christian believer who is competent to assess the origin and meaning of Christianity but also the ordinary human self, which can belong to any human being of any or no religious persuasion whatsoever. This can only strengthen Mancuso's conviction that Christianity is indeed only *a* religion among others and even if he professes his adherence to this particular religion, Christianity is a world phenomenon that can be fathomed by any human being regardless of whether he or she has in-depth awareness of its fundamental tenets.[25] It is clear in Mancuso that the capacity of the self to investigate religion is beyond question; the self uses reason to do a thorough search of religion as he seeks God, and what he finds is a wide range of reasonable doctrines that, while leading to God or rather to the idea of God, are nevertheless totally diversified and different from one another.[26] The self soon realizes that even if the same reason has been used by different individual selves, the religious results—which eventually end up in the establishment of particular religions—are remarkably varied. Moreover, the self also notices that while some selves reached the conclusion that God existed, others concluded that there was no God at all, and their totally opposed conclusions were issued as a result of using the very same human reason.[27]

The rational investigation of the self discloses that reason leads not only to belief or unbelief but also to almost totally opposed views within the same religion, and it is here that Mancuso makes reference to the manifold traditions of the church even if it is not clear whether he means the Roman Catholic Church only or the Christian Church in general, including non-Catholic confessions. Thus, while the Roman Catholic Church—through its Magisterium—says that God can be reached by using the natural light of reason, other Christian traditions—and Mancuso refers especially to Christian mysticism—seem to be convinced of the contrary, namely, that God cannot be known with absolute certainty if man uses only his natural reason.[28] The holy mystics of Christianity were more than clear in saying that it is actually impossible to know God through means that are merely natural, so using reason is out of the question in one's pursuit of God. Nevertheless, although Mancuso clearly illustrates reason's incapacity to discover God all by itself, he says nothing about what could eventually assist reason in reaching faith in God. A preliminary assessment of Mancuso's perspective should normally lead to the conclusion that the Roman Catholic Church is not exactly right when it says that natural reason can lead to faith in God. Mystical theology, on the other hand, seems to be closer to the fact that something more than mere reason is needed if one truly wants to find God.[29] Mancuso's conclusion, however, is astonishing because, at the end of his argument, he clearly says that the self should believe both the church *and* the mystics. In other words, the self should use both reason *and* something else to investigate the possibility of God's existence and—to come closer to Mancuso's second aspect concerning religion—the meaning and origin of Christianity as a religion of the world.

At this point, he does not shed any light on what is reason's aid in searching God, but he does point out—through a rhetorical question once again—that faith and the knowledge of God are depicted by means of two totally diverse languages that, although specific to the Catholic tradition, can nevertheless transcend its dogmatic boundaries.[30] It is a bit later that Mancuso discloses the assistance of reason in the self's quest for God; reason is helped by the idea of pure good, which moves the self innerly to faith in God.[31] The idea of good, however, must be understood in connection with the notion of grace—seen as gratuity—because it is only the unconditional adherence to doing the good in a gratuitous way that produces faith in God. For Mancuso, there is no rational motivation for man to adhere to faith and explicitly to faith in God. This is why reason needs the prop of the idea of good or the will to [do] good, which is at the same time the essence of true theology, the very foundation of truth.[32]

It must be noted here that Mancuso's foundation of faith, which he sees as the good and the will to good, is clearly subjective. He thus dismisses the objective character of faith as professed by traditional theology through the ontological reality of God's transcendental and metaphysical existence; faith is not based on whom and what God is in reality but on what man subjectively understands as good or the good.[33] Consequently, in Mancuso, while faith retains the idea of truth, it is disconnected from the objective truth of God's metaphysically onto-logical reality in order to be tied to the subjective truth of man's will to do the good. It appears that Mancuso postulates the existence of an objective reality of the good, which is transcendent to the natural experience of humanity, and can be accessed by various religions. The transcendence of the objective reality of the good does not seem to be ontological in the sense that it exists in some form of personal or non-personal existence. It is rather a theological or philosophical concept, which rises above humanity, and which can have access to it for as long as the will to good is there. This may lead to the conclusion that all religions are objectively true and equally valid to the extent that they profess their willingness to do the good.[34] On the other hand, Chris-tianity is superior only subjectively in the sense that Mancuso himself believes it to be so because it manages to understand and practice the good in a better way than other religions. To be sure, Christianity is not superior to other religions due to its traditional doctrine of God, which acknowledges the metaphysically objective reality of God as a personal and eternal being, perfect, all-powerful, omniscient, and omnipresent. It is not a superiority that comes from above but rather a superiority that comes from below, from the theological and philo-sophical—in a word, intellectual—power of its representatives who were able to produce teachings that capture the idea and practice of the good in a better way than other religions.[35] In other words, the fundamental difference between Christianity and other religions does not consist of their objective veracity (which religion presents *the right* God or *the right* kind of good) but in their subjective ability to access the reality of the good (which religion has *the best* intellectual skill to present God or the good).

This is how we reach the second feature of radical theology as seen in Mancuso, namely, the shift from the concept of God—conceived as a transcendent reality in traditional theology—to the notion of the good, which in radical theology translates or even replaces the tradi-tional concept of God. It is, however, crucial to know that in radical theology God is not transcendent; this is why the only explanation that could somehow elucidate the traditional concept of God to contemporary people is the idea of the good. As there is only one reality for radical theology—that of history and human experience—the only meaningful way to explain it is to use notions that pertain to the same reality; this is why the idea of the good that can be—although barely—connected to human experience is preferred over the traditional concept of God, which allows for a transcendent but equally ontological reality.

The Nature of Faith and Religion

The third aspect presented by Mancuso regarding the way we should see religion today concerns the nature of faith as a gift of God.[36] For Mancuso, the idea that faith is a gift of God, which he associates with traditional theology, means in fact that faith is a supernatural virtue.[37] This in turn leads to the idea that faith is given from above, when theology, including the idea of faith, should proceed from below, namely, from the reality of man's historical existence. Elaborating more on the idea that faith is supernaturally given to man from and by God as a gift, Mancuso makes it clear that—understood in this particular way—faith is given to man by grace.[38] He immediately asks what is this *grace* that has given man faith. To Mancuso, the question is at least partially rhetorical because he leaves the impression that he already knows the answer, which, however, he is not willing to disclose on the spot. Before giving his final word concerning the idea of grace that informs man's faith, Mancuso underlines the conviction that faith is supernaturally given by grace is an affirmation traditional Christianity cannot do without. For traditional theology, the doctrine of faith as given by grace is so fundamental it cannot be disposed of, precisely because it represents the absolute truth of its dogmatic system.[39]

At this point, Mancuso begins to present his own perspective on faith as given by grace, against which he presents his understanding of the nature of faith by means of a sequence of questions. Thus, he notices that the traditional teaching of faith as given by grace cannot avoid what he calls "a certain arbitrariness."[40] This is a clear sign, at least for Mancuso, that the idea of faith as given to man through God's supernatural grace is fatally flawed.[41] Then he discloses these flaws through three questions. If God loves each and every human being and each human being was created for salvation, how is it possible that God did not give the gift of grace to some of them (and, as Mancuso notices, the number of those who were left without God's

supernatural gift is anything but small)? Following this first question, the second arises: is it not weird that God created man only
to keep him away from the gift of faith, namely, away from the relationship with him and consequently away from salvation? Mancuso
notices that every now and then those who do not believe say, more
or less seriously, that the grace of faith was not given to them, and it
is because of this supernaturally intended situation that they actually
cannot believe. One can sense a veiled accusation in Mancuso's words
because the blame for this state of facts rests with the church, which
teaches that faith is God's supernatural gift. This unasserted accusation is immediately followed by a conclusion openly stating that,
according to Mancuso, theology—specifically traditional theology—
does not know how to answer why certain people are given salvation
and others are not.[42]

Such a position is clearly constructed on what Mancuso calls the
theology from below, which evaluates human reality from the standpoint of daily experience through the capabilities of reason. Thus,
Mancuso's first question is nothing but the conclusion of his empirical
observation concerning human experience, namely, that some people
have faith, or the gift of grace, while others do not have it. Corroborat-
ing this experiential observation, which is thoroughly valid, with the
traditional doctrine that God loves the entire world, Mancuso reaches
a deadlock because, at least in his theological framework, there should
be a perfect agreement between God's love for all people and the
idea of faith as a human reality. At this point, Mancuso seems to perceive traditional theology somewhat differently because he states that
God created each human being for salvation; whereas in traditional
theology God created each human being not for salvation—because
there was no need of salvation at the moment of man's creation—but
rather for God's own glory, for a relationship with himself. But why
does Mancuso include the idea of salvation in the doctrine of creation? A possible answer is his conviction that the traditional notion of
sin needs a dramatic reinterpretation, which should exclude the idea
of guilt in order to preserve only the image of metaphysical symbolism. Thus, sin—with reference to the original sin, which in traditional
theology connects creation and salvation—is the highest metaphysical symbolism, which designates the laceration of history and nature
(in the sense that history and nature are, at the same time, rooted in
God and afflicted by evil as well as suffering).[43] Thus, if original sin
is merely symbolic, then it does not ontologically affect the human
being but it rather pictures the reality of the human being. In other
words, man is not ontologically as well as inherently sinful and evil; on

the contrary, the human being is hit by evil and suffering. It is logical, therefore, to infer that creation includes in itself the idea of salvation, as Mancuso briefly mentions, which in turn leads to the conclusion that something is utterly wrong with the theology that preaches both God's love and the existence of faith as God's supernatural gift.[44]

Resuming his conviction that traditional theology has absolutely no answer to why faith appears in some people but not in others, Mancuso appears to see traditional theology as an attempt to quickly avoid a straight answer. Thus, as traditional theology cannot give a clear answer to why some people have faith while others do not, the standard official position of the church is that faith is given by God. In other words, the reality of man's faith is inscrutable as long as God himself decides who has and who does not have faith.[45] This also means that, from a human point of view, we actually do not know why some people have faith while others do not because the whole matter depends on God.

But this is traditional theology, and Mancuso does not agree with the fundamental tenets of traditional theology. This is mainly because traditional theology begins from above, so it has to do with the supernatural reality of God as well as of faith, while for Mancuso theology should proceed from below. When it comes to faith, Mancuso makes it explicitly clear that faith should not be concerned with the supernatural but rather with the world. The world is not the world in general but the human world, the very world of human beings, of human experience, and of human life.[46] So, as faith should be concerned with the world, it means that faith should be placed in the human experience of men and women.[47]

It turns out that this is the third characteristic of radical theology based on Mancuso's reflection: the radical redefinition of faith with the clear intention that the object of faith should be kept within the boundaries of human experience and history. So, for radical theology, it is not the notion or the reality of faith that presents a serious problem for contemporary men and women; it is the object of faith that can cause real problems. This is why faith should be redirected from the traditional concept of God, which points to a transcendent reality, to the world of history, which cements the existence of the single and unique reality of human experience. In other words, man should no longer believe in the traditional God who cannot offer relevant answers for today's problems; what man must do is believe in himself because this is the only way to make human life existentially relevant.

RELIGION AND SECULARIZED FAITH

Mancuso insists a lot on the idea of faith because when he defines it from the perspective of a theology that starts from below, the result is the secularization of faith. In other words, faith is no longer seen as the supernatural gift of God bestowed directly by God on some human beings of his own choice but rather as a feature or characteristic of human life. Faith is, therefore, detached from its traditional supernatural realm in order to be reattached to the reality of man's historical existence. Another consequence lies in the fact that faith is no longer theological—in the sense that it belongs to traditional theology—but is exclusively religious as it can be applied to any world religion. Faith, however, defined as a human religious feeling, exists for one reason and one reason alone, which in Mancuso is the idea of the good. Actually, he explains plainly that the idea of the good, which is actually man's will to do the good, is the *only* reason for man's adherence to faith. The sequence "the good—the will to [do] the good—the adherence to faith" or, in simpler words, "good—good-will—faith" is what actually defines fundamental theology. For him, fundamental theology is nothing but the ontology of the good and the ontology of truth. Mancuso could well have said that it is not only fundamental theology that is defined by the ontology of the good and of truth but also fundamental religion. As both the good and truth inform human faith from the exclusive perspective of man's historical existence, with actually no reference to anything that lies beyond it, it is perfectly logical to infer that such a definition of faith becomes diluted into a newer—evidently more religious than theological—presentation of the idea of faith.[48]

We should not lose sight of the fact that, in Mancuso, the object of faith is God because he does write that the unique motivation of faith *in* God is the unconditional adherence of the soul to the good. However, based on his previous affirmation that the only reason for man's adherence to faith is the good, it becomes clear that the object of faith is the good, which is also identified by Mancuso with the idea of God. In other words, the good is God or, to be sure, the idea of the good *is* the idea of God, so it is once again quite clear that, in Mancuso, God is stripped of his transcendent, metaphysical ontology. The existence of God is not above humanity but within it; God exists no longer above history but within it, so God is below his traditionally ascribed metaphysical realm. Defined as the good, God is no longer the God of traditional theology or the God of traditional Christian theology but specifically the God of fundamental theology, which to Mancuso means fundamental religion. God is the good of religion.[49]

Mancuso elaborates further on his basic theological sequence, which is "good—goodwill—faith," by explaining that the good is actually love. He writes that love, understood in its very essence, coincides with the good, and this can clearly be applied to any world religion. Mancuso also explains that the good and love are actually a single reality that can be looked at from two different perspectives. Thus, the good should be seen objectively and love subjectively but, at the same time, Mancuso recommends that subjective reality should be subordinated to objective reality.[50] In practical terms, this means that love is subordinated to the good. The reign of the objective good must always be enforced upon the subjective nature of love; otherwise love, "as a horse driven insane,"[51] can produce either good or evil consequences. Subjective love must be led by the idea of the good in order to produce the good; if not, love can cover itself in blood.

It is important to realize here that this is actually what Mancuso understands by religion. Religion must objectively promote the idea of the good and then apply it, by means of love, at the practical level of man's historical existence; it happens, though, that every now and then love is left without its objective tutelage, which results in an evil, even bloody, outcome. The idea and the practice of the good must be the goal of every religion because this is the only means whereby man's experience can go beyond the necessity of nature in order to reach the realm of the good and of eternity. Religion must occupy itself with the good because we all know what evil is. The problem of religion is not to define evil, but to define, understand, and practice the good. In this respect, Mancuso underlines, religion is closer to *the* truth than science and philosophy. Religion, as preoccupied with the idea and practice of the good (and of love), is able to have a deeper knowledge of things because the essence of everything is the human soul (*anima umana*) with its good as well as bad facets. Religion must serve the human soul by assisting it in applying the good in everyday life. So religion must be concerned with the actuality of man's historical existence, with his concrete experience of life. Religion can indeed come closest to truth because religion is truth. Mancuso writes that, in this particular sense, religion is truth as wisdom, as intelligence, even as the source of energy for actual life. The truth of religion, therefore, should not be searched in the metaphysical realm of an ontologically real God, as in traditional theology, but in the world of men and women, in the reality of concrete life. Consequently, truth must be looked for in the human soul because the good of humanity coincides with the good of the soul. At the same time, for Mancuso, religion is closer to the truth than philosophy and science because the truth is the good as well as whatever produces the good in order to help men and women face life. The truth of religion must help us confront the reality of life without fear.[52]

It is evident thus that Mancuso's theology is actually an attempt to define religion as the idea and application of the good, which is in fact *the* truth. Truth depends on man's historical existence but also on his actual, present, and daily experience. As truth is informed by human experience, the necessity of a metaphysical realm that transcends human history, as in traditional theology, is rendered useless. God is no longer outside humanity, as a personal, transcendental, and metaphysical being, but within us as an idea, which becomes concrete through another idea, namely, the idea of the good. This is why faith in God is no longer the belief in a metaphysical God who has an actual existence of his own but, as Mancuso clearly points out, faith in God means having a determined or fixed worldview. But if God is within us as the good and the truth, then there are no limits to what faith actually is. This is why Mancuso explains that faith should no longer be seen as obedience (to a metaphysical and ontologically real God) but as freedom (to understand human experience through the essence of the human soul). In other words, for Mancuso, faith is not in God but rather in man, and this is the central element of religion: the inner conviction of man that the world can be changed for the better through the practical application of the idea of the good to his actual experience with view to the development of man's capacity to live his life without anguish.

This perspective on faith, however, changes Mancuso's entire perspective on God and brings us to the fourth feature of radical theology: the secularization of faith and the dissolution of traditional metaphysics, including the doctrine of God as Trinity. Thus, Mancuso deconstructs the classical doctrine of the Trinity by offering separate discourses on the Father, the Son, and the Spirit while nevertheless clinging to the traditional language of the classical doctrine. This results in a dispersed Trinity, where the Father, Son, and Holy Spirit are seen as images of humanity and the spirit in general. Another obvious consequence of his theological enterprise is the dilution of metaphysics in the sense that the traditional metaphysical discourse about God should be understood in terms of the distinction between spirit and matter, where matter is the origin of the spirit. This is why his doctrine of God seeks to investigate human experience by making use of the Father, Son, and Holy Spirit in such a way that he defines God by means of the primacy of truth, the persistence of faith, and the necessity of knowing God as human love.

LOVE, HUMANITY, AND GOD

Any attempt to read Vito Mancuso's books will immediately lead to the observation that it is quite difficult to identify a distinct discourse on the doctrine of the Trinity. This is clearly the case because he is not interested in talking about the subject but rather in pointing to issues related to whatever ignites the concern of contemporary people. According to Mancuso, the foremost aspect of human reality that triggers the interest of people nowadays is love.[53] He actually says that in order to have money and success in today's world it is enough to be able to sing about love.[54] So love sells because it is a fundamental human feeling that enhances man's desire to live, exist, create, and enjoy life. As a basic human faculty, love augments the capacities of the self, so the very existence of the human being is essentially shaped by love.[55] Mancuso is keen to underline that, despite the obvious success of any human enterprise connected to love in some way, we should not lose sight of love as something more than a mere human feeling. Thus, love transcends the boundaries of physics and psychology in the sense that it is not a feeling that causes people to relate and increase their inner potential but rather the reality that shapes the being or even exists above or beyond the being itself. What interests Mancuso is love in its objective reality,[56] seen as the grounds of existence and not the subjective love of human sentiments. It is obvious therefore that in Mancuso, the idea of love leaves behind its sentimental aspects in order to embrace a much wider configuration, which presents love as *the* only possible meaning of human life; love is in the end the very light of humanity.[57]

This clarification of love is crucial because this is exactly what informs Mancuso's picture of the Trinity. In one of his very rare references to the Trinity—or rather to God as Trinity—Mancuso explains that it is only love that connects God, Christ, and the Spirit. It should be clear from the start that Mancuso does not like to use the term "Trinity"; what he prefers is to talk about God, Christ, and the Spirit as somehow distinct concepts. He does not exclude the fundamental connection between them because the only valid tie putting together God, Christ, and the Spirit is love.[58] Love is essentially a relationship, and it is in this capacity that love keeps God, Christ, and the Spirit within its encompassing domain. Nevertheless, and somehow regardless of the connection between God, Christ, and the Spirit,

Mancuso talks about each as distinct concepts. It has been made clear that love is fundamentally objective for Mancuso, but love must still have a practical application. What keeps God, Christ, and the Spirit together is love as expressed practically by means of *kenosis*.[59] Mancuso writes that Christ has never ceased to be God, but this fact was evident only in and through *kenosis*, which is the ultimate manifestation of love in the practical details of human life and existence. Christ always remained God because he acted "by virtue of the Spirit," or through the Spirit of God. But as God is love, Christ should be perceived as God as he acted in the Spirit of God, or in the spirit of love. Christ is God because he performed his activity with love.[60]

So love is God and God is love, but love must be seen practically if it is to be recognized as such. Love is God and God is love when we see Christ in his *kenosis*, when he is downtrodden, humiliated, and obscured, because in all these instances he acted in the Spirit of God, or out of love.[61] This proves that regardless of how we perceive God, Christ, and the Spirit, the only way to get a good grasp of what God really is remains the practical manifestation of love, which can be seen in Christ.[62] In other words, the reality of love and even the reality of objective love are useless without the practicality of human existence and experience. If we want to understand objective love, we must first take a careful look at our experience.[63]

This is the fifth characteristic of radical theology as seen in Mancuso: the reinterpretation of the traditional notion of God as love. There is no actual God who lives in a transcendent reality; radical theology only accepts a God who "lives" within human experience. As human experience is dominated by the reality of love, the idea of love becomes synonymous with the concept of God. Thus, radical theology transfers the classical notion of God from the metahistorical transcendence of traditional theology to the historicity of contemporary experience.

THEOLOGY, EXPERIENCE, AND SCIENCE

Mancuso is very careful to stress that theology must proceed from below, from the world of human experience. Theology must be about life and it must be concerned with real experience. According to Mancuso, theology must serve human life, with its good and bad experiences, if it aims to be useful at all. Unless theology depicts life as it is, unless it portrays human existence in all its wonderful as well as terrible manifestations, theology cannot be properly considered a useful tool in today's society. This, however, is not enough. Theology should not only see life in its beautiful and gruesome aspects; theology also must place itself in the service of humanity by permeating human experience with "positive energy," which takes the form of goodness and justice.[64] Therefore, for Mancuso, theology is an adequate discourse about God *exclusively* if it presents and serves human experience by promoting goodness and justice. To put it differently, theology is useful to us only if it starts from the reality of our lives and serves our experience. But theology should never stop at this point. In Mancuso, theology starts from below; it investigates our life and experience, but then it attempts to *clarify* or *explain* the good as well as the bad facets of whatever happens with us in the world. In short, theology begins from human experience in order to serve and explain it as part of the natural world.[65]

Mancuso's theology is drafted in such a way that it enters a dialogue with the world and its current interests. This also means that his theology is very open to science and lay consciousness; to put it in a nutshell, Mancuso's theology is a rational discourse about God.[66] He makes clear that there is a connection between theology, science, and God, but this connection is possible only if we start from the primordial phenomenon of life. Theology begins its journey from the Word of God, the doctrines of the church, and the traditional sources of its knowledge, but eventually it reaches the point when it has to say something concrete and real about the primordial phenomenon, which is life itself. Mancuso expresses his deep conviction that today it is virtually impossible to talk responsibly and realistically about life without taking science into account.[67] If we want to profess a true theology, we should carefully and diligently listen to what science or, even better, sciences have to tell us today. For theology, the dialogue with contemporary sciences is crucial. This dialogue, though, must be carried out in absolute faithfulness to the primary object of science and theology, namely, human life and its meaning. It should be obvious by now why for Mancuso theology begins from below and should not be seen as a creative act of God; theology stems from the internal or intrinsic harmony between matter and energy.[68]

In Mancuso, nothing exceeds the paramount importance of life. Thus, life is before theology, before philosophy, even before human thought, but the fact that theology starts from below is not a denial of God's creative act. Theology interprets God's creative act as proceeding from matter. It should be said here that, in Mancuso, matter is the mother (*mater*) of all things, so matter produces the spirit, produces life, and produces the being. This is why Mancuso sees absolutely no contrast between creation and evolution.[69] Actually, for Mancuso, evolution itself is the fact that everything starts from below, but evolution—like anything else—should be interpreted. When it comes to interpretation and especially to the theological interpretation of evolution, Mancuso stresses that evolution should be understood as a concrete manifestation of creation. At this point, Mancuso acknowledges that there are two types of theology. The first is the theology from above, namely, the theology that begins with the Bible, with the sources of tradition and the Magisterium, so this is the theology that attempts to interpret and understand human life from realities that are dogmatic rather than scientific. What is really important here is to notice that this particular type of theology, or the theology from above, considers the Bible—and consequently tradition and the Magisterium—as its primary object, not human life and experience. The second type of theology, and Mancuso especially makes clear that this is *his* theology, holds human life and experience as its primary object.[70] The theology from below makes use of the Bible, but it reads the Bible in light of human experience. Thus, the primacy of theology is not given by the Bible and the church's dogmas; the primacy of theology is given by human experience. In other words, theology begins from human experience and it ends with human experience. Mancuso underlines once more that *this* is his way of doing theology, which is in line with many illustrious representatives of modern thought and especially with Pierre Teilhard de Chardin.[71] It is quite clear that for Mancuso, the theology from above is utterly incapable of supporting a real dialogue with science. The theology from below can instead produce a valid dialogue with modern science, but it can never convince science of anything. Science has its own devices to convince itself, so it does not need theology to support its claims.

Theology, however, should never be concerned with convincing science; theology should give meaning to the information and the data provided by science. The task of science is to produce analyses and then, based on these analyses, to come up with theories. A totally different approach is enacted when scientific data and theories are put together in order to produce a worldview.[72] For Mancuso, this is the task of philosophy, which, having assembled the information and theories of science, brings forward a worldview that explains, to a certain degree, the realities of the natural realm. Theology is included in the definition of philosophy because, as Mancuso plainly shows, theology is a particular way of doing philosophy. Theology has its own worldview, a particular worldview but a worldview nonetheless. But science, as a way to approach the world, is one thing, while scientists, the people who work with science as a way to approach the world, are a totally different thing.

At this point, however, we come across the sixth feature of radical theology in Mancuso, which is the identification of theology with philosophy. Of course, the two do not overlap completely because theology has a specific type of discourse, but eventually both approach the same realities though from different angles: theology still uses the traditional language of God—though dramatically reinterpreted to fit today's human experience—while philosophy tends to offer valid explanations from a predominantly human perspective. Nevertheless, theology can be seen as a specific kind of philosophy because it attempts to offer relevant answers to the fundamental questions of humanity, which is nowadays confronted with the remarkable discoveries of contemporary science.

FINALITY, RELIGION, AND MEANING

Mancuso admits there is no such thing as a uniform or monolithic perspective on the world as produced by science; scientists themselves are divided into two camps: those who explain the world scientifically and those who look at natural reality in a more philosophical or even theological way. Thus, the first are convinced that there is an intrinsic finality of matter and energy, while the second believe there is a *law* or a *logos* that governs all things from outside, a *law* or a *logos* that is the foundation as well as the finality of the world. As compared to theology, science does not have—and does not want to have—the final word with reference to the reality of the world. Science analyzes data and comes up with theories, but it is not concerned with a worldview that must necessarily be *the* final image of the world we all live in. Science only produces words, distinct and separate words, which philosophy later puts together into a meaningful sentence or phrase. As part of philosophy or, even better, among various philosophical approaches, theology itself fosters its own way of putting together the words of science into a complete, coherent, and meaningful discourse.[73] In Mancuso, science or sciences, philosophy, and theology all provide information that eventually is integrated into a full, complete image of human experience. Individual human experience is legitimately endowed with meaning only to the extent that it is connected to the meaning of everything. So one's individual life is meaningful only if it is related to the ultimate meaning of natural reality.[74]

This is actually the essence of religion: being religious is being willing to connect one's most intimate individuality to the complete meaning of everything. Mancuso urges us to understand that there is something bigger than ourselves that brought us into existence;

we are religious when we tie our own freedom to the complete meaning of everything.[75] In Mancuso, this is the most important movement of religion: bringing together human individuality and common experience. He realizes that understanding what *is* the complete meaning of everything could be a problematic issue, so he comes up with an explanation.

The complete meaning of everything, which is bigger than any individual human experience, can be either the being or nothing. It is important to note here that, for Mancuso, there is no absolute final answer to this question. Each world religion gives its own answer to the question of ultimate meaning. As for Mancuso, he professes his allegiance to the religion of Christianity, which believes that the fundamental principle of the world is the *logos*. The *logos* should be understood as reason or, in Mancuso's exact words, as creative reason. This *logos* became flesh (*sarx*), so man is the *logos* of phenomenon.[76] In other words, creative reason finds its complete manifestation in the human flesh, or the human body, which is evidently the individual human being. This is the specificity of Christianity, which Mancuso says produced conviction even within himself: each phenomenon in the natural world has a *logos*, an intrinsic reason or logic that explains itself. Following this line of thought, even the human being can be conceived as a natural phenomenon, so we all have our own intrinsic reasons for being alive in the world; this is why Mancuso stresses once again that the *logos* finds its completeness in the human flesh. The human being reflects in himself this reason, this *logos*, and then it transmits it beyond himself or outside himself through ethics, aesthetics, social life, and politics.[77]

These are the things that express human love and cause human thinking. There is a common origin of humanity or at least of human thought, which means there must also be a common finality or conclusion with reference to human beings. In Mancuso's thought, this means that human beings can pursue various religions, which are historically different but originate within the same human intrinsic reason, as well as eventually come to the same fundamental conclusion. For Mancuso, this is the greatest consolation. There must be a parallel between religion and science because, very much like science, which manages to unite people by bringing together individuals of different nationalities, traditions, and cultures based on the same scientifically objective results, religion—as encompassing the great spiritual traditions of the world—must go beyond particular dogmatic systems in order to reach the essence of our humanity and thus unite all people.[78] Mancuso is convinced that such a reality can be achieved if, and only if, we always expose the truth.[79] The essence as well as the meaning of human life is never to tell lies when it comes to the understanding of reality. In other words, we should never accommodate within ourselves ideas, preconceptions or views not in accordance with concrete experience, so it is experience that regulates and informs theology, not the other way around. Religion is not the ultimate objective of human spirituality. Mancuso insists that we were not created by God in order to be religious because true or functional religion is the authenticity of life. In other words, we were not created for believing but rather for existing. Traditional theology can be maintained provided it supports the authenticity of life but excludes bigotry, immaturity, and imprisoned consciousness. It seems that for Mancuso, the authenticity of life is the essence of the human soul, understood as the vital principle that lives within us and transcends whatever nature and society produces within us.[80] The soul is what remains of ourselves beyond natural and social functionality, the most intimate dimension of ourselves, which both represents our most personal conviction (*fiducia*) and helps us go beyond our own deaths.[81] When we understand this kind of theology, our existence has indeed a true meaning.[82]

By offering this explanation, Mancuso points to the seventh feature of radical theology as depicted in his writings: man's personal conviction and the meaning of life must be sought within the inner reality of experience. When religion and science collide because of antagonistic interpretations of external reality, the only way to reach a compromise is to turn to our inner reality. Both the scientist and the theologian live in history, which constitutes the object of their scrutiny, so both interpret history as a reality external to them. Conflict cannot be avoided as the scientist turns to facts for answers, while the theologian uses concepts for the same purpose. Radical theology, however, suggests that the real meaning of our existence does not reside in the investigation of external realities but in the thorough search of what lies within ourselves. Such an endeavor, though, requires the fundamental redefinition of traditional concepts such as that of God as Trinity.

THE TRINITY, INCARNATION, AND THE ABSOLUTE VALUE OF MAN

The doctrine of the Trinity in Mancuso must be understood within the framework that he himself established for this theology. Thus, as matter is the mother of all things, and the spirit is the product of matter, it follows that even the being originates in the same matter.[83] It is clear that, for Mancuso, the traditional Christian discourse, which believes in the ontological reality of metaphysics, must be understood differently in order to fall within the lines of his theology from below. The immediate consequence is that any attempt to talk about metaphysics must necessarily begin with and from below, from the world of physics and humanity. Theology is the result of human experience, which informs doctrine,[84] so the Trinity as a traditional Christian dogma must undergo the same process.[85] The Trinity cannot and should not be thought of in terms of the Bible—at least not exclusively—because unless human experience does not make sense of its content, we should give it up as totally useless for our lives. Mancuso, however, does not discard the Trinity so easily; what he does is to read it in accordance with his conviction that matter is the origin of everything.[86] This reading of the doctrine of the Trinity transposes the whole doctrine from the ontology of traditional metaphysics to the ontology of contemporary philosophy and physics.

In Mancuso, the source of the doctrine of the Trinity is "the idea of the Son," with reference to Christ who, in traditional theology, is seen as the Son of God. Mancuso also explains that the idea of the Son makes sense if connected to the concept of incarnation. We should not lose sight of the fact that matter produces everything, including the spirit and the being, so even Christ or the Son must be understood within the same lines. Thus, Christ is a mere man even if we attach the idea of the incarnation to his person.[87] The incarnation should not be understood as in traditional theology, namely, as the divine action whereby the Son of God, revealed in Scripture to be the Christ, became flesh by assuming a human body and therefore was born into our world as Jesus of Nazareth. On the contrary, in Mancuso, the incarnation does not make any reference to supernatural or ontologically real metaphysical realities.[88] Incarnation is merely an indication that man has always been connected to God, in the sense that man has always been aware that there is something permanently above him or bigger than his particular individuality. Thus, the source of the doctrine of the Trinity is, according to Mancuso, the idea that man is permanently, and has always been, in touch with God.[89]

This is indeed a significant departure from the traditional doctrine of the Trinity, where the being of God who exists in three divine persons is utterly transcendent and thus has nothing to do with humanity. In traditional Christianity, God exists as a Trinity from eternity, so God was a Trinitarian being long before the physical reality of humanity came into existence as the result of the action of God. Therefore, while traditional Christianity professes the belief in the absolute metaphysical transcendence of God's ontology beyond the physical reality of humanity, Mancuso prefers to understand the Trinity as a way to picture man's physical existence as enriched by his awareness of a reality greater than his individual existence. Consequently, the Trinity becomes a symbol of humanity, which confirms man's experience is both physical and spiritual.[90]

For Mancuso, the Trinity is nothing but a step beyond mere monotheism. He explains that the Trinity is not a polytheistic belief because God is still *one* although in *three* persons. At this point, Mancuso does not elaborate on how the Trinity should be understood; what he does is to warn that the Trinity cannot be properly understood unless one comprehends the origin of the doctrine. Before releasing his perspective on the origin of the Trinity as doctrine, Mancuso uses a series of adjectives that offer a clear image on how he sees the Trinity. Thus, according to Mancuso, the doctrine of the Trinity is at first glance uncomfortable, troublesome, barely practical, and absurd. Nevertheless, a rereading of the doctrine based on a theology from below should present the Trinity in a much more favorable light. Mancuso is fully aware that such a rereading must not start from God, as in traditional theology, but rather from man, which would fit his belief that matter is the origin of the entire reality. This is why he writes that the origin of the Trinity is man and his absolute value with reference to the definition of divinity. In other words, the Trinity is a symbol of man's capacity to define God based on man's absolute value.[91]

It should be noted that the absolute value is not God, as in traditional theology, but man, who is even the origin of Trinity. Mancuso explains that God must always be thought of as starting from man because in what Mancuso believes to be true, Christian theocentrism must always be equated with anthropocentrism.[92] To draw the line, God is man but not in the sense of traditional Christianity where God became man in the person of Jesus of Nazareth. In Mancuso, God *is* man because man is always the true measure of whatever we say about God. Therefore, God and the Trinity or God as Trinity is a symbol of man's capacity to define himself as divine.[93] This is actually the very essence of the Trinity, which opposes both the Jewish religion and Islam, which see God as utterly transcendent and exclusively metaphysical. Christianity in turn, at least according to Mancuso, is the religion that brings God down to earth from his traditional ontology of absolute metaphysics to the contemporary experience of man's physical life. The difference between the Jewish religion and Islam, on the one hand, and Christianity, on the other, becomes even more evident when Mancuso stresses that in the Jewish religion and Islam God is unique and alone, while in Christianity God is trinitarian. He includes, besides the original idea of the monotheistic God, the concept of man and that of the spirit, which are the product of matter. At the end of the day, God as Trinity is the result of man's active thinking because the plenitude of divine mystery is the life and words of a man.[94] In Christianity's case, this man was Jesus of Nazareth but it seems that, for Mancuso, it could have well been any other human being.[95]

These considerations reveal the eighth feature of radical theology based on Mancuso's general overview, namely, the redefinition of the traditional doctrine of Trinity by means of a modified Christology. The detachment of Jesus from the notion of Christ is evident, as Mancuso believes that any other person could have filled Jesus's role in offering us a practical explanation of divine mystery. In radical theology, Jesus of Nazareth is not important for our contemporary theology; he is important for history and the past but when it comes to the experience of the present we must go beyond him in order to find—in ourselves—the power to see ourselves as divine. In other words, for radical theology, the source of the meaning of man's life is man himself due to his special capacity to see himself as divine, while Trinity is only a symbol that mediates this interpretation.

THE TRINITY, PREEXISTENCE, AND SPIRITUAL TRANSCENDENCE

The traditional doctrine of the Trinity is uncomfortable for the minds of modern people not only because it presents God as one in three persons but also because it includes the teaching of Christ's preexistence. It is obvious that Mancuso does not see Christ's preexistence in terms of Christ's metaphysical existence before he became incarnate in our physical world. For him, this is impossible given that theology is regulated by human experience and human experience does not confirm such a hypothesis. Thus, the traditional doctrine of Christ's preexistence must not be understood ontologically; on the contrary, it must be translated anthropologically and existentially, in the sense that the root of faith lies within us, not outside us.[96] If traditional theology tells us that the origin of faith is God as totally external to us, Mancuso believes that faith is exclusively a human phenomenon based on the idea of preexistence. Faith already exists within us even before we are aware of it because God himself as Trinity is a product of our experience (which includes our reasoning). But the ideas of preexistence and faith remain empty for Mancuso unless they are given a more practical content. So faith is man's desire to do good and justice, and this is the sign of our divine filiation.[97] We are children of God, and God is our Father if we have a burning desire to do good and justice, namely, confer meaning or even a new meaning to the existence and experience of other human beings. Mancuso stresses that men and women have always searched for God because they are, at least partially, divine. Again, man's divinity should not be understood as being connected in some mysterious way to God's absolute transcendence of traditional theology; man is divine because he has always nurtured within himself the desire to do good deeds as well as justice to his fellow humans, so divinity should not be deciphered theologically or metaphysically but rather anthropologically and existentially.[98]

As far as Mancuso is concerned, man has always been divine, which is confirmed by the idea of Christ's preexistence. The very same idea, however, proves in Mancuso's theology that God has always been human because the humanity of the Word (*logos*) preexists as compared to the incarnation.[99] Christ's incarnation is the practical consequence of his preexistence in the sense that the human being can practically "incarnate" his preexistent desire to do good and justice, which is once more a proof of his inner love. But why does Mancuso say that God has always been human? Because, if God became human, if God became incarnate, it means that he must have always been human. When traditional theology tells us that God created the world in Christ, we must understand that the idea of Christ contains and has always contained the notion of humanity. But if God created the world in Christ who contains the idea of humanity, it follows that humanity has always been part of God or of the idea of God.[100] Again, traditional theology informs us that the Son is not the same person as the Father but a being who exists, or rather subsists, personally and eternally as generated by the Father. In Mancuso, this means that the idea of the Son—namely, Christ—who embodies the divinity of humanity, has always been connected to the concept of God. At the same time, we must never forget that Christ is a mere man, so as a representative of the entire humanity he proves that human beings have always been divine. Mancuso is well aware that in traditional theology the communion between the Son and the Spirit is kept by the Spirit, which he translates as "love of ontological substance." The Spirit is not a person, as in traditional theology, but the love that characterizes the Father and the Son, namely, God and Christ, divinity and humanity. Thus, because of love, God is human and humans are divine but not with reference to transcendental metaphysics. God is human and humans are divine only to the extent that God explains the divinity of our humanity as deeply rooted in our physical, natural experience.[101]

In Mancuso, there is no place for the traditional doctrine of the Trinity, which defines God as a divine substance or being in three different, subsistent, and individual persons, whose eternal existence is characterized by an absolute metaphysical transcendence. Such a picture of God does not resemble human experience, which teaches us that matter is the source of everything. Thus, matter must be the source of what we call God, Christ (who represents man), and the Spirit, which is actually man's innermost feeling of love. Mancuso's Trinity is not ontologically real, metaphysical, and transcendent; it is physical, immanent, and spiritual—a symbol of man's eternal humanity. In his words, the face of God the Father, of Christ, and of man is the same, which is just another confirmation of the fundamental humanity of Mancuso's perspective on the Trinity.[102] So his Trinity is not ontological but rather spiritual, because it defines humanity as having a divine existence whenever it shows the practical side of love in doing good and justice. Even if he relocates the Trinity from the realm of traditional metaphysics to the world of our physical history, Mancuso seems reluctant to give up the concept. He continues to use the term "metaphysics," but its connotation is clearly not ontological, as in traditional theology, but outwardly spiritual. And, as metaphysics includes the idea of transcendence, Mancuso's man does not find himself in the position of being transcended by God's metaphysical existence; he only has to transcend himself in order to enter the realm of human spirituality, love, and justice.[103]

It is important to comprehend that, in Mancuso, the *locus* of God is the world, because, at the end of the day, God is human and humans are divine. The world was created by God but not in the traditional understanding of nature being created out of nothing by an ontologically real God who transcends it in an absolute way. For Mancuso, the world was created by God in the sense that nature is permeated by the idea of God, so it is destined to become divine. But if nature becomes divine, it also becomes more and more human because the world is bound to humanization. This means that the master of nature is man, but even if Mancuso had said that the master of nature was God, as the face of God and man are the same, it means that the master of nature is man.[104]

It is clear therefore that Mancuso's metaphysics becomes diluted in the physical reality of man's historical experience, which eventually produces a perspective that presents a dispersed Trinity. God the Father, the Son, and the Holy Spirit are no longer kept together in their absolute metaphysical transcendence, which lies beyond any human possibilities; the three persons of the traditional Trinity are scattered throughout the worldly reality of man's existence in history. God is no longer the Father whose eternal existence is depicted in traditional theology; he is only the face of humanity, which understands that this theoretical image can be made more practical by means of the idea of Christ's incarnation. Thus, man understands that his divine essence must be shown outwardly by "incarnating" his divinity in acts of love and justice. The Spirit is therefore a metaphor of human love, which elevates our desires beyond the physical realm of our existence to the "transcendent" spiritual experience of our historical humanity.

This posits the ninth characteristic of radical theology as seen in Mancuso: the reduction of the classical notion of the (Holy) Spirit—which in traditional theology is given a genuine ontological status as part of the Trinity—to the theoretical as well as practical reality of man's love. So the Spirit is not to be sought outside the human being but within it. It does not really matter for radical theology whether or not there is a spirit as such; what counts is the fact that love can be identified as a feeling with practical manifestations and this can explain the traditional idea of the (Holy) Spirit.

The immediate result of Mancuso's theology of the Trinity and of God in general is seen in his ethical as well as bioethical understanding of anthropology and particularly in his perspective on human disability. It has to be underlined from the start that he debates the issue of disability from a standpoint that opposes the traditional teaching of the Roman Catholic Church concerning anthropology in general. Thus, he is convinced that the Church is practically silent in this fundamental issue because, while it professes many doctrines and affirmations, it does not come up with valid ideas. Having gone through a series of anthropological considerations regarding the traditional Christian perspective on man as directly created by God and the practical reality of human disability, Mancuso postulates what he calls the "theological drama" in connection with the existence of evil as well as the image of God presented as both love and creator. Then he comes closer to a Christological approach with specific reference to the person of Jesus of Nazareth, who lies at the basis of the definition of disability as innocent suffering.

FROM PERSONAL EXPERIENCE TO THE PHILOSOPHY OF DISABILITY

The problem of disability in the theology of Vito Mancuso cannot be fully understood apart from his personal experience with the reality of disability. Although disability did not afflict him personally, his family suffered from an experience that had an abrupt and sad ending. It is important to note that his book on disability, entitled *Innocent Suffering: Disability, Nature and God*,[105] begins with a story that influenced his life and thought concerning the issue of disability. In 1997, his unborn son died in his mother's womb because of a genetic malady that put an end to his life in the fifth week of pregnancy. Mancuso gently mentions that the name of his unborn child would have been Federico, and his very short unborn existence produced a profound impact on his father, who began to approach theology from a different perspective. It seems that up to that moment, Mancuso was a traditionalist in the sense that he professed Christianity as a lay theologian who was more or less in line with the teaching of the Holy See. In connection with this aspect, he mentions that this unfortunate event took place at a time when the Vatican insisted that human life was sacred because it was a gift from God, as explained in John Paul II's *Donum Vitae*.[106] It seems Mancuso was deeply troubled both by the loss of his unborn son and the Vatican's conviction that human life was a gift from God. Even though at that time Mancuso had already been awarded a doctorate in systematic theology and published a dissertation[107] as well as other works, he was convinced that his theological apprehension of the whole situation was somehow lacking. As he felt his own expertise in the field was overcome by the competence of others, Mancuso decided to ask for advice from a friend. It is not very clear exactly what was Mancuso's question, but he seems to have asked his friend about the connection between the reality of disability and the fact that life is considered a personal gift from God, a gift bestowed upon us by God in a very personal way. Unfortunately, the friend appears to have bitterly disappointed Mancuso, who writes that he did not remember any worthwhile response but only some sort of ill-concealed embarrassment. The whole situation made Mancuso become suspicious but also worried because this did not push him toward losing his faith in God's existence; what happened in fact is that he now has doubts concerning the Church's dogmatic structure concerning faith and its ecclesiastical systematization. In other words, Mancuso is deeply dissatisfied with the Roman Catholic Church and with her capacity to manage faith dogmatically in such a way that faith is rendered meaningful to contemporary people. Mancuso seems to be convinced that the Church—or at least the Magisterium—is uncertain about the reality of human handicap to the point that she does not have sufficient dogmatic explanations with respect to the reality of disability.[108] In addition to this, at least according to Mancuso, the Church does not have the dogmatic capacity to speak about the terrible side of life, which includes the very serious and painful reality of disability.[109] Thus, Mancuso is convinced that if the teaching of the Church cannot explain both the beauty and the horror of life, then her teaching is not an adequate reflection of God. Actually, Mancuso asks the Church to introduce what he calls "positive energy"[110] into the beautiful and terrifying manifestations of life by means of "the good and justice"; otherwise, the Church fails to offer a meaningful explanation of the reality of God and human life.[111]

There is a tenth feature of radical theology that explains Mancuso's defense of what he calls "positive energy," that is, the necessity to use a positive language in presenting whatever is needed for man to find relevance for his existence. This means, by contrast, that the language of traditional theology carries with it a "negative energy," so concepts such as God, death for sin, repentance, and right morality, which tend to be negative and restrictive, should be abandoned. In turn, radical theology proposes the use of more positive terms—such as love, good, and justice—which do not restrict man's natural freedom and consequently can be relevant for man's existence.

DISABILITY, SUFFERING, AND THE PROBLEM OF SIN

Having presented his personal experience regarding the issue of human disability, Mancuso discloses that his enterprise seeks to find the meaning of the reality of God as well as the significance of human life as God's gift in close connection with the experience of disability. He actually admits that the Church can come forward with various responses concerning anthropology, but these are a matter of the past, which—for Mancuso—seems to be highly irrelevant when it comes to explaining disability in close relationship to the meaning of God and of life as gift of God.[112] At this point, it is crucial to see that Mancuso does not intend to explain disability from the standpoint of God but rather from the perspective of humanity and especially of the human persons who are afflicted by it. He discloses therefore that disability must be approached from a perspective that does not see the pain of handicap as reality that makes humans guilty in any way. The idea of guilt must be excluded from any attempt to explain disability based on the reality of guilt. This means that, for Mancuso, the traditional theological doctrine of "guilty suffering"[113] or "necessary suffering"[114] no longer satisfies the minds of contemporary men and women; there is a need, therefore, for a paradigm that makes pain and suffering meaningful to contemporary people. This is why in dismissing "guilty suffering" and "necessary suffering," he introduces the idea of "inno-cent suffering,"[115] which, of course, is not singular to Mancuso and has been used in Christian ethics and the problem of theodicy.[116]

It should be said here that the Church's traditional understanding of "guilty suffering" or "necessary suffering" is not intended to make suffering meaningful but to explain the reality of human existence.[117] In traditional theology, man's life is thoroughly afflicted by sin, which is always explained from the perspective of man's relationship to God. Man cannot lead his life apart from God; he may well want to exclude God from his intellectual horizon or belief in such a way that he no longer thinks of himself as being in a relationship with God. This, however, does not make God less existent or less real; it only means that man does not wish to have anything to do with life. The problem is that, in traditional theology, God exists anyway—whether human-ity likes it or not—and the state of sin, which affects not only man's thoughts and deeds but also his inner nature, is no less real. This is why traditional theology sees man as being guilty before God because he is born into this world in a state of guilt, and this has nothing to do with man's feelings about it. It is a reality of daily existence and man is invited to consider it. Whether he feels that this is right or wrong, or whether he believes this is utterly meaningless today is a totally different issue. The fact is that traditional theology understands and explains sin in close connection with the reality of salvation, which is provided by God in order to solve the problem of sin.[118]

This leads us to the eleventh feature of traditional theology as it appears in Mancuso: the complete reassessment of sin. Sin does not seem to make its way into Mancuso's thought—which is also the case with radical theology in general—at least not in the traditional sense of the concept. Thus, in radical theology, sin is not accusatory of man because it is devoid of the idea of guilt, which only makes sense for as long as it is conceived in close connection with the notion of God understood in terms of traditional theology. Inasmuch as sin is attached to the idea of guilt—from which it cannot be separated in tra-ditional theology—it should be avoided when it comes to explaining the reality of disability as part of human existence. This is, of course, in line with Mancuso's previously declared intention to explain disability without casting guilt on human persons. As he cannot accept both guilt and innocent suffering, Mancuso seems to be ready to give up sin in favor of a more rational explanation. Actually, he seeks a "new philosophy" that includes both physics and metaphysics with the pur-pose of building an ethics that becomes mature.

DISABILITY ETHICS AND HUMAN ONTOLOGY

The ethics based on physics and metaphysics must necessarily involve what Mancuso calls a "realistic perspective on nature." He does not forget theology in the process but theology must be based on philosophy. This philosophy must necessarily admit two fundamental realities when it comes to presenting the essence of disability: the reality of evil, because disabled persons suffers from something clearly wrong in their physical constitution, psychical constitution, or both, and the reality of objective good, because every human being afflicted by disability has the same ontologically real characteristics as a nondisabled person. This is to say that both disabled and nondisabled persons share the same humanity, and the degree of humanity in either group is no less existent in defining their ontology.[119] Ontology, however, must have a basis, and Mancuso is utterly preoccupied with finding it. So which is the basis of ontology, or what exactly makes human persons ontologically equal regardless of their physical and psychical inequality, even manifested as disability? Mancuso argues that neither theology, nor science, nor philosophy can fully demonstrate the ontological foundation of humanity. Theology is ultimately subjective because it is based on the idea of faith, which is appropriated in an individual way; thus, one's faith cannot always convince others. Biology is restrictive because it presents us as mere animals; therefore, if anything is wrong with our physical integrity we are no longer fit to survive among those who are fitter. Philosophy has its own problems in supporting human ontology because it shows that we are rational animals: if something goes wrong with our psychological capabilities it follows that our humanity is somehow fatally flawed.[120] The only answer that appears to be satisfactory for Mancuso has ultimately nothing to do with theology, science, or philosophy; it is neither theology, nor science, nor philosophy that renders human beings ontologically equal regardless of their physical or psychical integrity. Only love—the love of parents—can fully recognize one's complete humanity.[121] Mancuso admits that love is utterly subjective, but he explains that it is nonetheless essentially human and therefore cannot be discarded.[122]

As it turns out, this is the twelfth characteristic of radical theology revealed by Mancuso's analysis, namely, the exclusively human character of love. Put simply, there is only one kind of love, and this is human. This is an extreme position taken against traditional theology, which advocates the existence of love beyond the realm of created nature and history into the life of God himself. However, there is no such thing as divine love for radical theology. In order for today's men and women to understand their lives in a meaningful way, they must reconsider their definition of love and consequently restrict it solely to human experience. In radical theology, love can be considered divine only if divinity is defined as a special feature of humanity.

In this respect, it should be reiterated that Mancuso differs radically from traditional Christianity and especially its Roman Catholic confession. This is proved by the recent *Dignitas personae*,[123] which presents the Vatican's position on scientific issues pertaining to bioethics. *Dignitas personae* makes clear that the human being is created by God in his image and, even if it does not explicitly mention the reality of sin, it does say that our creation in the image of God is confirmed by the incarnation of God's Son, who made it possible for us to become sons of God and sharers of divine nature. This leads to the affirmation of the eternal vocation of man as well as of his calling to share in the trinitarian love of the living God [*DP* 7]. It means that this particular value is applied to every single human being without distinction or discrimination, but it must be underlined that creation of human beings is ordained by God only within the context of the family, namely, the marriage relationship between a man and a woman [*DP* 8]. What follows is the confirmation of the unconditional respect that must be granted to every human being [*DP* 9] based on his ontological dignity and value [*DP* 5, 6]. Thus, the human person's life, dignity, respect, and value are deeply anchored in the very being of God, who is presented as a metaphysically real person who exists in a realm beyond the physical horizon of our world. Unlike Mancuso, who roots human ontology in the love of one's parents, traditional theology sees the human being as the creation of God[124] in the context of the family as love between a man and a woman.[125] This is actually the marrow of what the *Dignitas personae* and traditional Christianity in general call the sacredness of human life [*DP* 7].

THE PROBLEM OF SIN BETWEEN HUMAN SUFFERING AND DILUTED METAPHYSICS

But it is the very sacredness of human life that is confuted by Mancuso. For him, the sacredness of human life is a traditional Christian concept that shows life does not have an absolute character. Thus, it is not life that is the absolute value but God. If God has and eventually *is* the absolute value, human life is only contingent and can be disposed of if needed (for instance, in case of legitimate defense). As far as Mancuso is concerned, Christianity, or rather traditional Christianity, is not a religion of life because God is seen as being above man, so the life of

God is not the life of man, which means that the existence of God is more important than the existence of man. In Mancuso, this means that God is not the being but is above the being, and it is clear that by "being" Mancuso understands the human being. One can conclude therefore that, for Mancuso, the reality of God should not be thought of in metaphysical terms but rather in connection with the reality of man's existence; God is man and the existence of God is actually the existence of man. It is this existence, the existence of man, that has absolute value. Nothing should prevail and be more important than man's life: neither God nor his will, it is only man, his life, and his will that have absolute value.[126] Mancuso seems to be quite irritated by the theological affirmations that present the human being as the direct result of God's creation.[127] In fact, he is not necessarily bothered by the fact that man can be perceived as the result of God's direct action but by the fact that the Church does not explain how disabled people can be created directly by God.[128]

It should be said here that Mancuso is partially right. *Dignitas personae* does not explain the reality of sin, which affects the human being to a larger or lesser extent from the moment of conception as created directly by God. Therefore, in *Dignitas personae*, the word "sin" is used only once with reference to "the sin of abortion" [*DP* 23] but apart from this instance, the word is totally ignored. On the other hand, even if *Dignitas personae* had indeed used the word "sin" to explain man's state of guilt in relationship to God, Mancuso would have rejected the concept because the suffering of the disabled is neither guilty nor necessary but only innocent. There is no way out between Mancuso's perspective on human life and disability, and traditional Christianity: it is that either Mancuso accepts the absolute value of God as creator of human life,[129] which he does not seem willing to do, or traditional Christianity accepts the absolute value of human life without the sovereign will of God,[130] which cannot happen without turning traditional Christianity into theological liberalism.

Mancuso resumes the idea of sin later in his *Innocent Suffering*, but he approaches it as if the sin of man were not so important because it is dependent or influenced by the sin of angels. The reality of sin is not concerned with highlighting the idea of guilt but rather with underlining the fact that sin is the result of one's will, not of one's intellect. Consequently, the essence of God—who seems to be a concept rather than a personal being—is not the intellect but the will, namely, the will to love and love itself. Love, however, has no meaning if it cannot be understood practically, or in the reality of history, and the idea of love as seen in history is presented by the image of Christ.

His life and death, however, should not be understood historically but metaphysically. For Mancuso, the cross of Christ is undoubtedly connected to the idea and reality of suffering, consequently to disability. So, according to Mancuso, Christianity faces a real "theological drama"[131] because it reportedly cannot reconcile the perfection, omnipotence, and love of God with the evil of human handicap.[132] God's love and human disability share a relationship of absurdity, so they must be somehow disconnected if the reality of suffering caused by disability is to make any sense. For Mancuso, this means that from the point of view of nature, God is absent because he vanishes or dissipates himself in human history.[133] This seems to mean that reality cannot be thought of in terms of metaphysics and physics because there is in fact only one reality: the physical reality that must be understood metaphysically as the rules that govern the world of physics must be exactly the rules that govern the realm of the spirit. In other words, there is no real distinction between spirit and matter or between metaphysics and physics; human reality is singular and it should be comprehended in terms of energy, so metaphysics becomes diluted into physics. The same should be true of God; thus, God should be understood as energy or as a gift of energy. God is energy that gives himself or rather itself.[134]

In this we come to the thirteenth characteristic of radical theology distinctly unfolded as a result of Mancuso's efforts to redefine traditional theology. In radical theology, God is no longer seen in ontologically metaphysical and metahistorical terms; on the contrary, God is perceived in *conceptually* metaphysical and metahistorical terms. Put simply, it means that God can no longer be understood as a being who lives beyond the physical world of history, which is God's classical definition in traditional theology; radical theology works with a completely different definition, which portrays God as a concept that is metaphysical and metahistorical only in the sense that it is not a physical object that exists in history. God is above physics and history because he is a concept, not a thing, but he is nevertheless part of the physical world of history. This is why for radical theology, transcendence and metaphysics are totally dependent on and inextricably linked to human history and experience.

The Quest for Salvation
between Spirit and Matter

The unicity and singularity of man's world means for Mancuso that the realm of human life is fundamentally natural in such a way that both good and evil pertain to it in a natural way. Mancuso is convinced disability pertains to the reality of natural evil, so the reality of disability should not be contemplated solely by the victim of disability and his or her family but by every man and woman as part of the world. Disability therefore should become internal to the consciousness of every human being. The natural character of disability is given by the close relationship between man's life and death. Thus, life and death are not only contradictory but also wedded because human life is not possible without death. Mancuso uses biology to prove his point and especially the phenomenon known as cellular suicide, or *apoptosis*,[135] which is necessary during human development in order for organs and limbs to take shape. Life and death should no longer be approached theologically and philosophically or by faith and by reason. Faith and reason must come together in a practical way that discloses human reality as experience. As far as Mancuso is concerned, faith and reason have no meaning without actual and practical existence. This is why he writes that man must first live before thinking (and consequently believing). The language of theology is not totally abandoned because Mancuso believes the idea of salvation continues to characterize human existence. It is not the traditional escape from the power and influence of sin but something unknown that represents the furthest point of hope for humanity, a hope that may or may not coincide with God.[136]

For Mancuso, disability is suffering, but this particular type of suffering must be understood against the background of the suffering of Christ.[137] Unless we comprehend Christ's suffering, which is essentially gratuitous, we cannot make sense of the suffering of disabled people. Mancuso argues that suffering inflicted by disability belongs to innocent suffering, which is best represented by Christ, as this particular suffering is part of the connection between life and death, which necessarily creates suffering. This is so because, in Mancuso, only suffering is capable of transforming the life that becomes death into another life. It is important to realize that whatever Christ does makes reference to spiritual life. Mancuso distinguishes between spirit and matter but not in order to discard matter. What he wants to do is make sure that the idea of the love of God and also that of the action of God is connected to the reality of the spirit, not the reality of the matter or of the body. Thus, God only acts with respect to the spirit, not the body, which basically means that God does not act in nature.[138] This has at least two implications: first, if God does not act with respect to the body it means that man can act upon the body, so all sorts of gene therapies are acceptable, and second, if God does not act with respect to the body then we can make full sense of what happened to all the children born with disabilities. God does not work within the realm of the natural world, but only within the sphere of the spiritual world. It is not very clear which is which, but it seems that for Mancuso any aspect of life that does not concern physics, matter, or bodies is spiritual, despite his conviction that the spirit cannot be separated from the daily and practical experience of humanity.[139]

It is here that Mancuso enters again into conflict with traditional theology. His conviction that God does not act within the realm of matter but only in that of the spirit is founded on his image of Christ who, as he was both divine and human, acted in the world only as an incarnated God, so his actions—which include miracles—were entirely contained by his humanity. Thus, miracles should be understood in human terms exactly the way religions other than Christianity profess their belief in miracles.[140] This is because, in Mancuso, both Christianity and other religions are perfectly right is saying that miracles can happen but only if understood in human terms. We may not understand them—for instance, miraculous healing—but they definitely pertain to the realm of humanity and its world. It is clear that such an understanding of Christology, which presents Christ as having the same importance as the founders of other religions, downplays or even cancels his unicity. Moreover, his humanity is fundamentally real but his divinity is somehow less visible in nature. What is visible of Christ's divinity seems to be his gratuitous love, but this has to do with the spirit, not the world. This is why gene therapy is allowed when it comes to the birth of children, which is totally against the instructions of *Dignitas personae*. While Mancuso is convinced that gene therapy can be used to help babies afflicted by genetic maladies, *Dignitas personae* explains that such techniques—with reference to the improvement of reproductive cells—fall within the category of *in vitro* fertilization and are morally unacceptable.[141] Mancuso even writes that science—namely, human science—can correct the work of God, which is once more against the traditional teaching of Christianity, which says that God is perfect and his actions are perfect, thus the world is perfect and the imperfections we now see in the world are not because of God but because of man's sin.[142] This is not acceptable for Mancuso because the world is separated from the action of God, who acts only in the realm of the spirit. There is no ontological transcendence attached to God in Mancuso's thought because even the idea of heaven is translated spiritually. Therefore, what the New Testament means by heaven is actually the spirit, or the spiritual dimension of man's existence. This means that in the realm of nature man is totally free, and the reality of handicap is the price humanity pays for its freedom. But freedom means fragility and exposure to nothingness. Nevertheless, for Mancuso, the frailty of human life is the only reality that accounts for the total freedom of men and women in the world.[143]

This prompts us to single out the fourteenth characteristic of radical theology as present in Mancuso, and this is the total freedom of the human being. Perceived generally as an illusion in traditional theology because of the reality of sin, the idea of total freedom is a precious commodity for radical theology mainly because of its capacity to convey meaning to human experience. Man is limited and his life is restricted in many ways—and radical theology is not unaware of human physicality—so the notion of total freedom is a promising solution for all those who seek a meaningful existence within the boundaries of the physical world.

THE PRIMACY OF HUMAN FREEDOM AND EXPERIENCE IN MEDICAL SCIENCE

This freedom seems to be absolute because man has the "sacred" freedom to die, so Mancuso defends euthanasia even if he does not use the word much. Man has the right to die the way he chooses, Mancuso writes, and there should be a law regulating the situation.[144] This is because human life and experience have primacy over anything else, including the Bible and consequently God as traditionally described in the Bible. Theology should proceed from below, Mancuso declares, because today's theology cannot ignore science in general or sciences in particular. The primacy of life and experience should be the first thing professed by theology in our time. So everything starts with experience and, even if we use the Bible and traditional ideas about God, we must return and end our enterprise with experience. Thus, experience is directly linked to matter and matter is the mother of all things; this also means that matter is the origin of the spirit. Actually, Mancuso says that matter produces the spirit,[145] it produces life and it produces the being, so there is an equality among the spirit, life, and being. At the end of the day, for Mancuso, the spirit is life itself as generated by matter, so the spirit is human experience.[146] Having said that, it becomes clear in Mancuso that science is kept separated from traditional theology. Science does not need theology to be convinced of what it holds true; science has its own ways to convince itself, so it does not need theology, or rather traditional theology, in any way. Mancuso's theology, however, reaches and actually ends up in the realm of contemporary science because of his conviction that the ultimate meaning of humanity or the finality of human life is to be found in the *logos*, which is creative reason, and this creative reason is embodied, or is made flesh (*sarx*) in every human being.[147] It follows then that the finality of humanity is life as it unfolds in human experience. Theology in particular and religion in general must comply with the actuality of practical experience. Resuming the language of traditional theology, Mancuso says that we were not created for believing but for existing or for being. Everything must serve the authenticity of life and of human experience. This leads to the idea that the human spirit is a principle that lives within us, the most intimate conviction that helps us go beyond death.[148]

Mancuso's theory ultimately proves that disability is somehow normal given human experience, which is neither good nor evil or good and evil. The reality of evil, seen in disability, is a feature of normality because the spirit of the human being is ultimately the essence of his experience. Moreover, experience is life and life is the final goal of human experience. Such theology must take into account whatever science says about human life and must do everything in order to produce and preserve it. This runs contrary to traditional Christian theology as expressed in *Dignitas personae*, which forbids certain medical techniques that cause and maintain life. Because of its tendency to highlight the primacy of human freedom and experience, Mancuso's theology has enough room for the medical procedures that are forbidden by *Dignitas personae*. Consequently, Mancuso's theology—which is prone to the production and preservation of life as experience (or practical experience) embodied in human flesh—could accept the latest techniques for assisting fertility, such as *in vitro* fertilization[149] and the deliberate destruction of embryos.[150] It could also accept intracytoplasmic sperm injection[151] and the freezing of embryos,[152] as well as the freezing of oocytes,[153] the reduction of embryos,[154] and preimplantation diagnosis.[155] At the same time, Mancuso's thought could easily embrace the latest discoveries concerning treatments that have to do with the manipulation of the embryo[156] or the human genetic patrimony. Thus, germ-line therapy seems acceptable within Mancuso's theological framework, and the same could be true of the use of embryonic stem cells, hybridization, and the use of human biological material of illicit origin.

While most of these medical techniques are considered morally illicit by traditional Christian theology and especially by the *Dignitas personae* based on the premise that they favor the prolongation and improvement of life, they nevertheless are not seen to produce "an invaluable service to the integral good of the life and dignity of every human being" [*DP* 3]. Another reason for their rejection, despite the fact that they sustain the life of individual human beings, is that they do not take into account the origin of human life in accordance with the metaphysical reality of God's actual existence. In other words, traditional Christianity is convinced that the "origin of human life has its authentic context in marriage and in the family,"[157] so "procreation which is truly responsible vis-a-vis the child to be born '*must be the fruit of marriage*'" (emphasis added) [*DP* 6]. Mancuso takes another approach, which, although he does not say anything directly pointed against family as he himself is a family man, perceives procreation as a reality that happens often beyond the limits of marriage. In fact, he warns that we should abruptly face the reality of sexual intercourse outside matrimony at younger ages.[158] He does not seem to approve this reality, but he definitely builds an image that allows for it within his theological system. This is why all the medical techniques rejected by the Vatican and *Dignitas personae* based on the traditional conviction that procreation is the fruit of marriage are eventually accommodated in Mancuso's thought as part of human experience. Based on this conviction, Mancuso's theology can virtually accept as fully moral almost all the latest medical discoveries and techniques that manage to preserve, improve, and prolong individual human life.

Mancuso's conviction fosters the fifteenth characteristic of radical theology, which is the promise of a new morality that no longer answers to God but only to man. A morality dependent on God, perceived as the creator of the entire universe and of human beings—which is the core of traditional theology—is highly restrictive for contemporary men and women who look for a meaningful life only within history. For radical theology, such a morality—deeply rooted in the total transcendence of God—is a factor that entails a high degree of risk. This is why the solution of radical theology proposes a morality that is in turn profoundly anchored in the actual experience of humanity. While traditional theology strongly rejects such a morality as it can predict its results based on God's revelation, for radical theology it remains to be seen whether or not this is an equally hazardous step toward a meaningful human ethics because—from an exclusively human perspective and in the total absence of God—what lies ahead is still for the future to tell.

CONCLUSION

Christian thought has gone through a series of complex developments with the result that its main doctrines were altered significantly enough for the church to witness a wide range of ecclesiastical unrest from misunderstandings and tensions to reforming initiatives and, at times, even serious schisms. The most important dogmatic shift that affected Christian thought occurred with the rise of Enlightenment rationalism and its corresponding brand-new worldview. The theology that, until then, had nurtured a profound belief in the metaphysical God whose ontologically personal existence went unquestioned was suddenly considered outdated by the new promoters of reason and its reportedly unlimited power. A new breed of theology was consequently born, but its teachings retained only the conceptual language of its older counterpart; its meaning, however, underwent crucial alterations from dramatic reinterpretation to complete cancelation. The new rational approach recycled some of the old doctrines—such as sin and salvation—while others were simply discarded as useless and irrelevant—for instance, the virgin birth. God was no longer seen as a personal being existing beyond the created universe; he slowly but surely turned into a concept that was accommodated and used by the more or less almighty reason. All the traditional doctrines went through the same radical change, so it became clear that old, traditional theology had been placed in an obvious contrast with the new, radical approach of rational thought.

This book attempts to present, in only six chapters, the two conflicting positions within Christian thought—traditional and radical—as they developed through some of the most important periods of church history. Thus, traditional Christian thought is followed in the first three chapters through late antiquity, early modernity, and postmodernity in specific works written by Gregory Nazianzen, Jean Calvin, and Ion Bria. Radical Christian thought is analyzed in the last three chapters as it unfolded gradually in postmodernity with exclusive reference to the twentieth and twenty-first centuries in authors Erich Fromm, Paul Ricoeur, and Vito Mancuso.

Chapter 1 presents the features of traditional Christian thought in late antiquity as identified based on Gregory Nazianzen's Christological spirituality in the fourth century. Gregory's primary source in this case was his *Letter to Nectarius, Bishop of Constantinople*, written against the dogmatic teachings of Apollinarians. A quick glance at this work will provide useful details about traditional theology, which takes the doctrines so seriously that any teaching contrary to them is considered like a disease that threatens the spiritual life of the church. These teachings, which are clearly antiorthodox in nature, are not treated exclusively as a disease; it is important to see that, for traditional theology, any dogma that goes beyond the orthodoxy of the established doctrine is seen as evil. This shows that doctrine is not a matter of personal choice for traditional theology; on the contrary, all believers must adhere to what has been delivered to them through the history of the community of faith. Nevertheless, the standard for doctrinal interpretation is not the individual assessment of Christian teachings but the belief that Jesus Christ, the man who lived in history, is also—and at the same time—the Logos of God, who existed beyond time and history even before the creation of the world. But as this belief can be constantly challenged by people who detach the Jesus of history from the existence of God's Logos, the church must be constantly vigilant in order to keep the integrity of its doctrine. Traditional theology also teaches that the human nature of Jesus Christ was not part of the metaphysical existence of God's Logos before incarnation. While it proclaims the complete personal identity between the Jesus of history and his existence as God's Logos before incarnation, traditional theology makes it clear that his physical life after incarnation is not to be mistaken for his metaphysically preexistent life before incarnation. So the Logos of God has an uninterrupted existence from eternity, which was entirely metaphysical before incarnation and then physical after it. This is why traditional theology insists on the fact that Jesus Christ's existence before incarnation, which shows forth his divinity, must be correctly kept in balance with his life after incarnation, which proves his humanity. Consequently, traditional theology opposes any attempt to distort either the divinity or the humanity of Christ by enhancing or diminishing one to the detriment of the other. It is very important at this point to realize that, for traditional theology, the divinity and humanity of Christ must be confessed as equally perfect in nature. In other words, Jesus Christ is fully divine and fully human at the same time, which means he is simultaneously true God and true man. This is the dogmatic confession of the church and of traditional theology in general, and no other teaching should replace it. This is an indication that, in the church, there is only one confession of faith, which proves that nobody has the right to proliferate different teachings within the community of faith. Freedom of speech is far less important than the faith of the church, so while everyone is free to say whatever he or she pleases outside the church, the confession of the brotherhood of faith is always the staunch belief in Jesus Christ's full divinity and full humanity.

Chapter 2 is concerned with traditional Christian thought in early modernity as reflected in Jean Calvin's theology of the sixteenth century. While the main interest of Gregory Nazianzen in late antiquity was to push the theology of the fourth century toward the realization that Jesus Christ was fully God and fully man, Jean Calvin's interest more than a thousand years later shifted more toward ecclesiology and the need to explain that those who believe in Christ belong to the same body of faith, so they must all share the same behavior within the church. This is why his interest in ecclesiastical discipline—as shown in his *Institutes of the Christian Religion*—was a constant element of his doctrine of the church. His interest, however, also presents us with some crucial characteristics of traditional theology, this time in connection with ecclesiology. Thus, we see that traditional theology must always be concerned with the necessity of church discipline, despite the fact that measures taken for the restoration of order in the church will constantly face opposition. The awareness that church discipline is needed should then be coupled with the willingness to act in order for discipline to be properly applied in the church. In other words, the values of the church must always be kept intact and detached from the values of the world, with which they are in permanent conflict. Ecclesiastical discipline, however, must never be enforced for the sake of punishing those who spell trouble within the church. On the contrary, traditional theology teaches that discipline must be applied based on doctrine—or on what the church actually holds as a confession of faith—and for the church this doctrine is always the Gospel of Christ. The fact that the Gospel of Christ is the core of ecclesiastical discipline and doctrine is vitally important because the very essence of church discipline is based on Christ's teachings. According to traditional theology, the very first step of church discipline is not rebuke but rather the correct preaching of the Gospel of Christ, so church discipline is not meant to hurt but to heal. Healing may involve hurting, but the pain caused by church discipline is always there to help us see Christ better and fight sin more effectively. The problem of sin is central to traditional theology because the church must not only be aware of the presence of sin within believers but also take all the necessary measures to counter the effects of sin in the lives of those who share the same faith in Christ. Irrespective of how difficult this may be, the church must constantly fight sin and therefore apply discipline to the point that discipline becomes a feature of ecclesiastical as well as spiritual normality. Nevertheless, as discipline always involves the correct preaching of the Gospel, it is clear that the teaching of Christ must become the fundamental characteristic of the church's spiritual life. For traditional theology, the application of church discipline has nothing to do with the infliction of pain and the enforcement of punitive action against troublemakers; on the contrary, church discipline is a call to holiness and to meet Christ personally through the hearing of his Gospel as well as through the constant submission to his teachings for the sake of a spiritually fulfilled life.

Chapter 3 is an investigation of traditional Christian thought in postmodernity, which discloses significant features of traditional theology in the pastoral ecclesiology of Ion Bria, one of the most famous Eastern Orthodox ecumenists of the twentieth century. His *Liturgy after the Liturgy* is an invitation to take Christian life and mission seriously based on the centrality of Jesus Christ. As we read through Bria's work, we understand that traditional theology is a constant call for reformation in the church. While it is true that he does not advocate a reformation that, as in the West, could end up in ecclesiastical schism, Bria nevertheless points to the need for the dramatic change of the believer's personal life and the necessity to extend Christian mission beyond the walls of the church. In other words, the believer must live liturgically in the world even after the liturgy itself has been spiritually performed in the church. This presupposes not only the reformation of one's life but also the awareness that his reformation must be done in full accordance with the integrity of doctrine. This reformation, however, cannot be achieved without conversion. In traditional theology, conversion is the foundation of Christian life, but it is important to realize that conversion does not apply exclusively to nonbelievers, but also to those who share the same trust in Jesus Christ. Conversion is crucial because it leads to a new morality, which is compulsory for the entire community of faith. This is why, in traditional theology, the necessity of conversion is based on the centrality of Jesus Christ seen as the Savior of the world according to the witness of Scripture. The key element at this point is faith and especially the necessity that faith should grow on a regular basis. Faith, however, cannot grow without the preaching of the Gospel, so in traditional theology, faith and the teaching of Christ are welded together because they lead not only to the awareness but also to the confession of sins. Faith, the reception of the Gospel, and the confession of sin lay the basis for the true spiritual life of the Christian, who is consequently a member of the church. One's membership in the church does not guarantee the reality or the quality of one's faith, so in traditional theology church membership and personal faith are two totally different realities. As this is true for every ordinary believer, it means that the ministers of the church must be even more concerned with living in accordance with the Gospel of Christ and, in doing so, they must dedicate themselves to solid training in all aspects of life—intellectual, spiritual, and moral—if they really want to serve the church properly. Therefore, the reality and the presence of sin in life must be faithfully acknowledged both by ordinary believers and by the ministers of the church; they must all confess their sins for the effective advancement of the church's mission in the world. This means that, according to traditional theology, the Gospel of Christ must be preached to everyone as a constant effort of the church to fight against the powerful secularizing tendencies of our contemporary society.

Chapter 4 approaches radical Christian thought in early postmodernity, so the research focuses on the first half of the twentieth century with special reference to Erich Fromm's psychoanalytical Christology as presented in his *The Dogma of Christ*. Fromm was influenced quite consistently by Adolf von Harnack's liberal approach to the history of Christian dogma, so his interpretation of the person and work of Jesus Christ is antagonistic to traditional theology. Thus, his understanding of Christology points to some basic features of radical theology, such as his deep conviction that every religion or theological concept can be changed if needed, so notions and doctrines can be corrected whenever that seems necessary. Normally, these changes occur when the context—social, intellectual, cultural, or economic—of certain categories of people undergoes significant alterations, so in radical theology human experience interprets the Bible, not the other way around. As human experience is informed by reason, the key concept of Christianity—that of Christ—must also change as compared with traditional theology. This is why, in radical theology, Christ is detached from the Jesus of history, so we now have two distinct concepts: Jesus of history, the man who lived in Palestine in the first century, and the Christ of faith or of doctrine, which is merely an image subject to change as time passes. It is important to notice that in radical theology this changing interpretation is needed in order for the social classes—both ruling and oppressed—to find a way to identify themselves with their particular condition. Consequently, because the theological concepts are subject to consistent change, Christianity as a world religion is not different in any way from other, equally valid religions. As a religion, Christianity is the product of the masses, and its concepts follow the trend imposed by the changing experience of the people in general. Resuming the dichotomy between Jesus and Christ, it should be stressed here that in radical theology Christ has no ontological status because he serves as a concept, so it is only Jesus that is acknowledged as having actually lived in history. This is a clear deconstruction of the traditional doctrine of Jesus Christ's hypostatic union, which is also an indication that radical theology challenges the teaching of Christ's full divinity. With a dead human Jesus and a Christ that is merely a concept that can change according to the experience of the masses, Christianity is left with a dogmatic system that can be altered whenever it travels from one geographical region to another. This happens because people everywhere—men and women belonging to various geographical regions and hence to specific social-cultural contexts—have deep inner needs that require psychological satisfaction. So in radical theology the image of Christ is meant to change in order to find a better way for the psychological satisfaction of various individuals. However, as the dead Jesus of history remains a significant figure for Christianity, radical theology still needs to deal with his divinity, but now the concept of divinity is attributed to any human characteristic that can be considered truly special. Human characteristics, though, are a conglomerate of an almost endless number of particularities, which can appear special to some and totally irrelevant to others. This is why, in radical theology, people tend to accept Christ and Christian doctrine in general somehow unconsciously. People may believe they have rational motives for accepting Christianity but, in radical theology, it turns out that the unconscious part of human psychology is oftentimes much more important than the ever so applauded rational decisions.

Chapter 5 is a detailed analysis of radical Christian thought in mid postmodernity as revealed by means of the fallibility theory formulated by Paul Ricoeur in his *Fallible Man* during the second half of the twentieth century. Ricoeur's interest in hermeneutics and anthropology led him to a very impressive investigation of human nature, as well as its relationship to the notion and reality of evil. His thorough research helps us identify some of the most important characteristics of radical theology, starting with his belief that the major traditional doctrines of Christianity should be interpreted through the idea of myth. Reason is fundamental to radical theology, so man should accept only the doctrines whose content falls within the limits of reason. Thus, supernatural aspects of specific doctrines can be accepted only as myths and interpreted in a rational way. This automatically modifies the traditional doctrine of God, who is no longer seen as a real spiritual being with an equally real and ontological existence; in radical theology, God can only "live" in nature and specifically in the human mind as a more or less crucial concept. In radical theology, humanity is left without the traditional ontology of God and of the spiritual world. Hence, evil has no ontology of its own even though it can be conceived as external to man. To be sure, evil transcends the human being not as an ontological reality but rather as a combination of multiple factors that have a direct influence on man's existence in general. So it is the context of man's life that is evil, not a spiritual force with a real metaphysical existence. If this is true, then radical theology must also find a way to redefine the traditional notion of the fall. For radical theology, the fall becomes a myth with no real connection with a past historical event. This is why the fall should be accepted only as a literary, philosophical, or even religious-theological device that informs us about the existence of evil in the world. At the same time, the myth of the fall is meant to warn us against irresponsible behavior due to the horrible consequences of evil. While dramatically reinterpreted, the fundamental concepts of traditional Christian thought retained their linguistic garment when used by radical theology. The linguistic form of each word that bears a concept with it is still the same in both traditional and radical theology. The fall is still the fall, evil is still evil, guilt is still guilt, so we must be sensitive to the concepts that lie beneath the words used by either traditional or radical theology. In radical theology, all these concepts are given a meaning that can be accepted rationally without reference to supernatural realities, so another notion that is reinterpreted in an equally drastic way is that of infinitude. While quite naturally the idea of infinitude points to the supernatural reality of God, in radical theology infinitude is deprived of any ontology whatsoever and is consequently interpreted as a symbol in order to fit man's rational assessment of his own experience. There is no reality beyond our natural existence in history, so this calls for the radical reassessment of another traditional concept, that of transcendence. In radical theology, transcendence falls within the same all-encompassing symbolism that reportedly makes sense in terms of our rational interpretation of human life. It is clear then that for radical theology, concepts like infinitude, transcendence, and God are symbols that explain human existence for as long as they are kept within the boundaries of rational hermeneutics.

Chapter 6 offers a discussion of radical theology's attempt to reassess faith in late postmodernity and especially in the writings of Vito Mancuso, an Italian theologian of liberal persuasion whose intention is to rebuild Christian theology based on human experience. Following in the footsteps of his world-famous predecessors, Mancuso wrote a series of books of significant impact in Italy such as *Innocent Suffering, Rebuilding Faith*, and *The Soul and Its Destiny*. He believes that Christianity is a religion like any other, which nevertheless is superior to other religions due to its capacity to offer better philosophical and theological explanations for man's fundamental questions. As Christianity is just another world religion, its concept of God cannot claim to be considered differently any longer; this is why in Mancuso—but also in radical theology—the idea of God is stripped of its ontological status in order to be reduced to the level of man's experience and particularly to the concept of the good. The immediate consequence is the radical reinterpretation of the notion of faith in the sense that the object of faith should no longer be placed beyond what we can perceive by reason and experience, so the object of faith should be kept within the realm of man's actual experience. Thus, in radical theology, man no longer believes in God as creator of the universe; man now believes in himself and the good that he is able to achieve for the benefit of the entire humanity. In other words, radical theology leads to the secularization of faith and to the corresponding dissolution of traditional metaphysics. The doctrine of God as Trinity is deconstructed, so radical theology uses the concepts of Father, Son, and Spirit only as images of humanity in its persistent attempt to provide us with rational explanations of traditional theological concepts. Everything—events, facts, people, and even concepts—is reduced to the world of history and, as this is the only true material reality, everything originates in matter. In other words, matter is the source of everything—including concepts—so all theological notions must be understood in material, human terms.

Another logical consequence is the redefinition of God's love, which is no longer the love of the supreme, ontologically real being but only the love of the human being. Therefore, radical theology identifies theology with philosophy because the supernatural discourse of traditional theology was brought down to earth into the realm of man's historical existence. So, because both theology and philosophy seek the meaning of life, man should channel his efforts to investigate his own existence if he wants to find any significance for his life in the world. In doing so, man is advised to find exceptional examples of persons—such as Jesus of Nazareth—who lived for the benefit of their fellow men. Jesus was such a special human being that people thought he was divine, but in radical theology this is only an indication of man's special ability to do good in order to help others. Radical theology urges us to see ourselves as divine or as having the capacity to implement the idea of the good in the complex situations of our lives. In order to do this, we must be led by the same spirit, which is no longer the Holy Spirit of God as in traditional theology but man's capacity to love his fellow men. In radical theology, the spirit is man's solidarity in the face of adversity, which should be a constant source of "positive energy" for all those who want to lead a better, more meaningful life. Thus, the negative language of traditional theology based on concepts such as sin and guilt should be given up entirely in favor of positive urges that reportedly inspire courage and support. One possible way to achieve this desiderate is to reconsider the idea of sin by detaching it from the corresponding notion of guilt. For radical theology, sin should no longer oppress and scare people but rather help them understand the complexity of suffering and death as part of man's experience in the world. This cannot be done without a new understanding of love, which in radical theology is exclusively human and pretty much the only human feature that can be considered "divine." A redefinition of God's transcendence is therefore inevitable, so God can no longer be accepted in terms of ontological metaphysics but only in terms of conceptual metaphysics. In other words, the idea of God can remain transcendent in radical theology, but this transcendence has nothing in common with an actual reality beyond our historical existence. God is transcendent only as a concept that raises above the physical character of our lives while it remains deeply rooted in our earthly existence. Consequently, radical theology promotes the idea that—despite its physical and social limitations—the human being enjoys total freedom as well as the possibility to build a morality no longer controlled by the restrictive God of traditional theology but by the emancipated man himself and his so-called capacity to harness it rationally.

Notes

Chapter 1

1. For details about this letter, see Christopher A. Beeley, *Gregory of Nazianzus on the Trinity and the Knowledge of God: In Your Light We Shall See Light* (Oxford: Oxford University Press, 2008), 60.
2. John Behr, *The Nicene Faith: Formation of Christian Theology* (Crestwood, NY: St. Vladimir's Seminary Press, 2004), 2:401–2.
3. Alloys Grillmeier, *Christ in Christian Tradition: From the Apostolic Faith to Chalcedon* (Louisville, KY: Westminster John Knox Press, 1975), 1:329–30.
4. N. McLynn, "*Curiales* into Churchmen: The Case of Gregory Nazianzen," in *Le trasformazioni delle élites in età tardoantica*, ed. Rita L. Testa (Rome: Libreria Editrice Romana Monumenti Arte di Bretschneider, 2006), 288.
5. Edward R. Hardy, ed., *Christology of the Later Fathers* (Louisville, KY: Westminster John Knox Press, 1954), 124.
6. But no later than 388, when all Apollinarians were banned from Constantinople. See, for instance, Nicholas Constas, *Proclus of Constantinople and the Cult of the Virgin in Late Antiquity: Homilies 1–5; Texts and Translations* (Leiden, NL: Brill, 2003), 33n95.
7. For details about Arius, see Rowan Williams, *Arius, Heresy and Tradition*, revised ed. (Grand Rapids, MI: Eerdmans, 2002).
8. Interesting details about Eudoxius can be found in Lacy O'Leary, *The Syriac Church and Fathers* (Piscataway, NJ: Gorgias Press, 2002), 51.
9. Gregory Nazianzen, "To Nectarius, Bishop of Constantinople," in *A Select Library of the Christian Church: Nicene and Post-Nicene Fathers*, ed. Philip Schaff and Henry Wace (Peabody, MA: Hendrickson Publishers, 2004), 7:438.1.
10. Also known as pneumatomachians, the promoters of Macedonianism believed that the Holy Spirit was not of the same substance with God the Father and God the Son. See, for details, Lewis Ayres, *Nicaea and Its Legacy: An Approach to Fourth Century Trinitarian Theology* (Oxford: Oxford University Press, 2006), 214–16.

11. Cf. Daniel Caner, *Wondering, Begging Monks: Spiritual Authority and the Promotion of Monasticism in Late Antiquity* (Berkeley, CA: University of California Press, 2002), 190–91.

12. See, for details, J. N. D. Kelly, *Early Christian Creeds*, 3rd ed. (London: Continuum, 2006), 341.

13. Also see R. P. C. Hanson, *The Search for the Christian Doctrine of God: The Arian Controversy, 318–381* (London: Continuum, 2005), 618–22.

14. Gregory Nazianzen, "To Nectarius, Bishop of Constantinople," 438.1.

15. For details about Nectarius, see Lewis Ayres, "Constantinople, First Council of," in *The New Westminster Dictionary of Church History*, ed. Robert Benedetto (Louisville, KY: Westminster John Knox Press, 2008), 168.

16. James M. Barnett, *The Diaconate: A Full and Equal Order* (London: Continuum, 1995), 107.

17. Gregory Nazianzen, "To Nectarius, Bishop of Constantinople," 438.1–438.2.

18. See also Donald K. McKim, *Theological Turning Points: Major Issues in Christian Thought* (Louisville, KY: Westminster John Knox Press, 1989), 34.

19. Stanley J. Grenz, *Theology for the Community of God* (Grand Rapids, MI: Eerdmans, 2000), 274.

20. Gregory Nazianzen, "To Nectarius, Bishop of Constantinople," 438.2.

21. See also Sergius Bulgakov, *The Lamb of God* (Grand Rapids, MI: Eerdmans, 2008), 9.

22. For details about Apollinarius's Christology, see Alan F. Johnson and Robert E. Webber, *What Christians Believe: An Overview of Theology and Its Biblical and Historical Development* (Grand Rapids, MI: Zondervan, 1993), 129–30.

23. G. W. H. Lampe, "Christian Theology in the Patristic Period," in *A History of Christian Doctrine*, ed. Hubert Cunliffe-Jones (London: Continuum, 2006), 124–25.

24. Gregory Nazianzen, "To Nectarius, Bishop of Constantinople," 438.2.

25. D. S. Wallace-Hadrill, *Christian Antioch: A Study of Early Christian Thought in the East* (Cambridge: Cambridge University Press, 1982), 132–34.

26. Oliver Crisp, *Divinity and Humanity: The Incarnation Reconsidered* (Cambridge: Cambridge University Press, 2007), 38.

27. J. N. D. Kelly, *Early Christian Doctrines*, 5th ed. (London: Continuum, 2000), 289–91.

28. Henry Chadwick, gen. ed., *Leontius of Jerusalem: Against the Monophysites; Testimonies of the Saints and Aporiae*, ed. and trans. Patrick T. R. Gray (Oxford: Oxford University Press, 2006), 123.

29. Gregory Nazianzen, "To Nectarius, Bishop of Constantinople," 438.2.

30. John Macquarrie, *Jesus Christ in Modern Thought* (London: SCM-Canterbury Press, 1990), 116–17.
31. Gregory Nazianzen, "To Nectarius, Bishop of Constantinople," 438.2.
32. Thomas F. Torrance, *The Christian Doctrine of God: One Being, Three Persons* (London: Continuum, 2001), 158–60.
33. Jaroslav J. Pelikan, *The Christian Tradition: A History of the Development of Doctrine* (Chicago: University of Chicago Press, 1989), 1:211–12.
34. Gregory Nazianzen, "To Nectarius, Bishop of Constantinople," 438.2.
35. Aidan Nichols, *The Shape of Catholic Theology* (Collegeville, MN: Liturgical Press, 1991), 276.
36. James Hastings and John A. Selbie, eds., *Encyclopedia of Religion and Ethics* (Whitefish, MT: Kessinger Publications, 2003), part 9:389.
37. Gregory Nazianzen, "To Nectarius, Bishop of Constantinople," 438.2.
38. Gregory Nazianzen, "To Nectarius, Bishop of Constantinople," 438.2.
39. As an interesting detail, Gregory was convinced that the sovereignty of Christ extended even over the Delphi oracle, which was silenced by Christ. See Paul Ciholas, *The Omphalos and the Cross: Pagans and Christians in Search of a Divine Centre* (Macon, GA: Mercer University Press, 2003), 125–26.
40. See also *The Church of England Magazine* XLVI (1859), 270.
41. Details about Gregory's way of presenting God can be found in Jostein Børtnes, "Rhetoric and Mental Images in Gregory," in *Gregory of Nazianzus: Images and Reflections*, ed. Jostein Børtnes and Tomas Hägg (Copenhagen: Museum Tusculanum Press, 2006), 54ff.
42. For more information about the correspondence between Gregory and Nectarius, see also Caroline Humfress, *Orthodoxy and the Courts in Late Antiquity* (Oxford: Oxford University Press, 2007), 260–61.
43. Sozomen, *The Ecclesiastical History of Sozomen, Comprising a History of the Church from AD 324 to AD 440. Translated from the Greek with a Memoir of the Author*, trans. Edward Walford (London: Henry G. Bohn, 1860), 293ff.
44. Gregory Nazianzen, "To Nectarius, Bishop of Constantinople,"438.2.
45. Edward Gibbon, *The History of the Decline and Fall of the Roman Empire* (New York: Cosimo, 2008), 3:151.
46. The emperor was Theodosius the Great. See Simon Swain, Introduction to *Approaching Late Antiquity: The Transformation from Early to Late Empire*, ed. Simon Swain and Mark Edwards (Oxford: Oxford University Press, 2006), 14.
47. Gregory Nazianzen, "To Nectarius, Bishop of Constantinople," 439.1.
48. John McGuckin, *Saint Gregory of Nazianzus: An Intellectual Biography* (Crestwood, NY: St. Vladimir's Seminary Press, 2001), 179n33.
49. See also Charles E. Raven, *Apollinarianism: An Essay on the Christology of the Early Church* (Cambridge: Cambridge University Press, 1923), 262.

50. For further historical details, see Philip Hughes, *A History of the Church* (London: Continuum, 1979), 1:228.

Chapter 2

1. Charles Partee, *The Theology of John Calvin* (Louisville, KY: Westminster John Knox Press, 2008), 270.
2. Sheldon S. Wolin, *Politics and Vision* (Princeton, NJ: Princeton University Press, 2004), 156.
3. William R. Estep, *Renaissance and Reformation* (Grand Rapids, MI: Eerdmans, 1986), 230.
4. In Geneva, this had immediate consequences on church attendance, which became equally compulsory even during Calvin's absence from the city from 1538 to 1541. See also Bernard Cottret, *Calvin: A Biography* (Grand Rapids, MI: Eerdmans, 2000), 146–47.
5. See also Christopher Elwood, *Calvin for Armchair Theologians* (Louisville, KY: Westminster John Knox Press, 2002), 106–8.
6. Jean Calvin, *Institutes of the Christian Religion*, trans. Henry Beveridge (Edinburgh: Calvin Translation Society, 1846), 4:453.
7. For details about the discipline of the clergy, see Harro Höpfl, *The Christian Polity of John Calvin* (Cambridge: Cambridge University Press, 1985), 91.
8. Elsie Ann McKee, "Calvin's Teaching on the Elder Illuminated by Exegetical History," in *John Calvin and the Church: A Prism of Reform*, by Timothy George, (Louisville, KY: Westminster John Knox Press, 1990), 153.
9. Calvin, *Institutes*, 4:453.
10. See also Janel Mueller, "Embodying Glory: The Apocalyptic Strain in Milton's *Of Reformation*," in *Politics, Poetics and Hermeneutics in Milton's Prose*, ed. David Loewenstein and James Grantham Turner (Cambridge: Cambridge University Press, 1990), 37 n21.
11. Calvin, *Institutes*, 4:453.
12. See also Ronald R. Stockton, *Decent and in Order: Conflict, Christianity and Polity in a Presbyterian Congregation* (Santa Barbara, CA: Greenwood Publishing Group, 2000), 77n6.
13. Calvin, *Institutes*, 4:453.
14. Earl S. Johnson, Jr., *Selected to Serve: A Guide for Church Officers* (Louisville, KY: Westminster John Knox Press, 2000), 81.
15. Partee, *The Theology of John Calvin*, 270.
16. Wulfert de Greef, *The Writings of John Calvin: An Introductory Guide*, expanded ed. (Louisville, KY: Westminster John Knox Press, 2008), 131.
17. See also T. H. L. Parker, *Calvin: An Introduction to His Thought* (Louisville, KY: Westminster John Knox Press, 1995), 145.

18. William G. Naphy, *Calvin and the Consolidation of the Genevan Reformation* (Manchester, UK: Manchester University Press, 1994), 56.

19. Calvin, *Institutes*, 4:453.

20. Raymond A. Mentzer, "The Genevan Model and Gallican Originality in the French Reformed Tradition," in *Adaptation of Calvinism in Reformation Europe: Essays in Honour of Brian G. Armstrong*, ed. Mack P. Holt (Aldershot, UK: Ashgate Publishing, 2007), 148.

21. For details, see Hugh Oliphant Old, "Why Bother with Church? The Church and Its Worship," in *Essentials of Christian Theology*, ed. William C. Placher (Louisville, KY: Westminster John Knox Press, 2003), 236.

22. Benjamin C. Milner, *Calvin's Doctrine of the Church* (Leiden, NL: Brill Publishers, 1965), 176.

23. Calvin, *Institutes*, 4:453.

24. For details about the relationship between discipline and doctrine, see Richard A. Muller, *After Calvin: Studies in the Development of a Theological Tradition* (Oxford: Oxford University Press, 2003), 57.

25. Loyal D. Rue, *By the Grace of Guile: The Role of Deception in Natural History and Human Affairs* (Oxford: Oxford University Press, 1994), 46.

26. See also I. John Hesselink, *Calvin's First Catechism: A Commentary* (Louisville, KY: Westminster John Knox Press, 1998), 163.

27. This could go as far as capital punishment. See Earl E. Cairns, *Christianity through the Centuries* (Grand Rapids, MI: Zondervan, 1996), 304.

28. Calvin, *Institutes*, 4:453.

29. Howard L. Rice, *Reformed Spirituality: An Introduction for Believers* (Louisville, KY: Westminster John Knox Press, 1991), 122.

30. This includes teaching and preaching from Scripture. See also William J. Bouwsma, *John Calvin: A Sixteenth Century Portrait* (Oxford: Oxford University Press, 1989), 90.

31. Calvin, *Institutes*, 4:453.

32. See also E. Brooks Holifield, *God's Ambassadors: A History of the Christian Clergy in America* (Grand Rapids, MI: Eerdmans, 2007), 26.

33. See Katherine Crawford, *European Sexualities, 1400–1800* (Cambridge: Cambridge University Press, 2007), 76.

34. George Steinmetz, *State/Culture: State Formation after the Cultural Turn* (Ithaca, NY: Cornell University Press, 1999), 163.

35. Calvin, *Institutes*, 4:454.

36. G. R. Elton, *Reformation Europe, 1517–1559* (Oxford: Wiley-Blackwell, 1999), 155.

37. F. Gerrit Immink, *Faith: A Practical Theological Reconstruction* (Grand Rapids, MI: Eerdmans, 2005), 110–11.

38. Calvin, *Institutes*, 4:454.

39. Michael F. Graham, *The Uses of Reform: 'Godly Discipline' and Popular Behavior in Scotland and Beyond, 1560–1610* (Leiden, NL: Brill, 1996), 21.
40. See also Peter G. Wallace, *The Long European Reformation* (New York: Palgrave Macmillan, 2004), 106.
41. See also Felix Herndon and Valerie J. Smith, "The Disenchantment of Modern Sexuality: Packaged by Media into Weber's 'Iron Cage,'" in *Sex, Religion, Media*, ed. Dane S. Claussen (Lanham, MD: Rowman and Littlefield, 2002), 222.
42. Calvin, *Institutes*, 4:454.
43. Crawford, *European Sexualities*, 76.
44. See also Roger Geiger, *History of Higher Education Annual* (Edison, NJ: Transaction Publishers, 1985), 12–14.
45. Cornelis P. Venema, *Accepted and Renewed in Christ: The «Twofold Grace of God» and the Interpretation of Calvin's Theology* (Göttingen, DE: Vanhenhoek and Ruprecht, 2007), 226.
46. Calvin, *Institutes*, 4:454.
47. Kenneth J. E. Graham, *The Performance of Conviction: Plainness and Rhetoric in the Early English Renaissance* (Ithaca, NY: Cornell University Press, 1994), 65.
48. Frits G. M. Broer, "A Pure City: Calvin's Geneva," in *The Quest for Purity*, ed. Walter E. A. Van Beek (Berlin: Walter de Gruyter, 1988), 44.
49. Venema, *Accepted and Renewed in Christ*, 226.
50. Calvin, *Institutes*, 4:454.

CHAPTER 3

1. Ion Bria, "The Liturgy after the Liturgy, 1978," in *The Ecumenical Movement: An Anthology of Key Texts and Voices*, ed. Michael Kinnamon and Brian E. Cope (Grand Rapids, MI: Eerdmans, 1997), 365.
2. It should be noted here that whenever Bria speaks about the church, he means the Orthodox Church.
3. For more details about what Bria means by the liturgy after the liturgy, see Ion Bria, *Liturghia după liturghie: O tipologie a misiunii apostolice si mărturiei crestine azi* (Bucharest: Editura Athena, 1996), 7–9.
4. See also Michael Plekon, "Mother Maria Skobtsova (1891–1945)," in *The Teachings of Modern Orthodox Christianity: On Law, Politics and Human Nature*, by John Witte Jr. and Frank S. Alexander (New York: Columbia University Press, 2007), 240.
5. This presents us with a radical redefinition of theology. See, for details, John S. Mbiti, "Dialogue between Eatwot and Western Theologians: A Comment on the Sixth Eatwot Conference in Geneva, 1983," in *Fullness of Life for All: Challenges for Mission in the Early 21st Century*,

ed. Inus Daneel, Charles van Engen, and Hendrik Vroom (Amsterdam: Rodopi, 2003), 95–96.

6. For details about what this new vision entails in Orthodox theology as defined by Stăniloae and Bria, see Charles Miller, *The Gift of the World: An Introduction to the Theology of Dumitru Stăniloae* (London: Continuum, 2000), 22. At this point it should be said that at least part of this new vision is that everything belonging to the church, doctrine and practice, must lead to Christ.

7. For the necessity of renewal in the Orthodox Church, see also Thomas E. Fitzgerald, *The Ecumenical Movement: An Introductory History* (Santa Barbara, CA: Greenwood Publishing Group, 2004), 149.

8. Bria, *Liturghia după liturghie*, 153–54.

9. Ion Bria, *Destinul Ortodoxiei* (Bucharest: Editura Institutului Biblic si de Misiune al Bisericii Ortodoxe Române, 1989), 321.

10. See also Jaroslaw Buciora, "Ecclesiology and National Identity in Orthodox Christianity," in *Orthodox Christianity and Contemporary Europe*, ed. Jonathan Sutton and Wil wan den Bercken (Leuven, BE: Peeters Publishers, 2003), 34.

11. J. Martin Bailey, "Commonwealth of Independent States (CIS)," in *Toward the 21st Century in Christian Mission*, ed. James M. Phillips and Robert T. Coote (Grand Rapids, MI: Eerdmans, 1993), 72.

12. Ion Bria, *Credinta pe care o mărturisim* (Bucharest: Editura Institutului Biblic si de Misiune al Bisericii Ortodoxe Române, 1987), 133.

13. See also Kallistos Ware, Foreword to *Orthodox Dogmatic Theology: The Experience of God*, by Dumitru Stăniloae, trans. Ioan Ioniță and Robert Barringer (London: Continuum, 1994), xviii.

14. Bria, *Credinta pe care o mărturisim*, 134.

15. Bria, *Liturghia după liturghie*, 155–58.

16. For a detailed definition of church mission as evangelization, see Bria, *Credinta pe care o mărturisim*, 133.

17. See also Anton C. Vrame, "An Overview of Orthodox Christian Religious Education," in *International Handbook of the Religious, Moral, and Spiritual Dimensions of Education*, ed. Marian de Souza, Kathleen Engebretson, Gloria Durka, Robert Jackson, and Andrew McGrady (Berlin: Springer, 2006), 281.

18. Bria, *Liturghia după liturghie*, 158.

19. See also Bria, *Credinta pe care o mărturisim*, 295.

20. Miller, *The Gift of the World*, 22.

21. Bria, *Liturghia după liturghie*, 159.

22. So the church must preach the Kingdom of God within society. See also Christine Lienemann-Perrin, *Mission und Interreligiöser Dialog*, Bensheimer Hefte 93: Ökumenische Studienhefte (Göttingen, DE: Vandenhoeck & Ruprecht, 1999), 114.

23. See also G. R. Evans, *The Church and the Churches* (Cambridge: Cambridge University Press, 2002), 154.

24. This is actually the work of salvation. See Magdalena Dumitrana, "In Quest of the Lost Ecumenism," in *Romanian Cultural Identity and Education for Civil Society*, ed. Magdalena Dumitrana (Washington, DC: Council for Research in Values and Philosophy, 2005), 251.

25. Bria, *Liturghia după liturghie*, 160–61.

26. Dumitrana, "In Quest of the Lost Ecumenism," 251.

27. Bria, *Credinta pe care o mărturisim*, 135.

28. Bria, *Destinul Ortodoxiei*, 281ff. In this book, Bria talks more about the saints as canonized individuals, while in his later *Liturghia după liturghie*, the saints are the ordinary believers, the members of the church.

29. Despite this reality, the Holy Spirit works in the church. See Bria, *Destinul Ortodoxiei*, 323.

30. For a brief comparison of Protestant and Orthodox ecclesiologies, see J. Martin Bailey, "Commonwealth of Independent States (CIS)," 72.

31. Bria, *Liturghia după liturghie*, 161.

32. See also Vladimir Feodorov, "Orthodox View on Theological Education as Mission," in *Theological Education as Mission*, ed. Peter F. Penner (Schwarzenfeld, DE: Neufeld Verlag, 2005), 80–90.

33. Bria, *Liturghia după liturghie*, 162.

34. Ross Langmead, *The Word Made Flesh: Towards an Incarnational Missiology* (Lanham, MD: University Press of America, 2004), 207.

35. Bria, *Liturghia după liturghie*, 163.

36. See, for instance, the case of the Mar Toma Church, which is part of Oriental Orthodoxy. Details can be found in Philip L. Vickeri, "The Mar Toma Christians of Kerala: A Study of the Relationship between Liturgy and Mission in the Indian Context," in *Christian Worship Worldwide: Expanding Horizons, Deepening Practices*, ed. Charles E. Farhadian (Grand Rapids, MI: Eerdmans, 2007), 88.

37. Bria seems to be more radical in singling out the utter importance of Scripture in his *Liturghia după liturghie* than he is in, for instance, his *Destinul Ortodoxiei*, where Scripture is placed at the same level with tradition. See Bria, *Destinul Ortodoxiei*, 275–76.

38. Cf. Jürgen Henkel, *Eros und Ethos. Mensch, gottesdienstliche Gemeinschaft und Nation als Adressaten theologischer Ethiek bei Dumitru Stanilaoe. Mit einem Geleitwort von Mitropolit Seraphim* (Berlin: LIT Verlag, 2003), 320.

39. Ion Bria, *The Sense of the Ecumenical Tradition: The Ecumenical Witness and Vision of the Orthodox* (Geneva: World Council of Churches Publications, 1991), 90.

40. Bria, *Credinta pe care o mărturisim*, 133.

41. Bria, *Liturghia după liturghie*, 164.

42. Bria, *Credinta pe care o mărturisim*, 133.

43. See also J. Andrew Kirk, *What Is Mission? Theological Explorations* (Minneapolis: Augsburg Fortress Press, 2000), 70.

44. Bria, *Liturghia după liturghie*, 165.
45. Cf. Carnegie Calian, "Challenges Facing Orthodox Theological Education in a Post-Communist, Post-Christian, Pluralistic World," in *Orthodox Christianity and Contemporary Europe*, ed. Jonathan Sutton and Wil wan den Bercken (Leuven, BE: Peeters Publishers, 2003), 47.
46. Bria, *Liturghia după liturghie*, 166.
47. Langmead, *The Word Made Flesh*, 208–9.
48. Bria, *Destinul Ortodoxiei*, 279.
49. Walter W. Sawatsky, "Without God We Cannot, without Us God Won't—Thoughts on God's Mission within CIS in the Future," in *Mission in the Former Soviet Union*, ed. Walter W. Sawatsky and Peter F. Penner (Schwarzenfeld, DE: Neufeld Verlag, 2005), 264.
50. Bria, *Liturghia după liturghie*, 166–67.
51. This is also true for Catholics. See Frederick M. Bliss, *Catholic and Ecumenical: History and Hope; Why the Catholic Church Is Ecumenical and What She Is Doing about It* (Lanham, MD: Rowman and Littlefield, 2007), 45.
52. Bria, *Liturghia după liturghie*, 167–68.
53. Bria also warns against taking for granted one's birth into a Christian family as well as one's education within the church's parochial context. See also Vrame, "An Overview of Orthodox Christian Religious Education," 281.
54. Bria, *Liturghia după liturghie*, 168.
55. See also Philip L. Vickeri, "The Mar Toma Christians of Kerala," 86–88.
56. For details about pastoral care within the Eastern theological setting, see Jeffrey Gross, Eamon McManus, and Ann Riggs, "Ecumenism and Ecclesial and Pastoral Proclamation," in *A History of Pastoral Care*, ed. G. R. Evans (London: Continuum, 2000), 441.
57. Some Protestants also highlighted the necessity of refounding church mission. See Jacques Gadille, "Introduction: Vingt-cinq ans de recherche missiologique. La naissance du CREDIC," in *Diffusion et acculturation du christianisme (XIXe-XXe s.): Vingt-cinq ans de recherches missiologieques*, ed. Jean Comby (Paris: Karthala, 2005), 14.
58. The thesis can be extended to all Christian churches as participants within the same evangelizing mission. See, for instance, Viorel Ioniță, "Ökumene und Mission aus orthodoxer Sicht," in *Gemeinschaft der Kirchen und gesellschaftliche Verantwortung. Die Würde des Anderen und das Recht anders zu denken*, ed. Lena Lybaek, Konrad Raiser, and Stefanie Schardien (Berlin: LIT Verlag, 2004), 62.
59. Bria, *Liturghia după liturghie*, 168–69.
60. For a brief but relevant definition of theology, see Bria's Preface to *Orthodox Dogmatic Theology*, by Dumitru Stăniloae, trans. Ioan Ioniță and Robert Berringer (London: Continuum, 2002), 2:xiii.
61. Bria, *Liturghia după liturghie*, 169.

62. See also Calian, "Challenges Facing Orthodox Theological Education," 47.
63. Bria, *Liturghia după liturghie*, 170.
64. Bria, *Credinta pe care o mărturisim*, 134.
65. For details about what education means in Orthodox theology, see Vrame, "An Overview of Orthodox Christian Religious Education," 281–82.
66. This points to the relativization of old canons. See also Sawatsky, "Without God We Cannot, without Us God Won't—Thoughts on God's Mission within CIS in the Future," 265.
67. Bria, *Liturghia după liturghie*, 170–71.
68. Details about what the Gospel means in Orthodoxy can be found in Langmead, *The Word Made Flesh*, 207–8.
69. See also Bria, *Credinta pe care o mărturisim*, 318.
70. Bria, *Liturghia după liturghie*, 171.
71. See also Leonie B. Liveris, *Ancient Taboos and Gender Prejudice: Challenges for Orthodox Women and the Church* (Aldershot, UK: Ashgate, 2005), 66.
72. Bria, *Destinul Ortodoxiei*, 274.
73. Bria, *Liturghia după liturghie*, 172.
74. This is crucial because the priests and the bishops have the duty to teach the Gospel to ordinary believers. See Bria, *Credinta pe care o mărturisim*, 319.
75. Bria, *Liturghia după liturghie*, 172–73.
76. Unlike the ancient period of the church, when education was a major concern of the church. See Betty J. Bailey and J. Martin Bailey, *Who Are the Christians in the Middle East?* (Grand Rapids, MI: Eerdmans, 2003), 9–10.
77. Bria, *Liturghia după liturghie*, 173.
78. These are good and effective only if their aim is social justice as proclaimed by the church. See Bria, *Credinta pe care o mărturisim*, 295.
79. Bria, *Liturghia după liturghie*, 174.
80. Spiritual effort is required for personal and community development. See Buciora, "Ecclesiology and National Identity in Orthodox Christianity," 35.
81. Miller, *The Gift of the World*, 47–48.
82. Bria, *Liturghia după liturghie*, 175.
83. See also Bria, *Credinta pe care o mărturisim*, 295.
84. Bria, *Liturghia după liturghie*, 176.
85. For the centrality of the Eucharist in the Orthodox tradition, see Emmanuel Clapsis, "Wealth and Poverty in Christian Tradition," in *Church and Society: Orthodox Christian Perspectives, Past Experiences and Modern Challenges*, ed. George P. Liacopoulos (Boston: Somerset Hall Press, 2007), 100.
86. Langmead, *The Word Made Flesh*, 207.

87. Bria, *Liturghia după liturghie*, 177.

88. See also Henkel, *Eros und Ethos*, 320.

89. Bria, *Liturghia după liturghie*, 178–79.

90. For a brief perspective on what Bria believed about church and politics before 1989, see Bria, *Destinul Ortodoxiei*, 10–11.

91. See also Bria, *Credinta pe care o mărturisim*, 297.

92. Bria, *Liturghia după liturghie*, 179.

93. Bria, *Credinta pe care o mărturisim*, 300.

94. The fight against these sins is the social justice imperative of the church. See Bria, *Credinta pe care o mărturisim*, 295.

95. Bria, *Liturghia după liturghie*, 180.

96. For an interesting discussion of the relationship between the church and the state with reference to the Russian and American contexts, see Anthony Ugolnik, *The Illuminating Icon* (Grand Rapids, MI: Eerdmans, 1989), 206.

97. See also Bria, *Credinta pe care o mărturisim*, 299.

98. John Witte Jr., *God's Joust, God's Justice: Law and Religion in the Western Tradition* (Grand Rapids, MI: Eerdmans, 2006), 91–92.

99. Bria, *Credinta pe care o mărturisim*, 294.

100. Bria, *Liturghia după liturghie*, 181–83.

101. The essence of the Gospel message is love, and it is love that the church must show to the world or to civil society. Bria, *Credinta pe care o mărturisim*, 300.

102. Bria, *Liturghia după liturghie*, 183–84.

CHAPTER 4

1. Erich Fromm, *The Dogma of Christ and Other Essays on Religion, Psychology and Culture* (1963; repr. Abingdon and New York: Routledge, 2004), 1–7.

2. For details about Fromm's perspective on psychoanalysis and what it should do, see Daniel Burston, *The Legacy of Erich Fromm* (Cambridge, MA: Harvard University Press, 1991), 1–8.

3. See also Rainer Funk, "Erich Fromm's Life and Work," in *Erich Fromm and Critical Criminology: Beyond the Punitive Society*, ed. Kevin Anderson and Richard Quinney (Champaign, IL: University of Illinois Press, 2000), 8.

4. Nicky Hayes, *Foundations of Psychology*, 3rd ed. (Andover, MA: Cengage Learning, 2000), 209.

5. Fromm, *The Dogma of Christ*, 1–2.

6. For details of Fromm's theory of psychoanalysis and its relationship with neurosis and religion, see J. M. Yinger, "Secular Alternatives to Religion," in *Man's Religious Quest: A Reader*, ed. Whitfield Foy (London: Open University Press, 1978), 551.

7. Fromm, *The Dogma of Christ*, 3–4.

8. For more information about the role of social psychology in interpreting the life and the teachings of Christ, see Antti Eskola, "How Many Social Psychologies Are There?" in *Blind Alleys in Social Psychology: A Search for Ways Out*, ed. Antti Eskola (Amsterdam: North Holland, 1988), 11–12.

9. Fromm, *The Dogma of Christ*, 5–6.

10. For details of Fromm's theory of impulses, also with reference to Freud's perspective, see Stephen A. Mitchell, *Influence and Autonomy in Psychoanalysis* (Hillsdale, NJ: Atlantic Press, 1997), 66.

11. Fromm, *The Dogma of Christ*, 7–11.

12. See also Ann Ulanov and Barry Ulanov, *Religion and the Unconscious* (Philadelphia: Westminster Press, 1985), 119–20.

13. For details about the role of religion from the perspective of psychoanalysis, see Arvind Sharma, *A Primal Perspective on the Philosophy of Religion* (Heidelberg: Springer, 2006), 76.

14. See also Monroe W. Strickberger, *Evolution*, 3rd ed. (Boston: Jones and Bartlett Publishers, 2005), 61.

15. Fromm, *The Dogma of Christ*, 12–17.

16. For details of Fromm's methodology, which combines Marxism with social psychology and psychoanalysis with reference to the conflicts between various social classes in antiquity and modernity, see Gino Germani, *Authoritarianism, Fascism, and National Populism* (New Brunswick, NJ: Transaction Books, 1978), 48–49.

17. Fromm, *The Dogma of Christ*, 18–28.

18. Stjepan G. Mestrović, *Durkheim and Postmodern Culture* (New York: Aldine de Gruyter, 1992), 105.

19. Fromm, *The Dogma of Christ*, 30.

20. See also George Novack, *Marxist Writings on History and Philosophy* (Broadway, NSW: Resistance Books, 2002), 246.

21. Rolf Wiggershaus, *The Frankfurt School: Its History, Theories, and Political Significance* (Cambridge, MA: MIT Press, 1995), 57.

22. Fromm, *The Dogma of Christ*, 31–36.

23. See also Kenneth Boa, *Augustine to Freud: What Theologians & Psychologists Tell Us about Human Nature and Why It Matters* (Nashville, TN: Broadman and Holman, 2004), 267n243.

24. David Nicholls, *Deity and Domination: Images of God and the State in the Nineteenth and Twentieth Centuries* (London: Routledge, 1994), 14.

25. Fromm, *The Dogma of Christ*, 37–44.

26. This can be seen as an attempt to highlight the strength of the human being by drawing it closer to God to the point of essential coincidence. See, for details, Maurice S. Friedman, *A Heart of Wisdom: Religion and Human Wholeness* (Albany, NY: State University of New York Press, 1992), 147–48.

27. W. L. Houser-Thomas, *An Era of Addiction: The Evolution of Dependency* (New York: Writers Club Press, 2002), 138.

28. Fromm, *The Dogma of Christ*, 45–49.

29. Details of the medieval order in Fromm can be found in Erich Fromm, *The Fear of Freedom* (London: Routledge, 2001), 219ff; and Harold Silver, *The Concept of Popular Education: A Study of Ideas and Social Movements in the Early Nineteenth Century* (London: Methuen & Co. Ltd, 1977), 21.

30. This illustrates the creative power of society. See also J. Guimón, *Relational Mental Health: Beyond Evidence-Based Interventions* (Heidelberg: Springer, 2003), 70.

31. Fromm, *The Dogma of Christ*, 50–56.

32. For details of the relationship between religion and social stability, see David R. Hodgin, "Religion and the Modern Mind," in *Religion and the Modern Mind: An Affirmation of Life and the Pursuit of Truth*, ed. Stanley South (Boone, NC: Parkway Publishers, 2006), 43.

33. Details of the complementary role of Mary in early Western Christianity in addition to that of the original Jewish God can be found in Miles Richardson, *Being in Christ and Putting Death in Its Place: An Anthropologist's Account of Christian Performance in Spanish America and the American South* (Baton Rouge, LA: LSU Press, 2006), 307.

34. Fromm, *The Dogma of Christ*, 57–64.

35. For more information about the supportive nature of religion, see Dianna Narciso, *Like Rolling Uphill: Realizing the Honesty of Atheism* (Tamarac, FL: Llumina Press, 2004), 56.

36. The idea of a secularized God is a combination of traditionalism and modernism in theology, a sort of middle way between belief and disbelief in God. Thus, God is portrayed as a human with divine qualities, a compromise between those who take for granted God's existence and those who take for granted God's nonexistence. See, for details, Richard C. McMillan, *Religion in the Public Schools: An Introduction* (Macon, GA: Mercer University Press, 1984), 30.

37. Fromm, *The Dogma of Christ*, 65.

38. For more information about Gnosticism as humanistic religion, see Paul C. Vitz, *Psychology as Religion: The Cult of Self-Worship*, 2nd ed. (Grand Rapids, MI: Eerdmans, and Carlisle, UK: Paternoster, 1994), 129.

39. For useful details about Gnosticism and its theory of creation, see Peter Lampe, *Christians at Rome in the First Two Centuries: From Paul to Valentinus* (London: Continuum, 2003), 292–93.

40. Fromm, *The Dogma of Christ*, 66–68.

41. See for further details Irving L. Horowitz, *Foundations of Political Sociology* (Edison, NJ: Transaction Publishers, 1997), 234.

42. Fromm, *The Dogma of Christ*, 69–71.

43. Arianism or, more exactly, its defeat marks the beginning of a new type of society, namely that of the Middle Ages, with a concept of God that was designed to inculcate respect for authority and the ruling class in general. See also Alfred Lévy and Erich Fromm. *Humanist zwischen Tradizion und Utopie* (Würzburg: Verlag Königshausen & Neumann, 2002), 56.

44. A good analysis of Fromm's perspective on the meaning of the father figure and its psychoanalytical meaning can be found in Thalia Anthony and Dorothea Anthony, "Psychologizing Criminals and the Frankfurt School's Critique," in *The Critical Criminology Companion*, ed. Thalia Anthony and Chris Cunneen (Annandale, NSW: Hawkins Press, 2008), 48–49.

45. Fromm, *The Dogma of Christ*, 72.

CHAPTER 5

1. See also Steven H. Clark, *Paul Ricoeur* (London: Routledge, 1991), 32.

2. David F. Klemm, "Philosophy and Kerygma: Ricoeur as Reader of the Bible," in *Reading Ricoeur*, ed. David M. Kaplan (Albany, NY: State University of New York Press, 2008), 65.

3. See Olav Bryant Smith, *Myths of the Self: Narrative Identity and Postmodern Metaphysics* (Lanham, MD: Lexington Books, 2004), 138.

4. Theodoor Marius van Leeuwen, *The Surplus of Meaning: Ontology and Eschatology in the Philosophy of Paul Ricoeur* (Amsterdam: Rodopi, 1981), 22.

5. Paul Ricoeur, *Fallible Man*, trans. Charles A. Kelbley (New York: Fordham University Press, 1986), xli.

6. For details of the relationship between fallibility and man's ontological structure, see John B. Thompson, "A Response to Paul Ricoeur," in *Paul Ricoeur: Hermeneutics and the Human Sciences*, ed. John B. Thompson (Cambridge: Cambridge University Press, 1998), 39.

7. Karl Simms, *Paul Ricoeur* (London: Routledge, 2003), 10.

8. Phillip Stambovsky, *Myth and the Limits of Reason* (Amsterdam: Rodopi, 1996), 60ff.

9. See Charles E. Reagan, *Paul Ricoeur: His Life and His Work* (Chicago: University of Chicago Press, 1998), 23. Here is what Ricoeur has to say about the idea of fault in connection with mythology: "Fault . . . is not a feature of fundamental ontology similar to other factors discovered by pure description . . . motives, powers, conditions and limits. Fault remains a foreign body in the eidetics [imagery, n.a.] of man. . . . The passage from innocence to fault is not accessible to any description, even an empirical one, but needs to pass through a *concrete mythics*. Thus the idea of approaching the empirics of the will by means of a concrete mythics was already formed, but we did not then realize the

reasons for this detour. Indeed, why can the 'passions', which affect the will, be spoken of only in the coded language of a mythics? How are we to introduce this mythics into philosophic reflection? How can philosophic discourse be resumed after having been interrupted by myth?" Ricoeur, *Fallible Man*, xli–xlii.

10. Patrick L. Bourgeois, *Extension of Ricoeur's Hermeneutic* (Dordrecht: Kluwer Academic Publishers, 1975), 63.

11. See John Wall, *Moral Creativity: Paul Ricoeur and the Poetics of Possibility* (Oxford: Oxford University Press, 2005), 29.

12. Dan R. Stiver, *Theology after Ricoeur: New Directions in Hermeneutical Theology* (Louisville, KY: Westminster John Knox Press, 2001), 54.

13. John B. Thompson, *Critical Hermeneutics: A Study in the Thought of Paul Ricoeur and Jürgen Habermas* (Cambridge: Cambridge University Press, 1983), 44.

14. In Ricoeur's words, "the *myths* of fall, chaos, exile, and divine blinding, all of which are directly accessible to a comparative history of religions, could not be inserted in their unrefined state into philosophic discourse. First they had to be put back into their own universe of discourse; for this reason I devoted several preparatory studies to its reconstruction. It then appeared that myths could be understood only as secondary elaborations of a more fundamental language that I call the language of avowal; this language speaks of fault and evil to the philosopher, and what is noteworthy in it is that it is *symbolic* through and through. It does not speak of stain, sin, or guilt in direct and proper terms, but in indirect and figurative terms. To understand this language is to bring into play an exegesis of the symbol, which calls for rules of deciphering: a hermeneutics. In this way the initial idea of a *mythics* of bad will has been expanded to the dimensions of a *symbolics of evil*. Now, in the center of this symbolics, the most speculative symbols, such as matter, body, and original sin, refer to mythical symbols such as the battle between the forces of order and the forces of chaos, the exile of the soul in a foreign body, the blinding of man by a hostile divinity, Adam's fall, and these refer to the primary symbols of stain, sin, and guilt." Ricoeur, *Fallible Man*, xlii.

15. Patrick L. Bourgeois, *Extension of Ricoeur's Hermeneutic*, 64.

16. See also Andrew Tallon, *Head and Heart: Affection, Cognition, Volition as Triune Consciousness* (New York: Fordham University Press, 1997), 89–90.

17. For details about the concept of "bad will," also in connection with Ricoeur, see Frank K. Flinn, "The Phenomenology of Symbol: Genesis I and II," in *Phenomenology in Practice and Theory*, ed. William S. Hamrick (Dordrecht: Martinus Nijhof Publishers, 1985), 227.

18. Ricoeur, *Fallible Man*, xlii.

19. For the connection between fallibility and knowledge in Ricoeur, see Thomas W. Ogletree, "Christian Social Ethics as a Theological

Discipline," in *Shifting Boundaries*, ed. Barbara G. Wheeler and Edward Farley (Louisville, KY: Westminster John Knox Press, 1991), 234.

20. Patrick L. Bourgeois, *Extension of Ricoeur's Hermeneutic*, 28.

21. Patrick L. Bourgeois and Frank Schalow, *Traces of Understanding: A Profile of Heidegger's and Ricoeur's Hermeneutics* (Amsterdam: Rodopi, 1990), 19.

22. Henry Isaac Venema, *Identifying Selfhood: Imagination, Narrative and Hermeneutics in the Thought of Paul Ricoeur* (Albany, NY: State University of New York Press, 2000), 54–55.

23. "The exegesis of these symbols prepares the myths for *insertion* into man's knowledge of himself. In this way a symbolics of evil is an initial step toward bringing myths nearer to philosophic discourse. In the present work this symbolics of evil occupies the second of three projected books. Now, in this second part, linguistic problems hold an important place. Indeed, the specific feature of the language of avowal has appeared more and more as one of the most astonishing enigmas of self-consciousness—making it seem as though man reached his own depth only by way of the royal road of analogy, as though self-consciousness could be expressed only in riddles and would necessarily require a hermeneutics. While the meditation on the mythics of bad will was unfolding into a *symbolics of evil*, reflection was pushing on in another direction: what is the human 'locus' of evil, what is its point of insertion in human reality? In order to reply to that question I wrote the outline of philosophical anthropology placed at the beginning of this work. This study is centered on the theme of fallibility: the constitutional weakness that makes evil possible. By means of the concept of fallibility, philosophical anthropology comes, as it were, to the encounter of the symbolics of evil, just as the symbolics of evil brings myths closer to philosophic discourse. With the concept of fallibility, the doctrine of man approaches a threshold of intelligibility wherein it is understandable that evil could "come into the world" through man. Beyond this threshold begins the enigma of an upheaval in which discourse is only indirect and ciphered." Ricoeur, *Fallible Man*, xliii.

24. David E. Klemm, "Searching for a Heart of Gold: A Ricoeurian Meditation on Moral Striving and the Power of Religious Discourse," in *Paul Ricoeur and Contemporary Moral Thought*, ed. John Wall, William Schweiker, and W. David Hall (London: Routledge, 2002), 102–3.

25. For details, see Bernard P. Dauenhauer, *Paul Ricoeur: The Promise and Risk of Politics* (Lanham, MD: Rowman and Littlefield, 1998), 61.

26. Details of Ricoeur's view of finitude can be found in Walter Lowe, *Theology and Difference: The Wound of Reason* (Bloomington, IN: Indiana University Press, 1993), 156.

27. Eugene T. Long, *Twentieth Century Western Philosophy of Religion, 1900–2000* (Dordrecht: Kluwer Academic Publishers, 2003), 431.

28. Karl Simms, *Paul Ricoeur*, 15–16.

29. Don Ihde, *Hermeneutic Phenomenology: The Philosophy of Paul Ricoeur* (Evanston, IL: Northwestern University Press, 1980), 161.

30. "The elaboration of the concept of fallibility has provided an opportunity for a much more extensive study of the structures of human reality. The duality of the voluntary and the involuntary is brought back into a much vaster dialectic dominated by the ideas of man's disproportion, the polarity within him of the finite and the infinite, and his activity of intermediation or mediation. Man's specific weakness and his essential fallibility are ultimately sought within this structure of mediation between the pole of his finitude and the pole of his infinitude. . . . By preceding the symbolics of evil with an elucidation of the concept of fallibility, I was confronted with the difficulty of incorporating the symbolics of evil into philosophic discourse. . . . This philosophic discourse leads to the idea of the possibility of evil or fallibility, and it receives new life and considerable enrichment from the symbolics of evil. But this is achieved only at the price of a revolution in method, represented by the recourse to a hermeneutics, that is, to rules of deciphering applied to a world of symbols. Now, this hermeneutics is not of the same nature as the reflective thought that led to the concept of fallibility. The rules for transposing the symbolics of evil into a new type of philosophic discourse are outlined in the last chapter of the second part under the title 'The symbol gives thought.' The text is the pivotal point of the whole work. It shows how we can both respect the specific nature of the symbolic world of expressions and think, not at all 'behind' the symbol but 'starting from' the symbol." Ricoeur, *Fallible Man*, xliii–xliv.

31. Clark, *Paul Ricoeur*, 32.

32. Thompson, *Critical Hermeneutics*, 46.

33. Dauenhauer, *Paul Ricoeur*, 74.

34. For an analysis of alienation in Ricoeur, see Jacques Ellul, *The Ethics of Freedom* (Grand Rapids, MN: Eerdmans, 1976), 28.

35. See also William David Hall, *Paul Ricoeur and the Poetic Imperative: The Creative Tension between Love and Justice* (Albany, NY: State University of New York Press), 2007, 66.

36. Ricoeur, *Fallible Man*, xlv.

37. David Tracy, *Blessed Rage for Order: The New Pluralism in Theology* (Chicago: University of Chicago Press, 1996), 213–14.

38. William Kerrigan, *The Sacred Complex: On the Psychogenesis of* Paradise Lost (Cambridge, MA: Harvard University Press, 1983), 100.

39. Ricoeur, *Fallible Man*, xlvi.

40. Wolfhart Pannenberg, *Anthropology in Theological Perspective* (London: Continuum, 2004), 118.

41. See also Richard Kearney, "Ricoeur," in *A Companion to Continental Philosophy*, ed. Simon Critchley and William Schroeder (Oxford: Blackwell, 1999), 444.

42. To quote Ricoeur: "To try to understand evil by freedom is a grave decision. It is the decision to enter into the problem of evil by the strait gate, holding evil from the outset for 'human, all too human.' Yet we must have a clear understanding of the meaning of this decision in order not to challenge its legitimacy prematurely. It is by no means a decision concerning the root origin of evil, but is merely the description of the place where evil appears and from where it can be seen. Indeed, it is quite possible that man is not the radical source of evil, that he is not the absolute evil-doer. But even if evil were coeval with the root origin of things, it would still be true that it is manifest only in the way it *affects* human existence. Thus, the decision to enter into the problem of evil by the strait gate of human reality only expresses the choice of a center of perspective: even if evil came to man from another source which contaminates him, this other source would still be accessible to us only through its relation to us, only through the state of temptation, aberration, or blindness whereby we would be *affected*. In all hypotheses, evil manifests itself in man's humanity." Ricoeur, *Fallible Man*, xlvi.
43. Ursula King, *Religion and Gender* (Oxford: Blackwell, 1995), 80.
44. See also Kevin J. Vanhoozer, *Biblical Narrative in the Philosophy of Paul Ricoeur* (Cambridge: Cambridge University Press, 1990), 239. Here is Ricoeur's explanation: "It may be objected that the choice of this perspective is arbitrary, that it is, in the strong sense of the word, a pre-judgment; such is not the case. The decision to approach evil through man and his freedom is not an arbitrary choice but suitable to the very nature of the problem. For in point of fact, evil's place of manifestation is apparent only if it is recognized, and it is recognized only if it is taken up by deliberate choice. The decision to understand evil by freedom is itself an undertaking of freedom that takes evil upon itself. The choice of the center of perspective is already the declaration of a freedom that admits its responsibility, vows to look upon evil as evil committed, and avows its responsibility to see that it is not committed. It is this *avowal* that links evil to man, not merely as its place of manifestation, but as its author. This act of taking-upon-oneself creates the problem; it is not a conclusion but a starting point. Even if freedom should be the author of evil without being the root origin of it, the avowal would place the problem of evil in the sphere of freedom. For if man were responsible for evil only through abandon, only through a kind of reverse participation in a more radical source of evil than his freedom, it would still be the avowal of his responsibility that would permit him to be in contact with that root origin." Ricoeur, *Fallible Man*, xlvi–xlvii.
45. See also Ernest Keen, *Depression, Self-Consciousness, Pretending and Guilt* (Westport, CT: Greenwood Publishing Group, 2002), 90.
46. David Wood, *On Paul Ricoeur*, 116.
47. Venema, *Identifying Selfhood*, 56.

48. Ricoeur, *Fallible Man*, xlvi–xlviii.

49. Cf. Wood, *On Paul Ricoeur*, 121.

50. For details, see also van Leeuwen, *The Surplus of Meaning*, 156.

51. Simms, *Paul Ricoeur*, 25.

52. Here is Ricoeur's explanation: "The main enigma of this symbolics lies in the fact that the world of myths is already a broken world. The myth of the fall, which is the matrix of all subsequent speculations concerning the origin of evil in human freedom, is not the only myth. It does not encompass the rich mythics of chaos, of tragic blinding, or of the exiled soul." Ricoeur, *Fallible Man*, xlix.

53. See, for details, Patrick Downey, *Serious Comedy: The Philosophical and Theological Significance of Tragic and Comic Writing in the Western Tradition* (Lanham, MD: Lexington Books, 2000), 106.

54. Keen, *Depression*, 90.

55. For a good analysis of Ricoeur's myth of the fall, see Thomas L. Brodie, *Genesis as Dialogue: A Literary, Historical and Theological Commentary* (Oxford: Oxford University Press, 2001), 146.

56. Simms, *Paul Ricoeur*, 21.

57. Hall, *Paul Ricoeur and the Poetic Imperative*, 66.

58. See, for further details, Rosalyn W. Berne, *Nanotalk: Conversations with Scientists and Engineers about Ethics, Meaning, and Belief in the Development of Nanotechnology* (London: Routledge, 2005), 267.

59. For an interesting discussion of the postulation of evil, which brings Ricoeur closer to Kant, see Wall, *Moral Creativity*, 83.

60. "Even if the philosopher gambles on the superiority of the myth of the fall because of its affinity with the avowal that freedom makes of its responsibility, even if taking the myth of the fall as the central reference point allows us to regroup all other myths, the fact remains that the myth of the fall does not succeed in abolishing or reducing them. Moreover, the exegesis of the myth of the fall directly brings out a tension between two significations: evil comes into the world insofar as man posits it, but man posits it only because he *yields* to the siege of the Adversary." Ricoeur, *Fallible Man*, xlix.

61. See also Anthony C. Thiselton, *The Hermeneutics of Doctrine*, 263.

62. See also Ursula King, *Religion and Gender*, 80.

63. Also check Anthony C. Thiselton, *Thiselton on Hermeneutics* (Grand Rapids, MN: Eerdmans, 2007), 48. For Ricoeur, "the limitation of an ethical vision of evil and of the world is already signified in the ambiguous structure of the myth of the fall: by positing evil, freedom is the victim of an Other. It will be the task of philosophic reflection to *recapture* the suggestions of that symbolics of evil, to extend them into all the domains of man's consciousness, from the human sciences to speculations on the slave-will. If 'the symbol gives thought,' what the symbolics of evil gives to thought concerns the grandeur and limitation of any

ethical vision of the world. For man, as he is revealed by this symbolics, appears no less a victim than guilty." Ricoeur, *Fallible Man*, xlix.

64. Kearney, *On Paul Ricoeur*, 18.
65. Ricoeur, *Fallible Man*, xlviii–xlix.
66. Venema, *Identifying Selfhood*, 54.
67. "In maintaining that fallibility is a concept, I am presupposing at the outset that pure reflection—that is, a way of understanding and being understood that does not come through image, symbol, or myth—can reach a certain threshold of intelligibility where the possibility of evil appears inscribed in the innermost structure of human reality. The idea that man is by nature fragile and liable to err is . . . an idea wholly accessible to pure reflection; it designates a characteristic of man's being." Ricoeur, *Fallible Man*, xlx.
68. Venema, *Identifying Selfhood*, 41.
69. See David M. Rasmussen, *Symbol and Interpretation* (Dordrecht: Kluwer Academic Publishers, 1974), 43.
70. Andrew Cutrofello, *Continental Philosophy: A Contemporary Introduction* (London: Routledge, 2005), 255.
71. See also Wall, *Moral Creativity*, 29.
72. For details about man's complexity and how it should be approached as far as Ricoeur is concerned, see Theodoor Marius van Leeuwen, *The Surplus of Meaning*, 38.
73. "But how can this idea of man's fallibility be made clear? We shall have to be prepared to formulate a series of approaches that, although partial, will in each case grasp a global disposition of human reality (or the condition) in which this ontological characteristic is inscribed. . . . this global disposition consists in a certain non-coincidence of man with himself: this 'disproportion' of self to self would be the *ratio* of fallibility. 'I should not be surprised' if evil has entered the world with man, for he is the only reality that presents this unstable ontological constitution of being greater and lesser than himself." Ricoeur, *Fallible Man*, 1.
74. See also Vanhoozer, *Biblical Narrative in the Philosophy of Paul Ricoeur*, 21.
75. Simms, *Paul Ricoeur*, 16.
76. Also see Paul Varo Martinson, *A Theology of World Religions: Interpreting God, Self, and World in Semitic, Indian, and Chinese Thought* (Minneapolis: Augsburg Fortress Publishing, 1987), 107.
77. Dan R. Stiver, *Theology after Ricoeur: New Directions in Hermeneutical Theology* (Louisville, KY: Westminster John Knox Press, 2001), 26.
78. See also Stephen David Ross, *Inexhaustibility and Human Being: An Essay on Locality* (New York: Fordham University Press, 1989), 137.
79. "We are certainly not in a position to deal directly with this ontological characteristic of man, for the idea of *intermediacy* that is implied in the idea of disproportion is also very misleading. For to say that man is situated *between* being and nothingness is already to treat human

reality as a region, an ontological locality, or a place lodged *between* other places. Now, this schema of intercalation is extremely deceptive: it tempts us to treat man as an object whose place is fixed by its relation to other realities that are more or less complex, intelligent, and independent than man. Man is not intermediate because he is between angel and animal; he is intermediate within himself, within his selves. He is intermediate because he is a mixture, and a mixture because he brings about mediations. His ontological characteristic of being-intermediate consists precisely in that his act of existing is the very act of bringing about mediations between all the modalities and all the levels of reality within him and outside him." Ricoeur, *Fallible Man*, 2.

80. For details about human reality in Ricoeur, see Wood, *On Paul Ricoeur*, 48–50.

81. See Vanhoozer, *Biblical Narrative in the Philosophy of Paul Ricoeur*, 211.

82. See also Paul Gifford, *Love, Desire and Transcendence in French Literature: Deciphering Eros* (Aldershot, UK: Ashgate, 2005), 45–48.

83. Jeffrey W. Robbins, *Between Faith and Thought: An Essay on the Onto-theological Condition* (Charlottesville, VA: University of Virginia Press, 2003), 104.

84. See Charles A. Kelbley, Introduction to *History and Truth: Essays*, by Paul Ricoeur (Evanston, IL: Northwestern University Press, 1965), xix.

85. For further insights into Ricoeur's idea of mediation, see Wood, *On Paul Ricoeur*, 26–27.

86. For details, see Domenico Jervolino, "Paul Ricoeur and Hermeneutic Phenomenology," in *Phenomenology World-Wide*, ed. Anna-Teresa Tymieniecka, 394.

87. Wall, *Moral Creativity*, 29.

88. For details about transcendence and immanence in Ricoeur, see Richard L. Lanigan, *Speaking and Semiology: Maurice Merleau Ponty's Phenomenological Theory of Existential Communication* (Berlin: Walter de Gruyter Verlag, 1991), 93.

89. Scott Lash, *Another Modernity, a Different Rationality* (Oxford: Blackwell, 1999), 158.

90. See also Vanhoozer, *Biblical Narrative in the Philosophy of Paul Ricoeur*, 132.

91. Cf. Richard Freadman, *Threads of Life: Autobiography and the Will* (Chicago: University of Chicago Press, 2001), 318.

92. Here is what Ricoeur has to say about the way we should understand the idea of transcendence with reference to man: "The question is whether man's transcendence is merely transcendence *of* finitude or whether the converse is not something of equal importance: as will be seen, man appears to be no less discourse than perspective, no less a demand for totality than a limited nature, no less love than desire. The

interpretation of the paradox beginning with finitude does not seem to us to have any privilege over the opposed interpretation. According to the latter, man is infinitude, and finitude is a sign that points to the *restricted* nature of this infinitude; conversely, infinitude is a sign of the *transcending* of finitude. Man is no less destined to unlimited rationality, to totality, and beatitude than he is limited to a perspective, consigned to death, and riveted by desire. Our working hypothesis concerning the paradox of the finite-infinite implies that we must speak of infinitude as much as of human finitude. The full recognition of this polarity is essential to the elaboration of the concepts of intermediacy, disproportion, and fallibility, the interconnections of which we have indicated in moving from the last to the first of these concepts." Ricoeur, *Fallible Man*, 3–4.

93. Simms, *Paul Ricoeur*, 19.
94. Van Leeuwen, *The Surplus of Meaning*, 188.
95. Cf. Rasmussen, *Symbol and Interpretation*, 43.
96. Reagan, *Paul Ricoeur*, 23.
97. Here is what Ricoeur has to say about fallibility as produced by the global view of humanity: "The question is how to begin. How can we determine the point of departure in a philosophical anthropology placed under the guiding idea of fallibility? We know only that we cannot start from a simple term, but must rather start from the composite itself, from the finite-infinite relation. Thus it is necessary to start from the whole of man, by which I mean from the global view of his noncoincidence with himself, his disproportion, and the mediation he brings about in existing. But is it not likely that this global view would exclude all progression and logical sequence? There remains the possibility that progress and order might develop in the course of a series of viewpoints or approaches that would in each case be a viewpoint on and approach to the totality." Ricoeur, *Fallible Man*, 4.
98. Ihde, *Hermeneutic Phenomenology*, 87.
99. Vanhoozer, *Biblical Narratives in the Philosophy of Paul Ricoeur*, 58.
100. Van Leeuwen, *The Surplus of Meaning*, 39.
101. See also Venema, *Identifying Selfhood*, 57. In Ricoeur's words, "Now, if the development of thought in a philosophical anthropology never consists in going from the simple to the complex, but always moves within the totality itself, this can only be a development in the philosophical elucidation of the global view. This totality, therefore, must first be given in some way prior to philosophy, in a precomprehension that lends itself to reflection. Consequently, philosophy has to proceed as a second-order elucidation of a nebula of meaning that at first has a prephilosophical character. This means that we must completely dissociate the idea of method in philosophy from the idea of a starting point. Philosophy does not start anything independently: supported by the non-philosophical, it derives its existence from the substance of

what has already been understood prior to reflection. However, if philosophy is not a radical beginning with regard to its sources, it may be one with regard to its method. Thus, through this idea of a difference of potential between the non-philosophical precomprehension and the methodical beginning of elucidation, we are brought closer to a well-defined working hypothesis. But where should we look for the precomprehension of fallible man? In the *pathétique of 'misery'*. This pathos is, as it were, the matrix of any philosophy that makes disproportion and intermediacy the ontic characteristic of man. Yet it is necessary to take this pathos at its highest point of perfection. Even though it is prephilosophical, this *pathétique* is precomprehension, and it is that insofar as it is perfect speech, perfect in its order and on its level. Accordingly, we shall look for some of those excellent expressions which tell of man's precomprehension of himself as 'miserable.'" Ricoeur, *Fallible Man*, 4.

102. Ricoeur, *Fallible Man*, 5–6.
103. Aloysius Rego, *Suffering and Salvation: The Salvific Meaning of Suffering in the Later Theology of Edward Schillebeeckx* (Leuven, BE: Peeters, 2006), 325.
104. Edward Schillebeeckx, *Christ, the Christian Experience in the Modern World* (London: SCM Press, 1990), 31–32.
105. Marguerite Abdul-Masih, *Edward Schillebeeckx and Hans Frei: A Conversation on Method and Christology* (Waterloo, ON: Wilfrid Laurier University Press, 2001), 88–89.
106. Edward Schillebeeckx, *Christ, the Sacrament of the Encounter with God* (Lanham, MD: Rowman and Littlefield, 1963), 64.
107. These experiences have authority; see Kathleen McManus, *Unbroken Communion: The Place and Meaning of Suffering in Edward Schillebeeckx* (Lanham, MD: Rowman and Littlefield, 2003), 34.
108. Schillebeeckx, *Christ, the Christian Experience*, 35.
109. See Erik Borgman, *Edward Schillebeeckx: A Theologian in His History* (London: Continuum, 2004), 210.
110. Schillebeeckx, *Christ, the Sacrament*, 65.
111. Edward Schillebeeckx, *God the Future of Man* (London: Sheed and Ward, 1968), 56.
112. Schillebeeckx, *World and Church*, 25.
113. Schillebeeckx, *God the Future of Man*, 180–81.
114. Edward Schillebeeckxand Ramona Simuţ, ed., "Reinterpreting Traditional Theology: An Interview with Edward Schillebeeckx," in *Perichoresis* 5:2 (2007), 275–76.
115. Edward Schillebeeckx, *Church, the Human Story of God* (London: SCM Press, 1990), 5–6.
116. John Westerdale Bowker, *The Sacred Neuron: Extraordinary New Discoveries Linking Science to Religion* (London: IB Tauris Publishers, 2005), 188n19.

117. Don Cupitt, *Sea of Faith: Christianity in Change* (Cambridge: Cambridge University Press, 1988), 251.

118. Cupitt, *Sea of Faith*, 31.

119. Cupitt, *Sea of Faith*, 41.

120. Cupitt, *Is Nothing Sacred? The Non-Realist Philosophy of Religion: Selected Essays* (New York: Fordham University Press, 2002), 96–97.

121. Cupitt, *Is Nothing Sacred?*, 101.

122. Cupitt, *Sea of Faith*, 253.

123. Cupitt, *Is Nothing Sacred?*, 103.

124. Gavin Hyman, *The Predicament of Postmodern Theology*, 46–47.

125. See, for details, Don Cupitt, *Creation out of Nothing* (London: SCM Press, 1990), 129.

CHAPTER 6

1. David Lehmann, "Religion and Globalization," in *Religions in the Modern World*, ed. Linda Woodhead, Paul Fletcher, Hiroko Kawanami, and David Smith (London: Routledge, 2004), 348–49.

2. E. J. Ashworth, "Religious Pluralism," in *The Routledge Encyclopaedia of Philosophy*, ed. Edward Craig (London: Taylor and Francis, 1998), 260–67.

3. See also Roger Trigg, *Rationality and Religion* (Oxford: Wiley-Blackwell, 1998), 168.

4. A useful tool for the investigation of the relationship between religion and human experience, which of course includes science, is James D. Proctor, ed., *Science, Religion and Human Experience* (Oxford: Oxford University Press, 2005).

5. For details about Christianity as a world religion, see Clive Erricker, *Teaching Christianity: A World Religions Approach*, 2nd rev. ed. (Cambridge: James Clarke & Co., 1987).

6. Lancelot L. Whyte, *The Universe of Experience: A Worldview beyond Science and Religion* (Edison, NJ: Transaction Publishers, 2003), 1–18.

7. Curtis Hutson, *Great Preaching on the Resurrection* (Murfreesboro, TN: Sword of the Lord Publishers, 2000), 72.

8. Jeffrey A. Kottler, *Doing Good: Passion and Commitment to Helping Others* (London: Routledge, 2000), 117.

9. Mary A. Stenger and Ronald H. Stone, *Dialogues with Paul Tillich* (Macon, GA: Mercer University Press, 2002), 13.

10. Luke T. Johnson, "Religious Rights and Christian Texts," in *Religious Human Rights in Global Perspective: Religious Perspectives*, ed. John Witte Jr. and Johan D. van der Vyer (Dordrecht: Martinus Nijhoff Publishers, 1996), 80.

11. Vito Mancuso, *Rifondazione della fede* (Milan: Mondadori, 2008), 26.

12. For details about intolerance within Christianity and some possible solutions, see Ian S. Markham, *Plurality and Christian Ethics* (Cambridge: Cambridge University Press, 1994), 1–17.

13. See also Wolfhart Pannenberg, *Systematic Theology* (Grand Rapids, MI: Eerdmans, 1991), 1:129.

14. Mancuso, *Rifondazione della fede*, 27.

15. Also see David Tracy, *Plurality and Ambiguity* (Chicago: University of Chicago Press, 1994), 91–92.

16. Mancuso, *Rifondazione della fede*, 36.

17. John Hick, *Dialogues in the Philosophy of Religion* (New York: Palgrave Macmillan, 2001), 196.

18. For a contrary view, see Geoffrey W. Bromiley, "Christianity," in *The International Standard Bible Encyclopedia*, ed. Geoffrey W. Bromiley (Grand Rapids, MI: Eerdmans, 1979), 660–61.

19. Mancuso, *Rifondazione della fede*, 26, 28.

20. For details, see Fred R. Dallmayr, *Margins of Political Discourse* (Albany, NY: State University of New York Press, 1989), 200–1.

21. Details about the *Filius Dei* can be found in Gerald J. Bednar, *Faith as Imagination: The Contribution of William F. Lynch, SJ* (Lanham, MD: Rowman and Littlefield, 1996), 7.

22. For details, see Mancuso, *Rifondazione della fede*, 28–29.

23. It must be stressed here that Mancuso's criticism is directed specifically against the tenets of the First Vatican Council. Further information about the light of reason in Vatican I can be read in Gianfranco Fioravanti, "Nationalism," in *Encyclopedia of Christian Theology*, ed. Jean-Yves Lacoste (London: CRC Press, 2004), 1:1104-6.

24. For further information about the meaning of the experience of the self in connection with the concept of God, see Harold G. Coward, *Jung and Eastern Thought* (Albany, NY: State University of New York Press, 1985), 129–30.

25. See also Peter Williamson, *Catholic Principles for Interpreting Scripture* (Leuven, BE: Peeters, 2001), 104–5.

26. For details about the capacity of the self to investigate religion, see Wayne Proudfoot, *God and the Self: Three Types of Philosophy of Religion* (Cranbury, Associated University Presses, 1976).

27. Mancuso, *Rifondazione della fede*, 29.

28. For the issue of pluralism within a distinctive religion, see Paul Helm, *Faith and Understanding* (Grand Rapids, MI: Eerdmans, 1997), 62–64.

29. See also Denys Turner, *Faith, Reason and the Existence of God* (Cambridge: Cambridge University Press, 2004), xiii.

30. Mancuso, *Rifondazione della fede*, 30–31.

31. It seems that, in using the idea of the pure good as attached to the self who has the capacity to exercise his reason with view to the knowledge of God, Mancuso actually demythologizes even Catholic mysticism.

For details about Catholic mysticism, see Evelyn Underhill, *Mysticism: A Study in the Nature and Development of Spiritual Consciousness* (Mineola, NY: Dover Publications, 2002), 205.

32. Mancuso, *Rifondazione della fede*, 36–37.

33. For a discussion of man's subjectivity in perceiving the good, see Robert M. Wallace, *Hegel's Philosophy of Beauty, Freedom, and God* (Cambridge: Cambridge University Press, 2005), 302.

34. An informative book that debates the claims of truth of various religions, also in connection with Christianity, is Gavin D'Costa, *The Meeting of Religions and the Trinity* (London: Continuum, 2000).

35. Strangely enough, Mancuso seems to be quite medieval in his conviction despite his evident modernistic impetus because, during the Middle Ages, the intellectual superiority of Christianity was defended against other religions, especially Judaism. See Gillian R. Evans, *Fifty Key Medieval Thinkers* (London: Routledge, 2002), 85.

36. For an interesting discussion of faith as a gift of God, by a nontraditional theologian, see Mark C. Taylor, *After God* (Chicago: University of Chicago Press, 2007), 60–62.

37. This is the definition of faith also according to Vatican I. See Avery R. Dulles, *The Assurance of Things Hoped For: A Theology of Christian Faith* (Oxford: Oxford University Press, 1997), 186.

38. Donald W. Wuerl, Thomas C. Lawler, and Ronald Lawler, eds., *The Gift of Faith: A Question and Answer Version of the Teaching of Christ* (Huntington, IN: Our Sunday Visitor, 2001), 83.

39. See Thomas R. Edgar, "Through the Written Word, Spiritual Truth Can Be Known," in *The Fundamentals of the Twenty-First Century: Examining the Crucial Issue of the Christian Faith*, ed. Mal Couch (Grand Rapids, MI: Kregel Publications, 2000), 43–47.

40. Mancuso, *Rifondazione della fede*, 33.

41. For an excellent discussion of God's grace and how it acts within the human being, see Michael R. Miller, "Freedom and Grace," in *Gathered for the Journey: Moral Theology in Catholic Perspective*, ed. David M. McCarthy and M. Therese Lysaught (Grand Rapids, MI: Eerdmans, 2007), 191–96.

42. See, for instance, Karl Barth, *Church Dogmatics* (London: Continuum, 1969), II.2:128.

43. Mancuso, *Il dolore innocente*, 150–52.

44. Such as Evangelical Reformed theology. See, for example, Roger E. Olson, *The Westminster Handbook to Evangelical Theology* (Louisville, KY: Westminster John Knox Press, 2004), 183.

45. Mancuso, *Rifondazione della fede*, 36.

46. Mancuso, *Rifondazione della fede*, 40.

47. This could mean that, at the end of the day, everyone has faith in something. See, for instance, Rob Bell, *Velvet Elvis: Repainting the Christian Faith* (Grand Rapids, MI: Zondervan, 2006), 19–20.

48. For the distinction between religious faith and theological faith, see also John D. Caputo, Kevin Hart, and Yvonne Sherwood, "Epoché and Faith: An Interview with Jacques Derrida," in *Derrida and Religion: Other Testaments*, ed. Yvonne Sherwood and Kevin Hart (London: Routledge, 2005), 39.

49. For an interesting parallel, see Eric D. Perl, *Theophany: The Neoplatonic Philosophy of Dionysius the Areopagite* (Albany, NY: State University of New York Press, 2007), 41–42.

50. For Mancuso, however, objective reality is still some sort of subjectivity: a communitarian subjectivity as opposed to and higher than individual subjectivity. For a good discussion of subjectivity and objectivity within the theological and philosophical discourse within modernity, see A. K. Min, "Phillips on the Grammar of «God»," in *Ethics of Belief: Essays in Tribute to D. Z. Phillips*, ed. Eugene T. Long and Patrick Horn (Berlin: Springer, 2008), 137.

51. Mancuso, *Rifondazione della fede*, 37.

52. Mancuso, *Rifondazione della fede*, 41–42.

53. See also Bruno Forte, "Gnosi di rittorno e linguaggio consolatorio", *L'Osservatore Romano*, February 2, 2008. Although Forte is extremely critical of Mancuso he nonetheless notices the paramount importance of love in Mancuso's theological discourse.

54. Christian songs contain innumerable references to love, and especially to God's love or Christian love. See Erik Routley, *A Panorama of Christian Hymnody* (Chicago: GIA Publications, 2005).

55. See also Cornelius A. Buller, *The Unity of Nature and History in Pannenberg's Theology* (Lanham, MD: Rowman and Littlefield, 1996), 187.

56. In this respect, Mancuso comes very close to Charles S. Pierce; see Peter Ochs, "Charles Sanders Pierce," in *Founders of Constructive Postmodern Philosophy: Pierce, James, Bergson, Whitehead, and Hartshorne*, ed. David R. Griffin et al. (Albany, NY: State University of New York Press, 1993), 75.

57. Mancuso, *Rifondazione della fede*, 15.

58. This classical formula shows that Mancuso does not totally give up traditional theology, but he uses its language, which he later translates into his rational "theology from below." See also David Bordwell, ed., *Catechism of the Catholic Church* (London: Burns and Oates, 2006), 170.

59. Kenotic theology became quite influential on the eve of the Second Vatican Council. For details, see Philip Kennedy, *Schillebeeckx* (Collegeville, MN: Liturgical Press, 1993), 100.

60. Mancuso, *Il dolore innocente*, 188–89.

61. Mancuso does not take his presentation of Christ further into a discussion about salvation and redemption. See Forte, "Gnosi di rittorno e linguaggio consolatorio."

62. Catholic feminism makes frequent use of the practical display of love in Christ's *kenosis*. For more information, see Tina Beattie, *New Catholic Feminism: Theology and Theory* (Oxford: Routledge, 2006), 160.

63. See also Terry Pinkard, *Hegel: A Biography* (Cambridge: Cambridge University Press, 2001), 142.

64. Mancuso is in full agreement here with the general pluralistic perspective of postmodern thought on world religions. See, for details, David W. Smith and Elizabeth G. Burr, *Understanding World Religions: A Road Map for Justice and Peace* (Lanham, MD: Rowman and Littlefield, 2007), xliii.

65. Mancuso, *Il dolore innocente*, viii.

66. Forte, "Gnosi di rittorno e linguaggio consolatorio."

67. Also see David O. Ahearn and Peter A. Gathie, eds., *Doing Right and Being Good: Catholic and Protestant Readings in Christian Ethics* (Collegeville, MN: Liturgical Press, 2005), 37.

68. Mancuso's approach at this point seems to bear a powerful resemblance to Oriental religious philosophies. See, for further information, Thomas P. Kasulis, ed., *Self as Body in Asian Theory and Practice* (Albany, NY: State University of New York Press, 1993), 190–91.

69. For further details about the relationship between creation and evolution in Christian theology, see J. P. Moreland, John Mark Reynolds, and Stanley N. Gundry, eds., *Three Views on Creation and Evolution* (Grand Rapids, MI: Zondervan, 1999), 8.

70. See also Edward O. de Bary, *Theological Reflection: The Creation of Spiritual Power in the Information Age* (Collegeville, MN: Liturgical Press, 2003), 23–24.

71. A detailed presentation of the basics of Pierre Teilhard de Chardin's theology can be found in Celia Deane-Drummond, "Theology and the Biological Sciences," in *The Modern Theologians: An Introduction to Christian Theology since 1918*, ed. David Ford (Oxford: Blackwell, 2005), 360.

72. F For useful details about worldview formation, with special reference to Husserl, see David K. Naugle, *Worldview: The History of a Concept* (Grand Rapids, MI: Eerdmans, 2002), 108–21.

73. At this point, Mancuso is very close to Schillebeeckx, who is convinced that, through the action of humans, the natural world or the world of phenomena turns into a realm for the giving of meaning. See Erik Borgman, *Edward Schillebeeckx: A Theologian in His History* (London: Continuum, 2004), 210.

74. See also Edward Schillebeeckx, *Christ, the Sacrament of the Encounter with God* (Lanham, MD: Rowman and Littlefield, 1963), 4.

75. For a thorough discussion of freedom and meaning, see Wilhelm Dupré, *Patterns in Meaning: Reflections on Meaning and Truth in Cultural Reality, Religious Traditions and Dialogical Encounters* (Leuven, BE: Peeters, 1994), 238–40.

76. See also Chiedozie Okoro, "Phenomenology for World Reconstruction," in Anna-Teresa Tymieniecka, ed., *Analecta Husserliana* (Dordrecht: Springer, 2006), XCII.5: 340–42.

77. In this respect, Mancuso comes close to Paul Tillich, who saw the *logos* as the essential structure of reality. Moreover, the *logos* reflects itself both in man's mind and in reality. Cf. John P. Dourley, *Paul Tillich and Bonaventure* (Leiden, NL: Brill, 1975), 176–77.

78. See also Swami Ranganathananda, *Human Being in Depth: A Scientific Approach to Religion* (Albany, NY: State University of New York Press, 1991), 3–4.

79. Mancuso's perspective on truth is criticized by Corrado Marucci, "L'anima e il suo destino secondo Vito Mancuso," *La Civiltà Cattolica*, February 2, 2008.

80. Mancuso's theory of the soul is also criticized by Marucci. See Marucci, "L'anima e il suo destino secondo Vito Mancuso."

81. Vito Mancuso, "Video intrevista a Vito Mancuso," June 16, 2008, http://www.associazioneasia.it/adon.pl?act=doc&doc=669 (accessed February 27, 2009).

82. Mancuso is fully aware that the promise of existence beyond individual death is one of the fundamental tenets of Christianity. See also Charley D. Hardwick, *Events of Grace: Naturalism, Existentialism and Theology* (Cambridge: Cambridge University Press, 1996), 13–14.

83. This aspect is part of Marucci's critique; see Marucci, "L'anima e il suo destino secondo Vito Mancuso."

84. Experience is the source of theology as, for instance, in Edward Schillebeeckx. For details, see Marguerite Abdul-Masih, *Edward Schillebeeckx and Hans Frei: A Conversation on Method and Christology* (Waterloo, ON: Wilfrid Laurier University Press, 2001), 2–6.

85. For an informative discussion of experience and how it influences theology, see Bruce D. Marshall, *Trinity and Truth* (Cambridge: Cambridge University Press, 2002), 81, 83, 84.

86. Mancuso does not say whether matter itself has an origin outside the world or it is the very origin of everything in the world. Nevertheless, it is logical to suppose that he makes reference to matter as the origin of everything *in the world*. For an interesting discussion of the origin of everything, see Roger Ellman, *The Origin and Its Meaning* (Santa Rosa, CA: Origin Foundation, 2004), 17–20.

87. Mancuso's theology is very similar to Teilhard de Chardin's thought, which is based on the conviction that there is no Christ without the cosmos and no spiritual being without matter. The incarnation is merely an indication that matter encompasses everything, including the spiritual realm. In other words, there is no spiritual realm without matter, which is explained through the idea of incarnation. See, for a detailed presentation, Anne Hunt Overzee, *The Body Divine: The Symbol of the*

Body in the Works of Teilhard de Chardin and Ramanuja (Cambridge: Cambridge University Press, 1992), 50–52.

88. Mancuso would agree with John Hick. See Brian Hebblethwaite, *Philosophical Theology and Christian Doctrine* (Oxford: Blackwell, 2005), 60–61.

89. Mancuso, *Rifondazione della fede*, 276.

90. See also Hans Dirk van Hoogstraten, *Deep Economy: Caring for Ecology, Humanity and Religion* (Cambridge: James Clarke and Co., 2001), 1–5.

91. This feature of Mancuso's theology resembles, to a high degree, both existentialism and Marxism. For details about existentialism and Marxism, see Robert B. Mellert, "Reconsidering the Medieval Concept of Nature in the Development of a Scientific Ethics," in *Miscellanea Medievalia* 13/2: Sprache und Erkenntnis im Mittelalter, ed. Jan P. Beckmann and Wolfgang Kluxen (Berlin: Walter de Gruyter, 1981), 609.

92. Mancuso is in agreement with Kant, who believed that the shift from theocentrism to anthropocentrism is man's transition from childhood to maturity. See Predrag Cicovacki, *Between Truth and Illusion: Kant at the Crossroads of Modernity* (Lanham, MD: Rowman and Littlefield, 2002), 124.

93. Mancuso's approach to the Trinity can be defined as psychological because it is man, or man's soul, who defines Trinity as symbol. This brings Mancuso closer to Jung; see C. L. Rothgeb, ed., *Abstracts of the Collected Works of C. G. Jung* (London: Karnac Books, 1992), 74.

94. See also Harold W. Percival, *Thinking and Destiny: The Descent of Man the Eternal Order of Progression* (New Delhi: Motilal Banarsidass Publishers, 2001), 596–97.

95. Mancuso, *Rifondazione della fede*, 276–77.

96. See John Macquarrie, *Stubborn Theological Questions* (London: SCM Press, 2003), 136–37.

97. As in Schillebeeckx, who believes that God is accessible only through justice and love. See Philip Kennedy, "God and Creation," in *The Praxis of the Reign of God: An Introduction to the Theology of Edward Schillebeeckx*, ed. Mary C. Hilkert and Robert J. Schreiter (New York: Fordham University Press, 2002), 52.

98. Mancuso, *Rifondazione della fede*, 277.

99. So Christ the man preexists his own incarnation as, for instance, in Robert Jenson. See, for details, Oliver D. Crisp, "Incarnation," in *The Oxford Handbook of Systematic Theology*, ed. John Webster, Kathryn Tanner, and Iain Torrance (Oxford: Oxford University Press, 2007), 167–69.

100. Mancuso's image of man looks like Auguste Comte's perspective on man as the Great Being, who replaces the traditional God. See Frederick C. Copleston, *A History of Philosophy: 19th and 20th Century French Philosophy* (London: Continuum, 2003), 95.

101. Mancuso, *Il dolore innocente*, 112–13.

102. Mancuso, *Il dolore innocente*, 113.

103. Man has the capacity to develop his own powers of love, reason, and justice, so spirituality exists only in man, not outside him. The development of man's capacity to understand spirituality as belonging exclusively to his own realm, which is the natural world, is the result of the process of human evolution, which confirms Mancuso's belief in the lack of contradiction between creation and evolution or between theology and science, provided creation and theology are understood only in terms of evolution and science. Man turns to himself because he knows or rather he learns how to love himself, first as individual then as humanity. This perspective resembles that of Erich Fromm, as in Pat D. Hutcheon, *Leaving the Cave: Evolutionary Naturalism in Social-Scientific Thought* (Waterloo, ON: Wilfrid Laurier University Press, 1996), 350–51.

104. Mancuso, *Il dolore innocente*, 114.

105. Mancuso, *Il dolore innocente*.

106. *Donum Vitae* was issued by the Congregation for the Doctrine of the Faith on February 22, 1987, and was signed by Cardinal Joseph Ratzinger.

107. Vito Mancuso, *Hegel teologo* (Casale Monferrato, IT: Edizioni Piemme, 1996).

108. Mancuso is not entirely right because, although the situation he signaled could be true in Italy, it is certainly not the case in the United States of America. See, for further information, Michelle N. Baum and Janice L. Benton, "The Evolution and Current Focus of Ministry with Catholics with Disabilities within the United States," in *Disability Advocacy among Religious Organizations*, ed. Albert A. Herzog (Philadelphia: Haworth Press, 2006), 39–54.

109. A book that seems to agree with Mancuso is Amos Yong, *Theology and Down Syndrome: Reimagining Disability in Late Modernity* (Waco, TX: Baylor University Press, 2007), 158–63. However, Mancuso's view is not supported by Hans S. Reinders, *Receiving the Gift of Friendship: Profound Disability, Theological Anthropology, and Ethics* (Grand Rapids, MI: Eerdmans, 2008), 88–90.

110. For an interesting perspective that equates God with energy, see Joseph Davydov, *God Exists: New Light on Science and Creation* (Rockville, MD: Schreiber Publishing, 2000), 125–40.

111. See for details, Mancuso, *Il dolore innocente*, vii–viii.

112. William E. May, *Catholic Bioethics and the Gift of Human Life: Celebrating the Beauty of Being* (Huntington, IN: Our Sunday Visitor Press, 2000), 16.

113. See also Robert L. Perkins, *Upbuilding Discourses in Various Spirits* (Macon, GA: Mercer University Press, 2005), 232.

114. Cf. Gregg Horowitz, *Sustaining Loss: Art and Mournful Life* (Palo Alto, CA: Stanford University Press, 2001), 50. For the medical connotation of the phrase, see Daniel Callahan, *The Troubled Dream of Life: In Search of a Peaceful Death* (Washington, DC: Georgetown University Press, 2000), 97.

115. Mancuso, *Il dolore innocente*, ix–x.

116. An informative work in this respect is Eduardo J. Echeverria, "The Gospel of Redemptive Suffering: Reflections on John Paul II's *Salvifici Doloris*," in *Christian Faith and the Problem of Evil*, by Peter van Inwagen (Grand Rapids, MI: Eerdmans, 2004), 111–47.

117. Kevin O'Rourke, "Pain Relief: Ethical Issues and Catholic Teaching," in *Birth, Suffering and Death: Catholic Perspectives at the Edges of Life*, ed. Kevin Wm. Wildes, Francesc Abel, and John C. Harvey (Dordrecht: Kluwer Publications, 1994), 157–70.

118. For more details, see Charles E. Curran, *The Catholic Moral Tradition Today* (Washington, DC: Georgetown University Press, 1999), 37–42.

119. Detailed information can be found in Robert Feduccia Jr., ed., with Jerry Windley-Daoust, Michael C. Jordan, and J. D. Childs, *Great Catholic Writings: Thought, Literature, Spirituality, Social Action* (Winona, MN: Saint Mary's Press, 2006).

120. Cf. Mancuso, *Il dolore innocente*, 17–23.

121. See also Stan van Hooft, *Life, Death and Subjectivity: Moral Sources in Bioethics* (Amsterdam: Rodopi, 2004), 137.

122. Mancuso, *Il dolore innocente*, 23–24.

123. *Instruction* Dignitas personae *on Certain Bioethical Questions* was approved by Benedict XVI on June 20, 2008.

124. Donald W. Wuerl, *The Teaching of Christ: A Catholic Catechism for Adults* (Huntington, IN: Our Sunday Visitor Press, 2004), 55.

125. See also Lisa Sowle Cahill, "Commentary on *Familiaris consortio* (*Apostolic Exhortation on the Family*), in *Modern Catholic Social Teaching: Commentaries and Interpretations*, ed. Kenneth R. Himes (Washington, DC: Georgetown University Press, 2005), 363–88.

126. Mancuso, *Il dolore innocente*, 25–31.

127. For the traditional view, see John A. O'Brien, *The Faith of Millions: The Credentials of the Catholic Religion* (Huntington, IN: Our Sunday Visitor Press, 1974), 438; and Kevin D. O'Rourke and Philip Boyle, *Medical Ethics: Sources of Catholic Teachings* (Washington, DC: Georgetown University Press, 1999), 249–50.

128. Mancuso, *Il dolore innocente*, 32.

129. Peter Williamson, *Catholic Principles for Interpreting Scripture: A Study of the Pontifical Commission's* The Interpretation of the Bible in the Church (Rome: Editrice Pontificio Istituto Biblico, 2001), 35.

130. See Hazel J. Markwell and Barry F. Brown, "Roman Catholic Bioethics," in *The Cambridge Textbook of Bioethics*, ed. Peter A. Singer and A. M. Viens (Cambridge: Cambridge University Press, 2008), 436–45.

131. Mancuso's "theological drama," which is essentially a way to describe the impossibility of reconciling God's love and omnipotence with human disability, has nothing in common with Hans Urs von Balthasar's "theological drama," which is a way to express the turmoil of faithful Catholics who are not properly understood by the churches they serve. See Aidan Nichols, *No Bloodless Myth: A Guide through Balthasar's Dogmatics* (London: Continuum, 2000), 127.

132. Mancuso, *Il dolore innocente*, 137–39.

133. A counter position is defended by Thomas J. Massaro, "From Industrialization to Globalization: Church and Social Ministry," in *Living the Catholic Social Tradition: Cases and Commentaries*, ed. Kathleen Maas Weigert and Alexia K. Kelley (Lanham, MD: Rowman and Littlefield, 2004), 56.

134. Mancuso, *Il dolore innocente*, 150–60.

135. For details of cellular suicide, see Jeffrey W. Myers, Marianne Neighbors, and Ruth Tannehille-Jones, *Pathophysiology and Emergency Medical Care* (Florence, KY: Thompson Cengage Learning, 2002), 16.

136. M Mancuso, *Il dolore innocente*, 161–75.

137. See also John Macquarrie, "Theological Reflections on Disability," in Marilyn Bishop, ed., *Religion and Disability: Essays in Scripture, Theology and Ethics* (Lanham, MD: Rowman and Littlefield, 1995), 44.

138. For a counter argument, see Paul S. Fiddes, *Participating in God: A Pastoral Doctrine of the Trinity* (Louisville, KY: Westminster John Knox Press, 2000), 312. See also James J. Walter, "Theological Parameters: Catholic Doctrine on Abortion in a Pluralist Society," in *Contemporary Issues in Bioethics: A Catholic Perspective*, ed. James J. Walter and Thomas A. Shannon (Lanham, MD: Rowman and Littlefield, 2005), 145–80. On this particular issue, Mancuso's attempt to isolate God from the world with reference to his direct acts is very similar to Malebranche's philosophical enterprise. See, for instance, Donald Rutherford, "Malebranche's Theodicy," in Steven M. Nadler, ed., *The Cambridge Companion to Malebranche* (Cambridge: Cambridge University Press, 2000), 165–89.

139. Mancuso, *Il dolore innocente*, 187–91.

140. See also Martin Michael, *Atheism: A Philosophical Justification* (Philadelphia: Temple University Press, 1992), 200–202.

141. For details about how Roman Catholicism perceives *in vitro* fertilization, see Tom Davis, *Sacred Work: Planned Parenthood and Its Clergy Alliances* (Rutgers, NJ: Rutgers University Press, 2005), 197–98. Not all traditional theology refutes *in vitro* fertilization. For instance, Protestants tend to accept it because medical techniques fall within the realm of general revelation, so humanity can carry its mandate to multiply, fill the earth, and exercise dominon over it. There is, however, one condition to the acceptance of *in vitro* fertilization in traditional Protestant theology, namely the necessity that the genetic material should

come from the spouses. See, for details, Scott B. Rae, *Moral Choices: An Introduction to Ethics*, 2nd ed. (Grand Rapids, MI: Zondervan, 2000), 150–52. The argument is that infertility is the consequence of the entering of sin into the world, and the evident result is the inability of the human reproductive system to work properly. This can be equated to other health problems that render various organs virtually useless, and the only way to restore their natural functions is by means of medical intervention.

142. This is a typical example of the difference between traditional theology and radical theology. Thus, while radical theology is convinced that—by means of modern science—we can actually correct the work of God, traditional Christianity holds that we can only correct the consequences of sin, which affect the work of God. In fact, these approaches stem from two different approaches of the idea of God: radical theology envisages God as nonmetaphysical in terms of ontological reality, while traditional Christianity understands God as utterly metaphysical when it comes to the reality of his actual existence. See, for details, Thomas J. J. Altizer, *The Genesis of God: A Theological Genealogy* (Louisville, KY: Westminster John Knox Press, 1993), 20; and Christopher Martin, ed., *The Philosophy of Thomas Aquinas: Introductory Readings* (London: Taylor and Francis, 1988), 99.

143. Mancuso, *Il dolore innocente*, 203–9.

144. Vito Mancuso, "La nostra sacra liberta di morire," in *Persona e danno*, August 29, 2008, http://www.personaedanno.it/cms/data/articoli/011333.aspx (accessed January 11, 2009).

145. See also William Stanley Dell, *Jung, Modern Man in Search of a Soul* (London: Routledge, 2001), 180.

146. Mancuso is hegelian at this point; see John Walker, "Hegel and Religion," in David Lamb, *Hegel and Modern Philosophy* (London: Routledge, 1987), 189–225.

147. Mancuso's thought is similar to that of Paul Tillich; see Paul Tillich, *Theological Writings* [Hauptwerke 6], ed. Gert Hummel and Carl Heinz Ratschow (Berlin: Walter de Gruyter Verlag, 1992), 308.

148. Vito Mancuso, "Video intrevista a Vito Mancuso."

149. Again, it should be highlighted that traditional Protestant theology tends to accept *in vitro* fertilization provided that the genetic material originates within the married couple. This means that medical technologies using the genetic material of the spouses are morally acceptable in general, such as gamete intrafallopian transfer (the so-called GIFT), the *in vitro* fertilization (IVF), and intrauterine insemination. The medical procedures that use genetic material from outside the married couple, like donor insemination, egg donation, and surrogate motherhood, are at least morally problematic if not unacceptable. See also Rae, *Moral Choices*, 154.

150. See Ted Peters, *Playing God? Genetic Determinism and Human Freedom* (London: Routledge, 2003), 185.

151. This is morally acceptable if the medical procedure facilitates the conjugal act and helps it reach its natural objectives, so the reproductive material must be collected from the spouses. See Todd A. Saltzman and Michael G. Lawler, *The Sexual Person: Toward a Renewed Catholic Anthropology* (Washington, DC: Georgetown University Press, 2008), 239.

152. Ruth Macklin, *Surrogates and Other Mothers: The Debates over Assisted Reproduction* (Philadelphia: Temple University Press, 1994), 34; and Lewis Petrinovich, *Human Evolution, Reproduction and Morality* (Cambridge, MA: MIT Press, 1998), 279.

153. For the risks of the procedure, see F. Shenfield and C. Sureau, "Ethics of Embryo Research," in *Ethical Dilemmas in Assisted Reproduction*, by F. Shenfield and C. Sureau (New York: Informa Healthcare, 1997), 15–22.

154. Leonardo de Castro, "Bioethics in the Philippines: An Overview of Developments, Issues, and Controversies," in *Regional Perspectives in Bioethics*, ed. John F. Peppin and Mark J. Cherry (London: Swets and Zeitlinger Publishers, 2003), 307.

155. Paul Flaman, *Genetic Engineering: Christian Values and Catholic Teaching* (Mahwah, NJ: Paulist Press, 2002), 92.

156. Traditional Protestant theology accepts gene therapy when it is meant to correct defects because it falls within the category of general revelation. As God does not intend either sin or its consequences for humanity, corrective gene therapy can be morally accepted. On the other hand, enhancement gene therapy, which is meant to improve the quality of genetic material, cannot be morally accepted. See Rae, *Moral Choices*, 175–77.

157. Pablo Gadenz, "The Church as the Family of God," in *Catholic for a Reason: Scripture and the Mystery of the Family of God*, ed. Scott Hahn and Leon J. Suprenant (Steubenville, OH: Emmaus Road Publishing, 1998), 80–82.

158. See Vito Mancuso, "La ragione vince, rifare la chiesa," *Il foglio*, January 22, 2008.

Bibliography

Abdul-Masih, Marguerite. *Edward Schillebeeckx and Hans Frei: A Conversation on Method and Christology.* Waterloo, ON: Wilfrid Laurier University Press, 2001.

Ahearn, David O., and Peter A. Gathie, eds. *Doing Right and Being Good: Catholic and Protestant Readings in Christian Ethics.* Collegeville, MN: Liturgical Press, 2005.

Altizer, Thomas J. J. *The Genesis of God: A Theological Genealogy.* Louisville, KY: Westminster John Knox Press, 1993.

Anthony, Thalia, and Dorothea Anthony. "Psychologizing Criminals and the Frankfurt School's Critique." In *The Critical Criminology Companion*, edited by Thalia Anthony and Chris Cunneen. Annandale, NSW: Hawkins Press, 2008.

Ashworth, E. J. "Religious Pluralism." In *The Routledge Encyclopaedia of Philosophy*, edited by Edward Craig. London: Taylor and Francis, 1998.

Ayres, Lewis. "Constantinople, First Council of." In *The New Westminster Dictionary of Church History.* Vol. 1, *The Early, Medieval and Reformation Eras*, edited by Robert Benedetto, ed. Louisville, KY: Westminster John Knox Press, 2008.

———. *Nicaea and Its Legacy; An Approach to Fourth Century Trinitarian Theology.* Oxford: Oxford University Press, 2006.

Bailey, Betty J., and J. Martin Bailey. *Who Are the Christians in the Middle East?* Grand Rapids, MN: Eerdmans, 2003.

Bailey, J. Martin. "Commonwealth of Independent States (CIS)." In *Toward the 21st Century in Christian Mission*, edited by James M. Phillips and Robert T. Coote. Grand Rapids, MN: Eerdmans, 1993.

Barnett, James M. *The Diaconate: A Full and Equal Order.* London: Continuum, 1995.

Barth, Karl. *Church Dogmatics.* Vol. 2: *The Doctrine of God.* London: Continuum, 1969.

Baum, Michelle N., and Janice L. Benton. "The Evolution and Current Focus of Ministry with Catholics with Disabilities within the United States." In *Disability Advocacy among Religious Organizations*, edited by Albert A. Herzog, 39–54. Philadelphia: Haworth Press, 2006.

Beattie, Tina. *New Catholic Feminism: Theology and Theory*. Oxford: Rout-ledge, 2006.

Bednar, Gerald J. *Faith as Imagination: The Contribution of William F. Lynch, SJ*. Lanham, MD: Rowman and Littlefield, 1996.

Beeley, Christopher A. *Gregory of Nazianzus on the Trinity and the Knowledge of God: In Your Light We Shall See Light*. Oxford: Oxford University Press, 2008.

Behr, John. *The Nicene Faith*, Volume 2, Part 2: *Formation of Christian Theology*. Crestwood, NY: St. Vladimir's Seminary Press, 2004.

Bell, Rob. *Velvet Elvis: Repainting the Christian Faith*. Grand Rapids, MN: Zondervan, 2006.

Berne, Rosalyn W. *Nanotalk: Conversations with Scientists and Engineers about Ethics, Meaning, and Belief in the Development of Nanotechnology*. London: Routledge, 2005.

Bliss, Frederick M. *Catholic and Ecumenical: History and Hope; Why the Catholic Church Is Ecumenical and What She Is Doing about It*. Lanham, MD: Rowman and Littlefield, 2007.

Boa, Kenneth. *Augustine to Freud: What Theologians & Psychologists Tell Us about Human Nature and Why It Matters*. Nashville, TN: Broadman and Holman, 2004.

Bordwell, David, ed. *Catechism of the Catholic Church*. London: Burns and Oates, 2006.

Borgman, Erik. *Edward Schillebeeckx: A Theologian in His History*. London: Continuum, 2004.

Børtnes, Jostein. "Rhetoric and Mental Images in Gregory." In *Gregory of Nazianzus: Images and Reflections*, edited by Jostein Børtnes and Tomas Hägg. Copenhagen: Museum Tusculanum Press, 2006.

Bourgeois, Patrick L. *Extension of Ricoeur's Hermeneutic*. Dordrecht: Kluwer Academic Publishers, 1975.

Bourgeois, Patrick L., and Frank Schalow. *Traces of Understanding: A Profile of Heidegger's and Ricoeur's Hermeneutics*. Amsterdam: Rodopi, 1990.

Bouwsma, William J. *John Calvin: A Sixteenth Century Portrait*. Oxford: Oxford University Press, 1989.

Bowker, John W. *The Sacred Neuron: Extraordinary New Discoveries Linking Science to Religion*. London: IB Tauris Publishers, 2005.

Bria, Ion. *Credinta pe care o mărturisim*. Bucharest: Editura Institutului Biblic si de Misiune al Bisericii Ortodoxe Române, 1987.

———. *Destinul Ortodoxiei*. Bucharest: Editura Institutului Biblic si de Misiune al Bisericii Ortodoxe Române, 1989.

———. *Liturghia după liturghie. O tipologie a misiunii apostolice si mărturiei crestine azi*. Bucharest: Editura Athena, 1996.

———. "The Liturgy after the Liturgy, 1978." In *The Ecumenical Movement: An Anthology of Key Texts and Voices*, edited by Michael Kinnamon and Brian E. Cope. Grand Rapids, MN: Eerdmans, 1997.

————. Preface. In *Orthodox Dogmatic Theology*. Vol. 2, *The World: Creation and Deification*, by Dumitru Stăniloae; translated by Ioan Ioniță and Robert Berringer. London: Continuum, 2002.

————. *The Sense of the Ecumenical Tradition: The Ecumenical Witness and Vision of the Orthodox*. Geneva: World Council of Churches Publications, 1991.

Brodie, Thomas L. *Genesis as Dialogue: A Literary, Historical and Theological Commentary*. Oxford: Oxford University Press, 2001.

Broer, Frits G. M. "A Pure City: Calvin's Geneva." In *The Quest for Purity*, edited by Walter E. A. Van Beek. Berlin: Walter de Gruyter, 1988.

Bromiley, Geoffrey W. "Christianity." In *The International Standard Bible Encyclopedia*, edited by Geoffrey W. Bromiley. Grand Rapids, MN: Eerdmans, 1979.

Buciora, Jaroslaw. "Ecclesiology and National Identity in Orthodox Christianity." In *Orthodox Christianity and Contemporary Europe*, edited by Jonathan Sutton and Wil wan den Bercken. Leuven, BE: Peeters Publishers, 2003.

Bulgakov, Sergius. *The Lamb of God*. Grand Rapids, MN: Eerdmans, 2008.

Buller, Cornelius A. *The Unity of Nature and History in Pannenberg's Theology*. Lanham, MD: Rowman and Littlefield, 1996.

Burston, Daniel. *The Legacy of Erich Fromm*. Cambridge, MA: Harvard University Press, 1991.

Cairns, Earl E. *Christianity through the Centuries*. Grand Rapids, MN: Zondervan, 1996.

Calian, Carnegie. "Challenges Facing Orthodox Theological Education in a Post-Communist, Post-Christian, Pluralistic World." In *Orthodox Christianity and Contemporary Europe*, edited by Jonathan Sutton and Wil wan den Bercken. Leuven, BE: Peeters Publishers, 2003.

Callahan, Daniel. *The Troubled Dream of Life: In Search of a Peaceful Death*. Washington, DC: Georgetown University Press, 2000.

Calvin, Jean. *Institutes of the Christian Religion*. Translated by Henry Beveridge. Edinburgh: Calvin Translation Society, 1846.

Caner, Daniel. *Wondering, Begging Monks: Spiritual Authority and the Promotion of Monasticism in Late Antiquity*. Berkeley: University of California Press, 2002.

Caputo, John D., Kevin Hart, and Yvonne Sherwood. "Epoché and Faith: An Interview with Jacques Derrida." In *Derrida and Religion: Other Testaments*, edited by Yvonne Sherwood and Kevin Hart; transcribed by Brook Cameron and Kevin Hart. London: Routledge, 2005.

Chadwick, Henry, gen. ed. *Leontius of Jerusalem: Against the Monophysites; Testimonies of the Saints and Aporiae*. Edited and translated by Patrick T. R. Gray. Oxford: Oxford University Press, 2006.

The Church of England Magazine XLVI (1859).

Cicovacki, Predrag. *Between Truth and Illusion: Kant at the Crossroads of Modernity*. Lanham, MD: Rowman and Littlefield, 2002.

Ciholas, Paul. *The Omphalos and the Cross: Pagans and Christians in Search of a Divine Centre.* Macon, GA: Mercer University Press, 2003.

Clapsis, Emmanuel. "Wealth and Poverty in Christian Tradition." In *Church and Society: Orthodox Christian Perspectives, Past Experiences and Modern Challenges,* edited by George P. Liacopoulos. Boston: Somerset Hall Press, 2007.

Clark, Steven H. *Paul Ricoeur.* London: Routledge, 1991.

Constas, Nicholas. *Proclus of Constantinople and the Cult of the Virgin in Late Antiquity: Homilies 1–5; Texts and Translations.* Leiden: Brill, 2003.

Copleston, Frederick C. *A History of Philosophy: 19th and 20th Century French Philosophy.* London: Continuum, 2003.

Cottret, Bernard. *Calvin: A Biography.* Grand Rapids, MN: Eerdmans, 2000.

Coward, Harold G. *Jung and Eastern Thought.* Albany: State University of New York Press, 1985.

Crawford, Katherine. *European Sexualities, 1400–1800.* Cambridge: Cambridge University Press, 2007.

Crisp, Oliver. *Divinity and Humanity: The Incarnation Reconsidered.* Cambridge: Cambridge University Press, 2007.

———. "Incarnation." In *The Oxford Handbook of Systematic Theology,* edited by John Webster, Kathryn Tanner, and Iain Torrance. Oxford: Oxford University Press, 2007.

Cupitt, Don. *Creation out of Nothing.* London: SCM Press, 1990.

———. *Is Nothing Sacred? The Non-Realist Philosophy of Religion: Selected Essays.* New York: Fordham University Press, 2002.

———. *Mysticism after Modernity.* Oxford: Blackwell Publishing, 1998.

———. *Sea of Faith: Christianity in Change.* Cambridge: Cambridge University Press, 1988.

Curran, Charles E. *The Catholic Moral Tradition Today.* Washington, DC: Georgetown University Press, 1999.

Cutrofello, Andrew. *Continental Philosophy: A Contemporary Introduction.* London: Routledge, 2005.

Dallmayr, Fred R. *Margins of Political Discourse.* Albany: State University of New York Press, 1989.

Dauenhauer, Bernard P. *Paul Ricoeur: The Promise and Risk of Politics.* Lanham, MD: Rowman and Littlefield, 1998.

Davis, Tom. *Sacred Work: Planned Parenthood and Its Clergy Alliances.* Rutgers, NJ: Rutgers University Press, 2005.

Davydov, Joseph. *God Exists: New Light on Science and Creation.* Rockville, MD: Schreiber Publishing, 2000.

D'Costa, Gavin. *The Meeting of Religions and the Trinity.* London: Continuum, 2000.

De Bary, Edward O. *Theological Reflection: The Creation of Spiritual Power in the Information Age.* Collegeville, MN: Liturgical Press, 2003.

De Castro, Leonardo. "Bioethics in the Philippines: An Overview of Developments, Issues, and Controversies." In *Regional Perspectives in*

Bioethics, edited by John F. Peppin and Mark J. Cherry. London: Swets and Zeitlinger Publishers, 2003.

De Greef, Wulfert. *The Writings of John Calvin: An Introductory Guide*. Louisville, KY: Westminster John Knox Press, 2008.

Deane-Drummond, Celia. "Theology and the Biological Sciences." In *The Modern Theologians: An Introduction to Christian Theology since 1918*, edited by David Ford. Oxford: Blackwell, 2005.

Dell, William Stanley. *Jung, Modern Man in Search of a Soul*. London: Routledge, 2001.

Donum Vitae, or *Instruction on Respect for Human Life and Its Origin, and on the Dignity of Procreation. Replies to Certain Questions of the Day*. February 22, 1987. http://www.vatican.va/roman_curia/congregations/cfaith/documents/rc_con_cfaith_doc_19870222_respect-for-human-life_en.html (accessed January 12, 2008).

Dourley, John P. *Paul Tillich and Bonaventure*. Leiden: Brill, 1975.

Downey, Patrick. *Serious Comedy: The Philosophical and Theological Significance of Tragic and Comic Writing in the Western Tradition*. Lanham, MD: Lexington Books, 2000.

Dulles, Avery R. *The Assurance of Things Hoped For: A Theology of Christian Faith*. Oxford: Oxford University Press, 1997.

Dumitrana, Magdalena. "In Quest of the Lost Ecumenism." In *Romanian Cultural Identity and Education for Civil Society*, edited by Magdalena Dumitrana. Washington, DC: Council for Research in Values and Philosophy, 2005.

Dupré, Wilhelm. *Patterns in Meaning. Reflections on Meaning and Truth in Cultural Reality, Religious Traditions and Dialogical Encounters*. Leuven: Peeters, 1994.

Echeverria, Eduardo J. "The Gospel of Redemptive Suffering. Reflections on John Paul II's *Salvifici Doloris*", in Peter van Inwagen, *Christian Faith and the Problem of Evil*. Grand Rapids, MN: Eerdmans, 2004.

Edgar, Thomas R. "Through the Written Word, Spiritual Truth Can Be Known", in Mal Couch, ed. *The Fundamentals of the Twenty-First Century. Examining the Crucial Issue of the Christian Faith*. Grand Rapids, MN: Kregel Publications, 2000.

Ellman, Roger. *The Origin and Its Meaning*. Santa Rosa: The Origin Foundation, 2004.

Ellul, Jacques. *The Ethics of Freedom*. Grand Rapids, MN: Eerdmans, 1976.

Elton, G. R. *Reformation Europe, 1517–1559*. Oxford: Wiley-Blackwell, 1999.

Elwood, Christopher. *Calvin for Armchair Theologians*. Louisville, KY: Westminster John Knox Press, 2002.

Erricker, Clive. *Teaching Christianity. A World Religions Approach*, 2nd revised edition. Cambridge: James Clarke & Co., 1987.

Eskola, Antti. "How Many Social Psychologies Are There?" In *Blind Alleys in Social Psychology: A Search for Ways Out* [Advances in Psychology 48], edited by Antti Eskola. Amsterdam: North Holland, 1988.

Estep, William R. *Renaissance and Reformation*. Grand Rapids, MN: Eerdmans, 1986.

Evans, G. R. *The Church and the Churches*. Cambridge: Cambridge University Press, 2002.

Evans, Gillian R. *Fifty Key Medieval Thinkers*. London: Routledge, 2002.

Feduccia, Robert, Jr., ed. *Great Catholic Writings: Thought, Literature, Spirituality, Social Action*. Winona, MN: Saint Mary's Press, 2006.

Feodorov, Vladimir. "Orthodox View on Theological Education as Mission." In *Theological Education as Mission*, edited by Peter F. Penner. Schwarzenfeld, DE: Neufeld Verlag, 2005.

Fiddes, Paul S. *Participating in God: A Pastoral Doctrine of the Trinity*. Louisville, KY: Westminster John Knox Press, 2000.

Fioravanti, Gianfranco. "Nationalism." In *Encyclopedia of Christian Theology*. Vol. 1, *A–F*, edited by Jean-Yves Lacoste. London: CRC Press, 2004.

Fitzgerald, Thomas E. *The Ecumenical Movement: An Introductory History*. Santa Barbara, CA: Greenwood Publishing Group, 2004.

Flaman, Paul. *Genetic Engineering: Christian Values and Catholic Teaching*. Mahwah, NJ: Paulist Press, 2002.

Flinn, Frank K. "The Phenomenology of Symbol: Genesis I and II." In *Phenomenology in Practice and Theory*, edited by William S. Hamrick. Dordrecht: Martinus Nijhof Publishers, 1985.

Forte, Bruno. "Gnosi di rittorno e linguaggio consolatorio." *L'Osservatore romano*, February 2, 2008.

Freadman, Richard. *Threads of Life: Autobiography and the Will*. Chicago: University of Chicago Press, 2001.

Friedman, Maurice S. *A Heart of Wisdom: Religion and Human Wholeness*. Albany, NY: State University of New York Press, 1992.

Fromm, Erich. *The Dogma of Christ and Other Essays on Religion, Psychology and Culture*. Abingdon and New York: Routledge, 2004, 1–7. First published 1963 by Routledge and Kegan Paul.

———. *The Fear of Freedom*. London: Routledge, 2001.

Funk, Rainer. "Erich Fromm's Life and Work." In *Erich Fromm and Critical Criminology: Beyond the Punitive Society*, edited by Kevin Anderson and Richard Quinney. Champaign, IL: University of Illinois Press, 2000.

Gadenz, Pablo. "The Church as the Family of God." In *Catholic for a Reason: Scripture and the Mystery of the Family of God*, edited by Scott Hahn and Leon J. Suprenant. Steubenville, OH: Emmaus Road Publishing, 1998.

Gadille, Jacques. "Introduction: Vingt-cinq ans de recherche missiologique. La naissance du CREDIC." In *Diffusion et acculturation du christianisme (XIXe–XXe s.). Vingt-cinq ans de recherches missiologieques*, edited by Jean Comby. Paris: Karthala, 2005.

Gavin, Hyman. *The Predicament of Postmodern Theology: Radical Orthodoxy or Nihilist Textualism?* Louisville, KY: Westminster John Knox Press, 2001.

Geiger, Roger. *History of Higher Education Annual.* Edison, NJ: Transaction Publishers, 1985.

Germani, Gino. *Authoritarianism, Fascism, and National Populism.* New Brunswick, NJ: Transaction Books, 1978.

Gibbon, Edward. *The History of the Decline and Fall of the Roman Empire.* Vol. 3. New York: Cosimo, 2008.

Gifford, Paul. *Love, Desire and Transcendence in French Literature: Deciphering Eros.* Aldershot, UK: Ashgate, 2005.

Graham, Kenneth J. E. *The Performance of Conviction: Plainness and Rhetoric in the Early English Renaissance.* Ithaca, NY: Cornell University Press, 1994.

Graham, Michael F. *The Uses of Reform. 'Godly Discipline' and Popular Behavior in Scotland and Beyond, 1560–1610.* Leiden: Brill, 1996.

Grenz, Stanley J. *Theology for the Community of God.* Grand Rapids, MN: Eerdmans, 2000.

Grillmeier, Alloys. *Christ in Christian Tradition.* Vol. 1, *From the Apostolic Faith to Chalcedon.* Louisville, KY: Westminster John Knox Press, 1975.

Gross, Jeffrey, Eamon McManus, and Ann Riggs. "Ecumenism and Ecclesial and Pastoral Proclamation." In *A History of Pastoral Care*, edited by G. R. Evans. London: Continuum, 2000.

Guimón, J. *Relational Mental Health: Beyond Evidence-Based Interventions.* Heidelberg: Springer, 2003.

Hall, William D. *Paul Ricoeur and the Poetic Imperative: The Creative Tension between Love and Justice.* Albany, NY: State University of New York Press, 2007.

Hanson, R. P. C. *The Search for the Christian Doctrine of God: The Arian Controversy, 318–381.* London: Continuum, 2005.

Hardwick, Charley D. *Events of Grace: Naturalism, Existentialism and Theology.* Cambridge: Cambridge University Press, 1996.

Hardy, Edward R., ed. *Christology of the Later Fathers.* Louisville, KY: Westminster John Knox Press, 1954.

Hastings, James, and John A. Selbie, eds. *Encyclopedia of Religion and Ethics.* Part 9. Whitefish, MT: Kessinger Publications, 2003.

Hayes, Nicky. *Foundations of Psychology*, 3rd ed. Andover, UK: Cengage Learning, 2000.

Hebblethwaite, Brian. *Philosophical Theology and Christian Doctrine.* Oxford: Blackwell, 2005.

Helm, Paul. *Faith and Understanding.* Grand Rapids, MN: Eerdmans, 1997.

Henkel, Jürgen. *Eros und Ethos. Mensch, gottesdienstliche Gemeinschaft und Nation als Adressaten theologischer Ethiek bei Dumitru Stanilaoe. Mit einem Geleitwort von Mitropolit Seraphim.* Berlin: LIT Verlag, 2003.

Herndon, Felix, and Valerie J. Smith. "The Disenchantment of Modern Sexuality. Packaged by Media into Weber's 'Iron Cage.'" In *Sex, Religion,*

Media, edited by Dane S. Claussen. Lanham, MD: Rowman and Little-field, 2002.

Hesselink, I. John. *Calvin's First Catechism: A Commentary*. Louisville, KY: Westminster John Knox Press, 1998.

Hick, John. *Dialogues in the Philosophy of Religion*. New York: Palgrave Macmillan, 2001.

Hodgin, David R. "Religion and the Modern Mind." In *Religion and the Modern Mind: An Affirmation of Life and the Pursuit of Truth*, edited by Stanley South. Boone, NC: Parkway Publishers, 2006.

Holifield, Brooks. *God's Ambassadors: A History of the Christian Clergy in America*. Grand Rapids, MN: Eerdmans, 2007.

Höpfl, Harro. *The Christian Polity of John Calvin*. Cambridge: Cambridge University Press, 1985.

Horowitz, Gregg. *Sustaining Loss: Art and Mournful Life*. Palo Alto, CA: Stanford University Press, 2001.

Horowitz, Irving L. *Foundations of Political Sociology*. Edison, NJ: Transaction Publishers, 1997.

Houser-Thomas, W. L. *An Era of Addiction: The Evolution of Dependency*. New York: Writers Club Press, 2002.

Hughes, Philip. *A History of the Church*. Vol. 1, *The World in which the Church Was Founded*. London: Continuum, 1979.

Humfress, Caroline. *Orthodoxy and the Courts in Late Antiquity*. Oxford: Oxford University Press, 2007.

Hunt Overzee, Anne. *The Body Divine: The Symbol of the Body in the Works of Teilhard de Chardin and Ramanuja*. Cambridge: Cambridge University Press, 1992.

Hutcheon, Pat D. *Leaving the Cave: Evolutionary Naturalism in Social-Scientific Thought*. Waterloo, ON: Wilfrid Laurier University Press, 1996.

Hutson, Curtis. *Great Preaching on the Resurrection*. Murfreesboro, TN: Sword of the Lord Publishers, 2000.

Hyman, Gavin. *The Predicament of Postmodern Theology*. Louisville: Westminster John Knox Press, 2004.

Ihde, Don. *Hermeneutic Phenomenology: The Philosophy of Paul Ricoeur*. Evanston, IL: Northwestern University Press, 1980.

Immink, F. Gerrit. *Faith: A Practical Theological Reconstruction*. Grand Rapids, MN: Eerdmans, 2005.

Instruction Dignitas personae *on Certain Bioethical Questions*. June 20, 2008. http://www.vatican.edu/roman_curia/congregations/cfaith/documents/rc_con_cfaith_doc_20081208_dignitas-personae_en.html (accessed January 12, 2009).

Ioniță, Viorel. "Ökumene und Mission aus orthodoxer Sicht." In *Gemeinschaft der Kirchen und gesellschaftliche Verantwortung. Die Würde des Anderen und das Recht anders zu denken*, edited by Lena Lybaek, Konrad Raiser, and Stefanie Schardien. Berlin: LIT Verlag, 2004.

Johnson, Alan F., and Robert E. Webber. *What Christians Believe: An Overview of Theology and Its Biblical and Historical Development.* Grand Rapids, MN: Zondervan, 1993.

Johnson, Earl S., Jr. *Selected to Serve: A Guide for Church Officers.* Louisville, KY: Westminster John Knox Press, 2000.

Johnson, Luke T. "Religious Rights and Christian Texts." In *Religious Human Rights in Global Perspective: Religious Perspectives,* edited by John Witte Jr. and Johan D. van der Vyer. Dordrecht: Martinus Nijhoff Publishers, 1996.

Kasulis, Thomas P., ed. *Self as Body in Asian Theory and Practice.* Albany, NY: State University of New York Press, 1993.

Kearney, Richard. *On Paul Ricoeur: The Owl of Minerva.* Aldershot, UK: Ashgate, 2004.

———. "Ricoeur." In *A Companion to Continental Philosophy,* edited by Simon Critchley and William Schroeder. Oxford: Blackwell, 1999.

Keen, Ernest. *Depression, Self-Consciousness, Pretending and Guilt.* Westport, CT: Greenwood Publishing Group, 2002.

Kelbley, Charles A. Introduction to *History and Truth: Essays,* by Paul Ricoeur,. Evanston, IL: Northwestern University Press, 1965.

Kelly, J. N. D. *Early Christian Creeds,* 3rd ed. London: Continuum, 2006.

———. *Early Christian Doctrines,* 5th ed. London: Continuum, 2000.

Kennedy, Philip. "God and Creation." In *The Praxis of the Reign of God: An Introduction to the Theology of Edward Schillebeeckx,* edited by Mary C. Hilkert and Robert J. Schreiter. New York: Fordham University Press, 2002.

———. *Schillebeeckx.* Collegeville, MN: Liturgical Press, 1993.

Kerrigan, William. *The Sacred Complex: On the Psychogenesis of* Paradise Lost. Cambridge, MA: Harvard University Press, 1983.

King, Ursula. *Religion and Gender.* Oxford: Blackwell, 1995.

Kirk, J. Andrew. *What Is Mission? Theological Explorations.* Minneapolis: Augsburg Fortress Press, 2000.

Klemm, David E. "Philosophy and Kerygma: Ricoeur as Reader of the Bible." In *Reading Ricoeur,* by David M. Kaplan. Albany, NY: State University of New York Press, 2008.

———. "Searching for a Heart of Gold: A Ricoeurian Meditation on Moral Striving and the Power of Religious Discourse." In *Paul Ricoeur and Contemporary Moral Thought,* edited by John Wall, William Schweiker, and W. David Hall. London: Routledge, 2002.

Kottler, Jeffrey A. *Doing Good: Passion and Commitment to Helping Others.* London: Routledge, 2000.

Lampe, G. W. H. "Christian Theology in the Patristic Period." In *A History of Christian Doctrine,* edited by Hubert Cunliffe-Jones. London: Continuum, 2006.

Lampe, Peter. *Christians at Rome in the First Two Centuries: From Paul to Valentinus.* London: Continuum, 2003.

Langmead, Ross. *The Word Made Flesh: Towards an Incarnational Missiology.* Lanham, MD: University Press of America, 2004.

Lanigan, Richard L. *Speaking and Semiology: Maurice Merleau Ponty's Phenomenological Theory of Existential Communication.* Berlin: Walter de Gruyter Verlag, 1991.

Lash, Scott. *Another Modernity, a Different Rationality.* Oxford: Blackwell, 1999.

Lehmann, David. "Religion and Globalization." In *Religions in the Modern World*, edited by Linda Woodhead, Paul Fletcher, Hiroko Kawanami, and David Smith. London: Routledge, 2004.

Lévy, Alfred. *Erich Fromm: Humanist zwischen Tradizion und Utopie.* Würzburg: Verlag Königshausen & Neumann, 2002.

Lienemann-Perrin, Christine. *Mission und Interreligiöser Dialog*, Bensheimer Hefte 93: Ökumenische Studienhefte. Göttingen: Vandenhoeck & Ruprecht, 1999.

Liveris, Leonie B. *Ancient Taboos and Gender Prejudice: Challenges for Orthodox Women and the Church.* Aldershot, UK: Ashgate, 2005.

Long, Eugene T. *Twentieth Century Western Philosophy of Religion, 1900–2000.* Dordrecht: Kluwer Academic Publishers, 2003.

Lowe, Walter. *Theology and Difference: The Wound of Reason.* Bloomington, IN: Indiana University Press, 1993.

Macklin, Ruth. *Surrogates and Other Mothers: The Debates over Assisted Reproduction.* Philadelphia: Temple University Press, 1994.

Macquarrie, John. *Jesus Christ in Modern Thought.* London: SCM-Canterbury Press, 1990.

———. *Stubborn Theological Questions.* London: SCM Press, 2003.

———. "Theological Reflections on Disability." In *Religion and Disability: Essays in Scripture, Theology and Ethics*, edited by Marilyn Bishop. Lanham, MD: Rowman and Littlefield, 1995.

Mancuso, Vito. *L'anima e il suo destino.* Milan: Raffaelo Cortina, 2007.

———. *Il dolore innocente: L'handicap, la natura e Dio*, 2nd ed. Milan: Mondadori, 2008.

———. *Hegel teologo.* Casale Monferrato, IT: Edizioni Piemme, 1996.

———. "La nostra sacra liberta di morire." In *Persona e danno*, August 29, 2008.

———. "La ragione vince, rifare la chiesa." In *Il foglio*, January 22, 2008.

———. *Rifondazione della fede.* Milan: Mondadori, 2008.

———. "Video intrevista a Vito Mancuso." http://www.associazioneasia.it/adon.pl?act=doc&doc=669 (accessed January 11, 2009).

Markham, Ian S. *Plurality and Christian Ethics.* Cambridge: Cambridge University Press, 1994.

Markwell, Hazel J., and Barry F. Brown. "Roman Catholic Bioethics." In *The Cambridge Textbook of Bioethics*, edited by Peter A. Singer and A. M. Viens. Cambridge: Cambridge University Press, 2008.

Marshall, Bruce D. *Trinity and Truth*. Cambridge: Cambridge University Press, 2002.

Martin, Christopher, ed. *The Philosophy of Thomas Aquinas: Introductory Readings*. London: Taylor and Francis, 1988.

Martinson, Paul V. *A Theology of World Religions: Interpreting God, Self, and World in Semitic, Indian, and Chinese Thought*. Minneapolis: Augsburg Fortress Publishing, 1987.

Marucci, Corrado. "L'anima e il suo destino secondo Vito Mancuso." *La Civiltà Cattolica*, February 2, 2008.

Massaro, Thomas J. "From Industrialization to Globalization: Church and Social Ministry." In *Living the Catholic Social Tradition: Cases and Commentaries*, edited by Kathleen Maas Weigert and Alexia K. Kelley. Lanham, MD: Rowman and Littlefield, 2004.

May, William E. *Catholic Bioethics and the Gift of Human Life: Celebrating the Beauty of Being*. Huntington, IN: Our Sunday Visitor Press, 2000.

Mbiti, John S. "Dialogue between Eatwot and Western Theologians: A Comment on the Sixth Eatwot Conference in Geneva, 1983." In *Fullness of Life for All: Challenges for Mission in the Early 21st Century*, edited by Inus Daneel, Charles van Engen, and Hendrik Vroom. Amsterdam: Rodopi, 2003.

McGuckin, John. *Saint Gregory of Nazianzus: An Intellectual Biography*. Crestwood, NY: St. Vladimir's Seminary Press, 2001.

McKee, Elsie A. "Calvin's Teaching on the Elder Illuminated by Exegetical History." In *John Calvin and the Church: A Prism of Reform*, by Timothy George. Louisville, KY: Westminster John Knox Press, 1990.

McKim, Donald K. *Theological Turning Points: Major Issues in Christian Thought*. Louisville, KY: Westminster John Knox Press, 1989.

McLynn, N. "*Curiales* into Churchmen: The Case of Gregory Nazianzen." In *Le trasformazioni delle élites in età tardoantica*, edited by Rita L. Testa. Rome: Libreria Editrice Romana Monumenti Arte di Bretschneider, 2006.

McManus, Kathleen A. *Unbroken Communion: The Place and Meaning of Suffering in Edward Schillebeeckx*. Lanham, MD: Rowman and Littlefield, 2003.

McMillan, Richard C. *Religion in the Public Schools: An Introduction*. Macon, GA: Mercer University Press, 1984.

Mellert, Robert B. "Reconsidering the Medieval Concept of Nature in the Development of a Scientific Ethics." In *Miscellanea Medievalia* 13/2: Sprache und Erkenntnis im Mittelalter, edited by Jan P. Beckmann and Wolfgang Kluxen. Berlin: Walter de Gruyter, 1981.

Mentzer, Raymond A. "The Genevan Model and Gallican Originality in the French Reformed Tradition." In *Adaptation of Calvinism in Reformation Europe: Essays in Honour of Brian G. Armstrong*, edited by Mack P. Holt. Aldershot, UK: Ashgate Publishing, 2007.

Mestrović, Stjepan G. *Durkheim and Postmodern Culture*. New York: Aldine de Gruyter, 1992.

Michael, Martin. *Atheism: A Philosophical Justification.* Philadelphia: Temple University Press, 1992.

Miller, Charles. *The Gift of the World: An Introduction to the Theology of Dumitru Stăniloae.* London: Continuum, 2000.

Miller, Michael R. "Freedom and Grace." In *Gathered for the Journey: Moral Theology in Catholic Perspective*, edited by David M. McCarthy and M. Therese Lysaught. Grand Rapids, MN: Eerdmans, 2007.

Milner, Benjamin C. *Calvin's Doctrine of the Church.* Leiden: Brill Publishers, 1965.

Min, A. K. "Phillips on the Grammar of «God»." In *Ethics of Belief: Essays in Tribute to D. Z. Phillips*, edited by Eugene T. Long and Patrick Horn. Berlin: Springer, 2008.

Mitchell, Stephen A. *Influence and Autonomy in Psychoanalysis.* Hillsdale, NJ: Atlantic Press, 1997.

Moreland, J. P., John Mark Reynolds, and Stanley N. Gundry, eds. *Three Views on Creation and Evolution.* Grand Rapids, MN: Zondervan, 1999.

Mueller, Janel. "Embodying Glory: the Apocalyptic Strain in Milton's *Of Reformation*." In *Politics, Poetics and Hermeneutics in Milton's Prose*, edited by David Loewenstein and James Grantham Turner. Cambridge: Cambridge University Press, 1990.

Muller, Richard A. *After Calvin: Studies in the Development of a Theological Tradition.* Oxford: Oxford University Press, 2003.

Myers, Jeffrey W., Marianne Neighbors, and Ruth Tannehille-Jones. *Pathophysiology and Emergency Medical Care.* Florence, KY: Thompson Cengage Learning, 2002.

Naphy, William G. *Calvin and the Consolidation of the Genevan Reformation.* Manchester, UK: Manchester University Press, 1994.

Narciso, Dianna. *Like Rolling Uphill: Realizing the Honesty of Atheism.* Tamarac, FL: Llumina Press, 2004.

Naugle, David K. *Worldview: The History of a Concept.* Grand Rapids, MN: Eerdmans, 2002.

Nazianzen, Gregory. "To Nectarius, Bishop of Constantinople." In *A Select Library of the Christian Church: Nicene and Post-Nicene Fathers.* Vol. 7, *Cyril of Jerusalem, Gregory Nazianzen*, 2nd series, edited by Philip Schaff and Henry Wace. Peabody, MA: Hendrickson Publishers, 2004.

Nicholls, David. *Deity and Domination: Images of God and the State in the Nineteenth and Twentieth Centuries.* London: Routledge, 1994.

Nichols, Aidan. *No Bloodless Myth: A Guide through Balthasar's Dogmatics.* London: Continuum, 2000.

———. *The Shape of Catholic Theology.* Collegeville, MN: Liturgical Press, 1991.

Novack, George. *Marxist Writings on History and Philosophy.* Broadway, NSW: Resistance Books, 2002.

O'Brien, John A. *The Faith of Millions: The Credentials of the Catholic Religion.* Huntington, IN: Our Sunday Visitor Press, 1974.

O'Leary, Lacy. *The Syriac Church and Fathers.* Piscataway, NJ: Gorgias Press, 2002.

O'Rourke, Kevin. "Pain Relief: Ethical Issues and Catholic Teaching." In *Birth, Suffering and Death: Catholic Perspectives at the Edges of Life*, edited by Kevin Wm. Wildes, Francesc Abel, and John C. Harvey. Dordrecht: Kluwer Publications, 1994.

O'Rourke, Kevin D., and Philip Boyle. *Medical Ethics: Sources of Catholic Teachings.* Washington, DC: Georgetown University Press, 1999.

Ochs, Peter. "Charles Sanders Pierce." In *Founders of Constructive Postmodern Philosophy: Pierce, James, Bergson, Whitehead, and Hartshorne*, edited by David R. Griffin et al. Albany, NY: State University of New York Press, 1993.

Ogletree, Thomas W. "Christian Social Ethics as a Theological Discipline." In *Shifting Boundaries: Contextual Approaches to the Structure of Theological Education*, edited by Barbara G. Wheeler and Edward Farley. Louisville, KY: Westminster John Knox Press, 1991.

Okoro, Chiedozie. "Phenomenology for World Reconstruction." In *Analecta Husserliana* XCII. Book Five, *Logos of Phenomenology and Phenomenology of the Logos*, edited by Anna-Teresa Tymieniecka. Dordrecht: Springer, 2006.

Oliphant Old, Hugh. "Why Bother with Church? The Church and Its Worship." In *Essentials of Christian Theology*, edited by William C. Placher. Louisville, KY: Westminster John Knox Press, 2003.

Olson, Roger E. *The Westminster Handbook to Evangelical Theology.* Louisville, KY: Westminster John Knox Press, 2004.

Pannenberg, Wolfhart. *Anthropology in Theological Perspective.* London: Continuum, 2004.

———. *Systematic Theology.* Vol. 1. Grand Rapids, MN: Eerdmans, 1991.

Parker, T. H. L. *Calvin: An Introduction to His Thought.* Louisville, KY: Westminster John Knox Press, 1995.

Partee, Charles. *The Theology of John Calvin.* Louisville, KY: Westminster John Knox Press, 2008.

Pelikan, Jaroslav J. *The Christian Tradition: A History of the Development of Doctrine.* Vol. 1, *The Emergence of the Catholic Tradition, 100–600.* Chicago: University of Chicago Press, 1989.

Percival, Harold W. *Thinking and Destiny: The Descent of Man the Eternal Order of Progression.* New Delhi: Motilal Banarsidass Publishers, 2001.

Perl, Eric D. *Theophany: The Neoplatonic Philosophy of Dionysius the Areopagite.* Albany, NY: State University of New York Press, 2007.

Peters, Ted. *Playing God? Genetic Determinism and Human Freedom.* London: Routledge, 2003.

Petrinovich, Lewis. *Human Evolution, Reproduction and Morality.* Cambridge: MIT Press, 1998.

Pinkard, Terry. *Hegel: A Biography.* Cambridge: Cambridge University Press, 2001.

Plekon, Michael. "Mother Maria Skobtsova (1891–1945)." In *The Teachings of Modern Orthodox Christianity: On Law, Politics and Human Nature*, by John Witte Jr., and Frank S. Alexander. New York: Columbia University Press, 2007.

Proctor, James D., ed. *Science, Religion and Human Experience*. Oxford: Oxford University Press, 2005.

Proudfoot, Wayne. *God and the Self: Three Types of Philosophy of Religion*. Cranbury, NJ: Associated University Presses 1976.

Rae, Scott B. *Moral Choices: An Introduction to Ethics*, 2nd ed. Grand Rapids, MN: Zondervan, 2000.

Ranganathananda, Swami. *Human Being in Depth: A Scientific Approach to Religion*. Albany, NY: State University of New York Press, 1991.

Rasmussen, David M. *Symbol and Interpretation*. Dordrecht: Kluwer Academic Publishers, 1974.

Raven, Charles E. *Apollinarianism: An Essay on the Christology of the Early Church*. Cambridge: Cambridge University Press, 1923.

Reagan, Charles E. *Paul Ricoeur: His Life and His Work*. Chicago: University of Chicago Press, 1998.

Rego, Aloysius. *Suffering and Salvation: The Salvific Meaning of Suffering in the Later Theology of Edward Schillebeeckx*. Leuven, BE: Peeters, 2006.

Reinders, Hans S. *Receiving the Gift of Friendship: Profound Disability, Theological Anthropology, and Ethics*. Grand Rapids, MN: Eerdmans, 2008.

Rice, Howard L. *Reformed Spirituality: An Introduction for Believers*. Louisville, KY: Westminster John Knox Press, 1991.

Richardson, Miles. *Being in Christ and Putting Death in Its Place: An Anthropologist's Account of Christian Performance in Spanish America and the American South*. Baton Rouge, LA: LSU Press, 2006.

Ricoeur, Paul. *Fallible Man*. Translated by Charles A. Kelbley. New York: Fordham University Press, 1986.

Robbins, Jeffrey W. *Between Faith and Thought: An Essay on the Ontotheological Condition*. Charlottesville, VA: University of Virginia Press, 2003.

Ross, Stephen D. *Inexhaustibility and Human Being: An Essay on Locality*. New York: Fordham University Press, 1989.

Rothgeb, C. L., ed. *Abstracts of the Collected Works of C. G. Jung*. London: Karnac Books, 1992.

Routley, Erik. *A Panorama of Christian Hymnody*. Chicago: GIA Publications, 2005.

Rue, Loyal D. *By the Grace of Guile: The Role of Deception in Natural History and Human Affairs*. Oxford: Oxford University Press, 1994.

Rutherford, Donald. "Malebranche's Theodicy." In *The Cambridge Companion to Malebranche*, edited by Steven M. Nadler. Cambridge: Cambridge University Press, 2000.

Saltzman, Todd A., and Michael G. Lawler. *The Sexual Person: Toward a Renewed Catholic Anthropology*. Washington, DC: Georgetown University Press, 2008.

Sawatsky, Walter W. "Without God We Cannot, without Us God Won't—Thoughts on God's Mission within CIS in the Future." In *Mission in the Former Soviet Union*, edited by Walter W. Sawatsky and Peter F. Penner. Schwarzenfeld, DE: Neufeld Verlag, 2005.

Schillebeeckx, Edward. *Christ, the Christian Experience in the Modern World.* London: SCM Press, 1990.

———. *Christ, the Sacrament of the Encounter with God.* Lanham, MD: Rowman and Littlefield, 1963.

———. *Church, the Human Story of God.* London: SCM Press, 1990.

———. *The Eucharist.* London: Continuum, 1968.

———. *God, the Future of Man.* London: Sheed and Ward, 1968.

———. *World and Church.* London: Sheed and Ward, 1982.

Schillebeeckx, Edward, and Ramona Simuţ, eds. "Reinterpreting Traditional Theology: An Interview with Edward Schillebeeckx." *Perichoresis* 5:2 (2007): 275–83.

Sharma, Arvind. *A Primal Perspective on the Philosophy of Religion.* Heidelberg: Springer, 2006.

Shenfield, F., and C. Sureau. "Ethics of Embryo Research." In *Ethical Dilemmas in Assisted Reproduction*, by F. Shenfield and C. Sureau. New York: Informa Healthcare, 1997.

Silver, Harold. *The Concept of Popular Education: A Study of Ideas and Social Movements in the Early Nineteenth Century.* London: Methuen, 1977.

Simms, Karl. *Paul Ricoeur.* London: Routledge, 2003.

Smith, David W., and Elizabeth G. Burr. *Understanding World Religions: A Road Map for Justice and Peace.* Lanham, MD: Rowman and Littlefield, 2007.

Smith, Olav B. *Myths of the Self: Narrative Identity and Postmodern Metaphysics.* Lanham, MD: Lexington Books, 2004.

Sowle Cahill, Lisa. "Commentary on *Familiaris consortio* (*Apostolic Exhortation on the Family*)." In *Modern Catholic Social Teaching: Commentaries and Interpretations*, edited by Kenneth R. Himes. Washington, DC: Georgetown University Press, 2005.

Sozomen. *The Ecclesiastical History of Sozomen, Comprising a History of the Church from AD 324 to AD 440. Translated from the Greek with a Memoir of the Author.* Translated by Edward Walford. London: Henry G. Bohn, 1860.

Stambovsky, Phillip. *Myth and the Limits of Reason.* Amsterdam: Rodopi, 1996.

Steinmetz, George. *State/Culture: State Formation after the Cultural Turn.* Ithaca, NY: Cornell University Press, 1999.

Stenger, Mary A., and Ronald H. Stone. *Dialogues with Paul Tillich.* Macon, GA: Mercer University Press, 2002.

Stiver, Dan R. *Theology after Ricoeur: New Directions in Hermeneutical Theology.* Louisville, KY: Westminster John Knox Press, 2001.

Stockton, Ronald R. *Decent and In Order: Conflict, Christianity and Polity in a Presbyterian Congregation*. Santa Barbara, CA: Greenwood Publishing Group, 2000.

Strickberger, Monroe W. *Evolution*, 3rd ed. Boston: Jones and Bartlett Publishers, 2005.

Swain, Simon. Introduction to *Approaching Late Antiquity: The Transformation from Early to Late Empire*, edited by Simon Swain and Mark Edwards. Oxford: Oxford University Press, 2006.

Tallon, Andrew. *Head and Heart: Affection, Cognition, Volition as Triune Consciousness*. New York: Fordham University Press, 1997.

Taylor, Mark C. *After God*. Chicago: University of Chicago Press, 2007.

Thiselton, Anthony C. *The Hermeneutics of Doctrine*. Grand Rapids, MN: Eerdmans, 2007.

———. *Thiselton on Hermeneutics: Collected Works with New Essays*. Grand Rapids, MN: Eerdmans, 2006.

Thompson, John B. *Critical Hermeneutics: A Study in the Thought of Paul Ricoeur and Jürgen Habermas*. Cambridge: Cambridge University Press, 1983.

———. "A Response to Paul Ricoeur." In *Paul Ricoeur: Hermeneutics and the Human Sciences*, edited by John B. Thompson. Cambridge: Cambridge University Press, 1998.

Tillich, Paul. *Theological Writings* [Hauptwerke 6]. Edited by Gert Hummel and Carl Heinz Ratschow. Berlin: Walter de Gruyter Verlag, 1992.

Torrance, Thomas F. *The Christian Doctrine of God: One Being, Three Persons*. London: Continuum, 2001.

Tracy, David. *Blessed Rage for Order: The New Pluralism in Theology*. Chicago: University of Chicago Press, 1996.

———. *Plurality and Ambiguity*. Chicago: University of Chicago Press, 1994.

Trigg, Roger. *Rationality and Religion*. Oxford: Wiley-Blackwell, 1998.

Turner, Denys. *Faith, Reason and the Existence of God*. Cambridge: Cambridge University Press, 2004.

Tymieniecka, Anna-Teresa, ed. *Phenomenology World-wide: Foundations, Expanding Dynamisms, Life-engagements—A Guide for Research and Study*. Dordrecht: Kluwer Academic Publishers, 2002.

Ugolnik, Anthony. *The Illuminating Icon*. Grand Rapids, MN: Eerdmans, 1989.

Ulanov, Ann, and Barry Ulanov. *Religion and the Unconscious*. Philadelphia: Westminster Press, 1985.

Underhill, Evelyn. *Mysticism: A Study in the Nature and Development of Spiritual Consciousness*. Mineola, NY: Dover Publications, 2002.

Van Hooft, Stan. *Life, Death and Subjectivity: Moral Sources in Bioethics*. Amsterdam: Rodopi, 2004.

Van Hoogstraten, Hans Dirk. *Deep Economy: Caring for Ecology, Humanity and Religion*. Cambridge: James Clarke and Co., 2001.

Van Leeuwen, Theodoor M. *The Surplus of Meaning: Ontology and Eschatology in the Philosophy of Paul Ricoeur*. Amsterdam: Rodopi, 1981.

Vanhoozer, Kevin J. *Biblical Narrative in the Philosophy of Paul Ricoeur*. Cambridge: Cambridge University Press, 1990.

Venema, Cornelis P. *Accepted and Renewed in Christ: The «Twofold Grace of God» and the Interpretation of Calvin's Theology*. Göttingen: Vanhenhoek and Ruprecht, 2007.

Venema, Henry I. *Identifying Selfhood: Imagination, Narrative and Hermeneutics in the Thought of Paul Ricoeur*. Albany, NY: State University of New York Press, 2000.

Vickeri, Philip L. "The Mar Toma Christians of Kerala: A Study of the Relationship between Liturgy and Mission in the Indian Context." In *Christian Worship Worldwide: Expanding Horizons, Deepening Practices*, edited by Charles E. Farhadian. Grand Rapids, MN: Eerdmans, 2007.

Vitz, Paul C. *Psychology as Religion: The Cult of Self-Worship*, 2nd ed. Grand Rapids, MI: Eerdmans, and Carlisle, UK: Paternoster, 1994.

Vrame, Anton C. "An Overview of Orthodox Christian Religious Education." In *International Handbook of the Religious, Moral, and Spiritual Dimensions of Education*, edited by Marian de Souza, Kathleen Engebretson, Gloria Durka, Robert Jackson, and Andrew McGrady. Berlin: Springer, 2006.

Walker, John. "Hegel and Religion." In *Hegel and Modern Philosophy*, by David Lamb. London: Routledge, 1987.

Wall, John. *Moral Creativity: Paul Ricoeur and the Poetics of Possibility*. Oxford: Oxford University Press, 2005.

Wallace-Hadrill, D. S. *Christian Antioch: A Study of Early Christian Thought in the East*. Cambridge: Cambridge University Press, 1982.

Wallace, Peter G. *The Long European Reformation*. New York: Palgrave Macmillan, 2004.

Wallace, Robert M. *Hegel's Philosophy of Beauty, Freedom, and God*. Cambridge: Cambridge University Press, 2005.

Walter, James J. "Theological Parameters: Catholic Doctrine on Abortion in a Pluralist Society." In *Contemporary Issues in Bioethics: A Catholic Perspective*, edited by James J. Walter and Thomas A. Shannon. Lanham, MD: Rowman and Littlefield, 2005.

Ware, Kallistos. Foreword to *Orthodox Dogmatic Theology: The Experience of God*, by Dumitru Stăniloae; translated by Ioan Ioniță and Robert Barringer. London: Continuum, 1994.

Whyte, Lancelot L. *The Universe of Experience: A Worldview beyond Science and Religion*. Edison, NJ: Transaction Publishers, 2003.

Wiggershaus, Rolf. *The Frankfurt School: Its History, Theories, and Political Significance*. Cambridge, MA: MIT Press, 1995.

Williams, Rowan. *Arius, Heresy and Tradition*, revised edn. Grand Rapids, MI: Eerdmans, 2002.

Williamson, Peter. *Catholic Principles for Interpreting Scripture*. Leuven, BE: Peeters, 2001.

———. *Catholic Principles for Interpreting Scripture: A Study of the Pontifical Commission's* The Interpretation of the Bible in the Church. Rome: Editrice Pontificio Istituto Biblico, 2001.

Witte, John, Jr. *God's Joust, God's Justice: Law and Religion in the Western Tradition*. Grand Rapids, MN: Eerdmans, 2006.

Wolin, Sheldon S. *Politics and Vision*. Princeton, NJ: Princeton University Press, 2004.

Wood, David. *On Paul Ricoeur: Narrative and Interpretation*. London: Routledge, 1992.

Wuerl, Donald W. *The Teaching of Christ: A Catholic Catechism for Adults*. Huntington, IN: Our Sunday Visitor Press, 2004.

Wuerl, Donald W., Thomas C. Lawler, and Ronald Lawler, eds. *The Gift of Faith: A Question and Answer Version of the Teaching of Christ*. Huntington, IN: Our Sunday Visitor Press, 2001.

Yinger, J. M. "Secular Alternatives to Religion." In *Man's Religious Quest: A Reader*, edited by Whitfield Foy. London: Open University Press, 1978.

Yong, Amos. *Theology and Down Syndrome: Reimagining Disability in Late Modernity*. Waco, TX: Baylor University Press, 2007.

Index